OXFORD STUDIES IN AFRICAN AFFAIRS

General Editors
JOHN D. HARGREAVES *and* GEORGE SHEPPERSON

THE HISTORICAL TRADITION
OF BUSOGA

MUKAMA AND KINTU

THE HISTORICAL
TRADITION OF
BUSOGA

Mukama and Kintu

BY

DAVID WILLIAM COHEN

CLARENDON PRESS · OXFORD

1972

Oxford University Press, Ely House, London W.1

GLASGOW NEW YORK TORONTO MELBOURNE WELLINGTON
CAPE TOWN IBADAN NAIROBI DAR ES SALAAM LUSAKA ADDIS ABABA
DELHI BOMBAY CALCUTTA MADRAS KARACHI LAHORE DACCA
KUALA LUMPUR SINGAPORE HONG KONG TOKYO

PRINTED IN GREAT BRITAIN
BY RICHARD CLAY (THE CHAUCER PRESS) LTD,
BUNGAY, SUFFOLK

To Susan and Jennifer

Preface

THE historical tradition of a people comprises all the verbal effects which historical experience generated in the past, which have been transmitted down to the present, and which survive as historically significant materials. Among traditionally literate peoples, these historically significant verbal materials are generally preserved and transmitted in written form. Among traditionally non-literate peoples whose historical tradition is of an entirely oral nature, the events of pre-colonial ages were not recorded in written documents deposited and preserved in archives. These events were, rather, recorded in the memories of men and the records of them transmitted by word of mouth from generation to generation. When conditions were favourable, these records were transmitted down to this century and are preserved in the minds, and transmitted through the lips, of the living. With the imposition of European rule in Africa, the written document became a significant means of record-keeping in societies where the written document was previously absent, and, in this century, a small percentage of these oral records have been set down in writing and thus are likely to be preserved for future generations.

This present work attempts to reconstruct the early history of an East African people, the Basoga of Uganda, through an analysis of their historical tradition. This analysis is based largely on the collection of testimonies recorded by the present writer in Busoga in 1966–7. The reconstruction focuses on that narrow but crucial period of momentous migrations in which the significant threads of historical tradition of Busoga were given shape and substance. These migrations are associated in Soga tradition with the *Adamic* figures Kintu and Mukama.

This is not the first work of historical reconstruction based on oral tradition. Over the past fifteen years, historians of Africa have become increasingly aware of the possibilities and problems of oral history research—both in attempting to recover the events of the pre–colonial past and in giving voice to sources of fresh perspective on the events of colonial and post-colonial Africa.[1]

[1] Notable work on pre-colonial history includes B. A. Ogot's *A History of the Southern Luo: Migration and Settlement* [Nairobi, 1967], a study of the migrations and settlements of the Padhola of eastern Uganda and the Luo of western Kenya.

Historians working within the Interlacustrine region, of which Busoga is a part, have generally been less interested in the composition, origins, and migrations of the peoples of the region than in the structure, origins, and changes in their political institutions. The importance and complexity of Interlacustrine state structures have attracted the attentions of both historians and social anthropologists, with a concomitant neglect of other features of Interlacustrine history and society. Associated with this concentration on political institutions is the problem of sources. Historians interested in the political structures of the region have been largely dependent on traditions bearing directly on the central institutions of the state—more often than not, 'official histories'. In the present work, emphasis is shifted away from these 'official' accounts and is placed instead on the traditions of the 'inarticulate' peasants and clients: the men of the clan, lineage, and family. The traditions of these groups often reflect the internal shape of the momentous migrations, and they occasionally detail the circumstances of contact between the heroic migrating families and the peasant families whom they found in Busoga, thereby throwing light on the very events and processes associated with the foundations of the states. From this same perspective of clan, lineage, and family, it is possible to reach some understanding of the nature of the emerging historical tradition and of the forces at work which have shaped the 'official' tradition—as the centripetal forces at work in Buganda and South Busoga have shaped 'official' or popular tradition of Kintu. Through such analysis, these two great *Adamic* traditions of Kintu and Mukama—central to the ethos of the peoples of Busoga past and present—can be set into historical context.

This study of the early history of Busoga, in a slightly different form, was presented and accepted as a dissertation for a Ph.D at the University of London in January 1970. I am most deeply indebted to Professor Roland Oliver for his patient guidance through the research and writing of the dissertation. I owe special thanks to Professors

Jan Vansina has used oral tradition in reconstructing state history in the Bushong kingdom of the Congo ['Recording the Oral History of the Bakuba', *Journal of African History*, i, 1 (1960), 45–54; i, 2 (1960), 257–80], and Rwanda [*L'Évolution du royaume rwanda des origines à 1900* (Brussels, 1962)]. Vansina has also produced a major work [*Oral Tradition: A Study in Historical Methodology* (London, 1965)] setting forth a methodological framework for the collection and interpretation of oral tradition.

Philip D. Curtin and Jan Vansina of the University of Wisconsin who, during my three years in Madison as an undergraduate, introduced me to the history of Africa. Professor Lyndon Harries and Mr. R. A. Snoxall provided me with the linguistic fundamentals, giving me a very necessary entry into the Lusoga language. Drs. Gideon Were, Mathias Kiwanuka, and Michael Twaddle were extremely helpful in the preparation for the research work. Grateful acknowledgement is made to the Central Research Fund, University of London, and to the School of Oriental and African Studies, both of which undertook, at early dates and with generous grants, to support the research.

The Uganda Government and the Busoga Local Government gave their permission, assistance, and encouragement, and without their co-operation the field research in Busoga, and therefore this present work, could not have been undertaken. In Uganda, Dr. Merrick Posnansky helped me over some early hurdles, offering assistance and hospitality in unstinting quantities. I am grateful also to Mrs. Petua Guina and Miss Mary Mance, headmistresses of the Wanyange Girls' Junior Secondary School (now part of Busoga College, Mwiri), who provided my wife and me with such a pleasant base for research.

The research on which this book is predominantly based could not have been done without the co-operation and interest of the people of Busoga themselves. The officers of the Local Government at the Bugembe headquarters and the *Ssaza* chiefs and *Ggombolola* chiefs in the eight counties of Busoga were unhesitatingly helpful. I am ever-lastingly grateful to the common people of Busoga who displayed a deep concern for their own past and who opened their homes and their heritage to my assistant, myself, and the tape recorder. Particular debt is owed Oweekitiibwa Y. K. Lubogo, Oweekitiibwa Y. K. M. Zirabamuzale, Omw. Sirimani Waiswa, Omw. Fenekansi Gabula ekiri, Omw. Yona Kalende, Omw. Zakayo Ntende, Omw. Zefaniya Kafuko, Omw. Samwiri Nkondho, and Omw. Y. K. Kabali who, perhaps without themselves realizing it, conveyed to me a concern for Busoga's past that fired my own interest in Busoga's history. Thanks are also due my assistants in the field: Mr. Charles Muganza, who travelled with me every day as my interpreter-assistant; Mr. Stephen A. Waiswa, who ably handled the work of transcription; and Mr. L. K. Bagimba, Mr. Gabriel Kunya, Mr. William Matagala, and Mr. G. W. Ntalo.

In the writing of this work, helpful advice was received from Dr. Richard Rathbone, Mr. Richard Levy, and Mr. Colin Freebrey. Miss

Johanna Freudenberg and Mrs. Laura Gordon assisted in the preparation of the maps.

Most of all, a debt of gratitude which can never be repaid is owed my parents, Wallace and Sylvia Cohen, who unselfishly gave of themselves so that I might be able to pursue studies and research far from home. The inspiration and comfort given to me over the past five years by Dr. and Mrs. Gideon Hadary are deeply appreciated. And to my wife Susan, who assisted at every point, and without whose devotion and support this work would never have been completed, I am especially grateful. The responsibility for what follows, however, is mine.

Acknowledgement

The Editors of the *Journal of African History* have kindly allowed the inclusion in Chapter II of sections of my article, 'A Survey of Interlacustrine Chronology', xi, 2 (1970), 177–201.

Contents

List of Maps

Orthography and Special Terms

EXCEPT where regular local and written usage vary, an attempt has been made to follow the modern Lusoga orthography as set forward by Gideon I. Byandala.[1]

For precision of meaning, certain Lusoga words and several terms recently adopted from Luganda are used in the text. They include:

butaka = ancestral lands; hereditary estate
ggombolola = (Luganda) sub-county
Katikkiro = (Luganda) chief minister of important chief or ruler
kisoko = sub-village area
mbuga = palace or residence of chief or ruler
musambwa = deity
mutaka (pl. *bataka*) − guardian of ancestral lands
mutala = rise of land between swamps; village area
muvule = hardwood tree, *iroko, Chlorophora excelsa*
muzimu = spirit of the deceased
mwise (pl. *baise*) = prefix to clan eponym meaning, 'person of the "father"...'
mwiwa (pl. *baiwa*) = child of daughter of a clan
nkuni = shrine dedicated to, and usually located at, ancestral settlement
ssaza = county; traditional state

[1] *The Lusoga Orthography* (Iganga, Uganda, 1963).

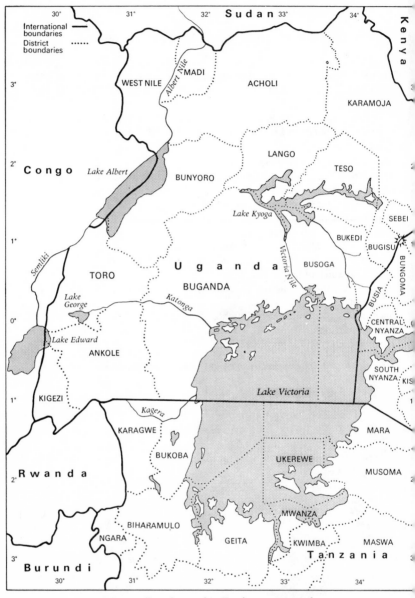

MAP I. Interlacustrine Region: present-day

CHAPTER I

The Busoga Setting

SINCE the 1890s, when the first European administrators defined as an administrative unit the lands lying between the Victoria Nile and the Mpologoma River and between Lake Kyoga and Lake Victoria, 'Busoga' has constituted an official political division of Uganda. Before the impact of colonial rule, this area, located on the eastern side of the Interlacustrine region of East Africa, consisted of several historical and cultural spheres which, in some measure, flowed across Busoga's present frontiers. Originally referring to a hill located in the south central part of the country, the term 'Busoga' later referred to a small kingdom along the Nile near Jinja. Still later, the name was applied to the region lying to the east of the Nile between Lake Kyoga and Lake Victoria. The early European visitors to the area adopted this usage and eventually the Mpologoma River was designated the eastern frontier.

The Interlacustrine region, comprising the lands from 2°N. to 4°S. and from 29° 30′E., to 34°E. and including Busoga,[1] has generally been considered an area of integrated historical activity. One of the unifying features of the region is the pattern of centralized kingdoms found throughout. These kingdoms, of which there were some sixty-eight in pre-colonial Busoga, were founded as a result of, or as a reaction to, the appearance of immigrant families reaching the region some four to eight centuries ago. Among these immigrants were Nilotic Lwo groups who pushed in from the north and are associated with the Mukama figure, and the Bantu speakers who were swept along in the backwash of Bantu expansion into the Mount Elgon region and who are associated with the Kintu figure.

This duality in the major traditions associated with the founding of the Soga states is also reflected in the longer view of Soga history. At the beginning of the nineteenth century, Busoga was really two worlds: the North, dominated by descendants of the early Lwo, evolving a singular historical tradition centering on the Mukama figure, and living in a world in which the Lwo pastoral contribution

[1] See MAP I.

was still marked; and the South, dominated by its associations with and through Lake Victoria, with rule in the hands of groups either associated with the Kintu figure or with processes similar to the back-wash experience from which the Kintu figure appears to have emerged.[2]

The Geographical Setting

Busoga District encompasses some 3,709 square miles of land area, and within this area two geographical zones are distinguishable. To a large extent these zones replicate the pre-nineteenth-century division of Busoga. The southern zone is dissected by a myriad of swampy valleys and streams. A number of hill-peaks reach 700 or 800 feet above the floors of the valleys. Apart from these more distinctive peaks, the country is dominated by the monotonous repetition of lower flat-topped hills marked off by the valleys and streams into nearly distinct tracts, most between two and six square miles in land area.

The northern zone is considerably larger than the southern and is flatter by comparison. Hills rise some 250 feet above the valley floors. There are a few hill-peaks and rocky outcrops, conspicuous by their rarity. Several rivers—among them the Naigombwa, the Kiko, the Lumbuye, and the Kitumbezi—divide the northern zone into large areas. These areas are, in turn, dissected by valleys and streams which cut off tracts of between fifteen and sixty square miles each. The physiographic features of both zones have a base elevation of between 3,400 and 3,600 feet above sea level, and both form part of wider physiographic regions.

Busoga is nearly completely surrounded by water, and the swampy shorelines along the Mpologoma River, Lake Victoria, and Lake Kyoga hinder communication with neighbouring lands to the north, east, and south. Floating papyrus islands give an ever-changing pro-file to the Mpologoma River and Lake Kyoga and occasionally clog parts of the Mpologoma system. While the river banks and lake shores are ill-defined swampland, there are occasional points of firm land where landings may be made and where ferriage is possible.

The mean annual rainfall is generally uniform throughout Busoga:

---

[2] In the nineteenth century, this earlier frontier between South and North—a frontier in terms of culture, tradition, population and political ethos—was eroded. A second volume on the pre-colonial history of Busoga will consider the after-math of the 'cataclysms' and the tumultuous changes evidenced in Busoga during the nineteenth century.

between forty and sixty inches a year. Significant year-to-year variations are uncommon and thirty-three or more inches of rainfall can
be expected in nine years out of ten.[3] The southern zone and the
southern margin of the northern zone are favoured by a more even
distribution of rainfall throughout the year. The northern zone and
the very south-eastern corner of present-day Busoga are faced with a
less favourable month-to-month distribution of rainfall, and a deficiency of effective moisture is a regular problem in the dry seasons.
Throughout Busoga the season of heaviest rains runs from March to
May, and there is a season of lesser rains between August and
December.

Located to the west of Busoga are the eastern counties of Buganda:
Bugerere County (formerly Bulondoganyi) to the north and Kyaggwe
County to the south. The Ssezibwa, a great swampy river flowing
parallel to the Nile, separates north-eastern Buganda from the central
Buganda region. The southern area is dominated by the vast Mabira,
a tropical forest which continues across the Nile into south-western
Busoga. A series of outstanding ridges just south of the Mabira flanks
the Lake Victoria coast.

To the south of the Busoga mainland are the numerous islands of
Lake Victoria, among the largest of which are Buvuma, Sigulu
[Kigulu], and Bugaya. The islands form part of an archipelago
stretching west to the Ssese Islands and east to the Nyanza coast of
Kenya.

To the east of Busoga is Bukedi district, encompassing present-day
Samia-Bugwe, West Budama, Bunyole, Budaka-Bugwere, and Pallisa
Counties. In topography and in rainfall distribution, Bukedi re-
sembles the northern zone of Busoga, though Bukedi is dissected by
rivers flowing westwards rather than northwards. Further east, the
land rises in fertile, natural terraces to the top of Mount Elgon
(14,178 feet).

The Traditional Economy

Basoga say, 'The hoe is my mother,'[4] and hoe cultivation has been
the principal subsistence activity. The environment is well suited to
such a way of life, and the banana is, in Busoga, the staple food. The

[3] David N. McMaster, *A Subsistence Crop Geography of Uganda* (Bude, Cornwall, England, 1962), pp. 13–16.
[4] 'Embago ni Mama', 'Selected Texts: Busoga Traditional History' [henceforth
referred to as STBTH], i, 20.

banana thrives where there is no harsh dry season and can, where there is a well-distributed annual rainfall, constitute a year-round staple.[5] In the central and southern part of Busoga the banana is able to thrive all year round. In the northern and south-eastern parts, where the dry season is drier, the banana has not been as important to the subsistence economy. Four general classes of banana are recognized—cooking [matooke], beer, roasting, and dessert. By-products of the plantain, such as leaves and fibres, were used in the making of all sorts of domestic articles.

An estimated date for the beginnings of banana cultivation in Busoga is difficult to establish. The banana has been associated with the expansion of Bantu speakers into the moister areas of southern, eastern, and central Africa, the beginnings of which have been dated to the first millennium A.D.[6] Soga traditions record a cataclysmic beginning for the banana. One popular theme relates that Kintu, the culture hero of Busoga and Buganda, carried the banana into Busoga from the east. The plant then became differentiated and spread from Bukyemanta in north-western Bukooli to the rest of the region.[7] Another tradition records that a fisherman in Lake Victoria found a banana shoot in his trap. His family, later called abaiseMugogo[8] after that plantain shoot, carried their discovery into the centre of Busoga from where it dispersed.[9] Both stories are very likely apochryphal; yet, as they are told, a relatively early presence of the plant in Busoga is suggested.[10]

Finger millet, or eleusine [bulo], is today a food of secondary importance in the areas of Busoga where the banana is favoured by

---

[5] McMaster, pp. 40–6.

[6] Roland Oliver, 'The Problem of the Bantu Expansion', *Journal of African History*, vii, 3 (1966), 368–9. The expansion of the Bantu is discussed in greater depth below, Chapter III, pp. 73–77.

[7] 'Collected Texts: Busoga Traditional History' [henceforth referred to as CTBTH], Texts 15, 487, 509, 610.

[8] *Mugogo* = Mr. Shoot.

[9] CTBTH, Texts 381, 383. Y. K. Lubogo, *A History of Busoga* (Jinja, 1960) [hereafter, Lubogo], records a similar tradition though one which gives the credit to hunters rather than fishermen (pp. 154–6).

[10] The banana was probably not the earliest staple in Busoga. Lubogo (p. 153) asserts that millet cultivation preceded banana cultivation. This is seemingly supported by the drumbeat slogan, 'Kisendo produces quite enough millet', of the abaiseKisendo (STBTH, i, 100), an early group in the centre of Busoga. Bryan Kirwan ['Place Names, Proverbs, Idioms and Songs as a Check on Traditional History', *Prelude to East African History*, ed. Merrick Posnansky (London, 1966), pp. 161–3] makes a strong case for the proposition that millet preceded the plantain as a staple in the region.

year-round moisture; but in the other areas one or two crops of millet may be raised a year, and in these areas, millet is more prominent. Millet requires a good two or three months of rainfall during the first part of its four month growing season. The traditional sowing time is therefore just before the heavy rain season running from March to May with harvesting in June or July. Millet stores well and can later be made into porridge or beer. It is very likely that millet preceded the plantain as a staple and was at an earlier time more important in Busoga—particularly northern Busoga—than it is at present.

The cassava and sweet potato are today important food crops. They are New World plants and therefore of estimably recent introduction. Both are easily stored, and neither requires a well-distributed annual rainfall. In poorer areas, they have from time to time constituted staples, and everywhere they have been and are being used as reserves against famine. Like the banana, their cultivation requires little labour.

Various other foods, including numerous varieties of peas, beans, and nuts, were cultivated and are grown today.

Cattle have been a vital economic and cultural factor, particularly in the less densely settled areas of northern Busoga where the environment is less favourable to banana cultivation. The areas of intensive banana cultivation appear to correspond to the areas of tsetse infestation. While South Busoga provided an environment apparently deadly to cattle, the northern part of Busoga was safe, and there pastoral traditions and customs were strong.

Fishing was and is significant in the areas adjacent to the lakes and major rivers. Various types of fish were caught by hook and line, and basket-net, dried fish were and are traded into the interior areas and fishing traditions were significant among clans associated with the fishing life.

Salt was traditionally extracted from the filtrate of burned papyrus pulled up from swamps. There were a few salt licks, but there is no evidence of any long-distance salt trade as in other parts of Africa.

Few deposits of iron-ore or other metal-bearing ore appear to have been found or exploited in Busoga. Iron for making tools and weapons came from smelting sites outside Busoga.

Hunting, which was apparently done for both food and for protection, is, in the historical traditions of Busoga, frequently associated with state-foundation. These hunters are recalled as winning clients and followers through exhibiting unusual skill and through providing gifts of meat.

Crafts such as drum-making, pottery, blacksmithing, and canoe-building were, and still are, of importance, and were traditionally the guarded specialities of particular clans. The items which these craftsmen produced were trade items. Such crafts as basketry and house-building were not typically specialist activities but rather were undertaken by everyone, excluding members of royal families for whom these services were rendered by commoners.

Trading within Busoga, and in particular within the South, was, and is today, significant. A number of villages in South Busoga are remembered as pre–colonial markets, and trade extended from some of these across Lake Victoria to the islands and neighbouring lands.

Traditional Social Organization

There were two principal institutions of social organization in pre–colonial Busoga: the clan, encompassing relationships of blood; and the state, encompassing political relationships. The two institutions were not mutually exclusive.

Clans in Busoga at the beginning of the colonial period, as today, were dispersed and corporately weak, though clearly this was not always the case. The clan [*ekika*] in Busoga was a patrilineal descent group, including all those who recognized a common ancestor through male lines, even if unable to trace their genealogy right back to the common ancestor.[11] Every Musoga belonged to a clan and the facts of his birth determined his membership. A child, male or female, belonged to the father's clan. A man's sons and daughters and a man's son's children were fellow clansmen, while his wife and his daughter's children belonged to a different clan.

A person was prohibited from marrying a member of his or her own clan or of his or her mother's clan. Every clan had a totem, but the sameness of totem did not necessarily mean that the groups recognized any kinship unity, nor did the sameness of totem play a part in determining the limits of exogamy as with the Ganda clans.[12]

[11] Most of this discussion of social organization is in the past tense, but this does not necessarily mean that what is described no longer exists. The use of the past tense reflects the attempt to achieve a synthetic understanding of Busoga society at an approximate 1892 baseline—the year in which European agents became seriously involved in the affairs of the Busoga states.

[12] This view, based upon an examination of a number of marriages, contradicts Fallers, who writes, 'It is the common totem . . . which defines the limits of

What distinguished one clan from all others was the name of the clan ancestor.[13] For example, one clan was called abaiseMusuubo, meaning, 'those of the father Musuubo'. The clan name identified that particular kinship group as entirely independent of all other groups. A mwiseMusuubo [singular] could not marry someone who also recognized Musuubo as his clan's eponymous ancestor.

Today, there are some 220 clans of significant size in Busoga. All of these were represented in the Busoga area in 1892. There are, in addition, 100 or so clans that appear to have migrated to Busoga since 1892. The earlier clans may be divided into two groups: those of royal bearing—that is, those ruling states in Busoga; and the commoner or peasant clans. Today, the clans of Busoga vary in size from the abaiseNgobi ruling clan, which must number more than 50,000 kinsmen, to the small clans numbering as few as 500. Most of the Soga clans probably number between 1,000 and 3,000 persons.[14]

Because the typical clan became widely dispersed around Busoga, and beyond Busoga as well, effective and unified action by the whole clan was virtually inconceivable. But within the structure of the clan there were effective, localized sub-units. The Soga clan segmented into lineages called *nda*. The *nda* typically included those kinsmen who could trace their genealogies through the male line to a common ancestor. At the outset of the colonial era, these lineages clearly were not as effective as they once had been, but they were considerably less dispersed than the clan and often were confined to a single Soga state. At this organizational level, collective action was possible. Members could join together at important occasions such as the death of a male lineage mate. The funeral of a kinsman provided the moment when the lineage was responsible for the fair and legitimate passage of property, wives, and children of the deceased.

There are instances today of several lineages attempting to join together to resurrect a wider corporate kinship body at the clan level. Before the colonial era this was impossible, as clans could not easily collect together members living in different states. For all intents and

---

exogamy.' Lloyd A. Fallers, *Bantu Bureaucracy* (Chicago and London, 1965) pp. 65–6.

[13] Or his son or father, as we shall see below.

[14] These are estimates. There has been no census by clan. The 1959 census reported 660,507 persons resident in Busoga District. Of these, 470,006 were 'Basoga'. There were also 'Basoga' living outside the District, particularly in the districts to the east. The 1969 census provisionally records 897,644 persons, including "non-Basoga", residing in Busoga District.

purposes, clan segments which left the main body and migrated into a different state became separate clans. The earlier eponymous ancestor might soon be disregarded with a new clan evolving from the new lineage or family head. With the Pax Britannica that settled over the country after 1892, communications across state frontiers became possible. Some clans refound their former unity. Others, formerly united, did not choose to reconstruct their traditional unit. Others are still seeking lost kinsmen in the far reaches of the district.

By the beginning of the colonial period, the most functional structure within the institution of the clan was typically the shallow patrilineage. At this level, the kinship group was able to maintain a common residence. The shallow lineage generally encompassed three or four generations: a father, his sons, and their sons and unmarried daughters. People tied by blood preferred to live close to one another. Land was relatively plentiful in the earliest times and the kin group, perhaps growing generation by generation, could expand their settlements as their numbers increased. Today, mutual defence and support are less important—individual enterprise more so—and the kin group living together tends to be even shallower.

Today, the activities of many clans are regulated by a hierarchy of clan officials. Many of these hierarchies were established in this century. Two types of hierarchy may be distinguished. One, which might be called the *authentic*, was constructed on the traditional framework of lineage and sub-lineage, with each described lineage unit having its traditional head. The other, the *inauthentic*, was constructed according to the plan of the modern administrative framework of Busoga, with the clan officials appointed to serve as clan heads at county, sub-county, and parish levels. A clan official's real importance has always been proportional to the corporateness of the group which he headed. Today, the inauthentic hierarchy tends to confuse the clan's functional organization, particularly at times when decisions relating to succession must be made.

Permanent cleavages in clans, whereby one clan became two, were apparently not uncommon. These cleavages can be traced to several causes. There are examples of cleavage resulting from infractions of the rule of exogamy. In order to safeguard, in the ritual sense, the clansmen and their descendants, the predicament was often resolved through recognition of the emergence of a new clan out of the chaos of alleged incest. Some cleavages occurred as a consequence of the migration of lineage segments into different states from that in which the main body resided, with the resultant difficulty of maintaining communications between the segments and the main lineage. The breakdown in contact among dispersed segments could lead to a complete breakdown in mutual corporateness. Fallers has given two reasons for such clan dispersal: the fertility of the land and consequent over-population; and the magnetism of rulers drawing sons-in-law and clients into their realms.[15] At times, cleavage occurred when a member of a lineage achieved great wealth and distinction; his descendants might remember him vividly and forget the former eponymous founder and, as a consequence, recognize an exclusive corporateness encompassing only the descendants of the wealthy and distinguished lineage head.

When a clan underwent cleavage, the new clan usually preserved the former totem. While there are some 220 significant clans in Busoga today, there are only some seventy different totems. Several clans may therefore have the same totem, and, while cleavage may explain some of these cases of clans having similar totems, cleavage does not explain them all; in a number of cases, clans with the same totems record entirely different 'origins'.[16]

While kinship arrangements often led to the fragmentation of clans, marriage functioned to establish links between kinship groups. Marriage was traditionally arranged by fathers and brothers of the boy and girl, and elopement, though common, was not considered the ideal approach to marriage.[17] The marriage was sealed with the payment of a bride-price by the bridegroom's family to the bride's family. This functioned both as a legitimization of the marriage and as an indemnity, an incentive for both groups to strive to support the marriage link. The bride-price was usually returned in the event of a separation. Besides the bride-price, the bridegroom had many continuing responsibilities to assist his wife's kin group. Although he could never be a member of his wife's clan, he could be called upon for help by any of his wife's kin. One generation below, a child had a special relationship with his or her mother's kinship group, though

[15] Fallers, pp. 65–6.

[16] The 'origins' of a clan can only be a relative designation. Most of the 'origins' of the Soga clans are traceable only within the Interlacustrine region, and in many cases, only within a small part of the region. There are certainly deeper origins which are much more difficult to trace.

[17] Elopement is mentioned as common in some early ethnographic works on Busoga: John Roscoe, *The Northern Bantu* (Cambridge, 1915), pp. 209–10; and J. F. Cunningham, *Uganda and its Peoples* (London, 1905), pp. 112–14.

the child was never a member of the mother's clan. The child played a crucial role in the funeral rites and burial of a member of the child's mother's clan.

For any clan, the marriage of a female member enlarged the body of men outside the clan whom they could rally in time of need. This was significant in respect to commoner clans and vital to the ruling clans.

Polygyny was the ideal marriage arrangement in Busoga, and the ideal form of polygyny was for a man to have as many wives as possible. In commoner marriages, the husband tended to try to strengthen the tie between his clan and his wife's clan by taking as his second wife the sister of the first. For a chief, marriage was a means of forging non-political links with the population at large. The chief's wives rallied their kinsmen to the side of the ruler. The possibility of a wife and her kinsmen being 'mother' to a successor ruler was of paramount importance to peasant groups in Busoga, as in Buganda, where it was at the same time the *raison d'être* and possible apex of a clan's organizing efforts within the political context.

Crucial to the maintenance of the lineage was the complex system of succession and inheritance. At the funeral of a married man, the lineage members gathered together, not only to celebrate the funeral rites, but also to ensure the legitimate passage of the deceased's property, home, and family. In Busoga, there were two successors: the *musika ow'enkoba*, 'the heir of the belt'; and the *musika ow'embisi*, 'the property heir'.[18] The *musika ow'enkoba* became the guardian of the deceased's immediate family and was expected to take the widow as his wife. He took over the belt, the spear, the stool, the *kanzu* [robe], and other symbols of the deceased, and he filled the role of the deceased in most situations. The *musika ow'enkoba* was a younger brother, whether collateral or real, of the deceased. The Soga kinship system was a classificatory one—kinship terms being applied to groups of kin on a collateral basis, cutting across family lines. One of the more important elements of the Soga kinship system was the classificatory arrangement of siblings. With the *ow'enkoba* succession, the deceased was succeeded by his immediate younger brother. The younger brother was in turn succeeded by *his* younger brother. When one immediate sibling group was exhausted, it was succeeded by its junior collateral sibling group; that is, the sons of the next younger

[18] Fallers calls *ow'embisi* the *musika atwala ebintu*, 'the heir who takes the things'. Fallers, p. 90.

brother of the last deceased's father. Within this junior sibling group, the eldest brother was the first successor, followed by his younger brother and so on right through the generation of collateral sibling groups and collateral brothers. When the generation of siblings ran out, or at least when no more junior collateral sibling groups could be found (and finding them under dispersed conditions was difficult), succession passed to the next generation and to the eldest sibling group in that generation; that is, the eldest son of the eldest sibling of the eldest sibling group of the preceding generation. When a sibling died before the responsibility of succeeding fell upon his shoulders, the deceased was succeeded by his younger brother, even though an elder brother or elder sibling groups might still be living. Succession eventually passed over the deceased collateral brothers to the living ones. In Busoga, when a married man died, it was said, 'He has broken the home.' It was this system of ow'enkoba succession which functioned to mend and maintain the 'home' of the deceased.

This musika ow'enkoba was not the property heir of the deceased; he took the symbols of his succession and his adopted family to his own home. The property of the deceased, typically land and livestock (and today, money and store-bought goods), went to the musika ow'embisi or musika atwala ebintu, usually a son of the deceased. The lineage members attending the funeral were responsible for the passage of this property to a son, generally the eldest. If there were no son, they chose a property successor from among the deceased's brothers. They might also carry through or reject a testament if the deceased had uttered one.

Thus in Busoga, succession and inheritance were, at least in the late nineteenth century, quite distinct. Family status passed horizontally, while land and livestock passed vertically. Fallers[19] suggests that this separation may have occurred in the late nineteenth century and may be attributed to the introduction of new trade goods from outside East Africa and to the emergence of a cash-crop economy. 'Perhaps in such situations individuals felt it desirable to preserve control of the new wealth within the direct line of descent rather than to see it dispersed throughout the wider lineage.'[20] Succession and inheritance may have earlier been a singular function, according to this hypothesis, with both passing collaterally; that is, following the present ow'enkoba pattern.

Fallers[21] has suggested that lineages might undergo fission when

[19] Fallers, pp. 90–2.   [20] ibid., p. 92.   [21] ibid., pp. 89–90.

the clansmen seeking the proper *musika ow'enkoba* excluded a lineage
from consideration, even when common descent was recognized.
This was more likely to happen when the appropriate successor was
not of an adjacent lineage but from the most distant collateral line.
Error in choosing the proper successor could also ignite intra-clan
conflict, but error did not itself cause clan cleavage. In this century,
the inauthentic hierarchy of clan officials has complicated the quest
for the proper successor lineage and has aroused considerable contention in a number of situations.[22]

Traditional Political Institutions

Before the colonial era, there existed no one political authority
having control over the whole of Busoga. Politically, Busoga was
parcelled into a number of independent chiefdoms or states. Lubogo
has listed forty-seven traditional states.[23] E. M. Woodward listed
forty-six states.[24] The present writer has been able to discern some
sixty-eight states which were significant before 1892.

In the southern part of Busoga, the area decimated by Sleeping
Sickness, the former state structures have been wiped away; yet this
was the area in which the greatest number of states existed. It is therefore difficult to offer a definitive analysis of the structure of these
states, as Fallers has done for the small Busambira state in the centre
of Busoga and the large Bulamogi state in the north-east.[25] While
some of these southern states clearly had their origins in the wake of
the arrivals of prestigious migrants, many apparently were little more
than transitional structures between clan organized polities and the
more complex state-types which Fallers has described.

The Soga states were in some ways similar to the Ganda and
Nyoro kingdoms. The royal clans of Busoga had the same proliferating and self-defeating characteristics as the Bito royal clan in Bunyoro, though the Soga royal houses were not endogamous. The Soga
peasant clans, like the Ganda clans, played a momentous role in the
royal succession struggles, the peasant clan supporting the candidacy
of their princely son-in-law.

---

[22] The dual succession system has frequently played havoc with dynastic succession; consequently, the problems of establishing dynastic chronologies are considerable. The problems of establishing a chronology for Busoga are discussed
below, in Chapter II, pp. 62–68.

[23] Lubogo, p. 4.   [24] *The Uganda Protectorate* (London, 1902), p. 42.

[25] Fallers, *Bantu Bureaucracy*. Bulamogi and Busambira were Fallers's two case
studies.

There are certain structural features and problems common to all the extant state structures in Busoga. Fallers has defined three principles around which the Soga states were traditionally organized: patrilineal kinship, ascribed status, and the patron-client relationship.[26] According to Fallers, 'The principle of ascribed rank set one patrilineal descent group—that of the ruler—above all others. Princes were, by birth, assigned higher status and an in-born fitness to rule.'[27] As in the kingdoms of western Uganda, a royal kinship group stood above the commoner clans in each state. The ruler was the representative of the royal clan, and, while all the princes of the royal clan had some of the ascribed status of the state ruler, the ruler's predominance was legitimized by the accession rites.

But ascribed status was not rulership. The ruler was constrained to delegate some of the authority which his status gave him. In Busoga, the ruler could delegate authority to his royal kinsmen—the princes—or he could delegate it to commoners. The bearers of delegated authority, whether princes or commoners, would find themselves within a hierarchical structure. At the highest level, the ruler appointed *bakungu* to administer territorial divisions or to serve in special palace posts, such as that of the *Kitukiro*,[28] the chief minister. In the larger states, the *bakungu* ruled over wide areas of the country. In the smaller states, the *bakungu* were village headmen and sub-village headmen, sometimes appointed by the ruler, sometimes appointed by a senior *mukungu*, and sometimes hereditary, with the ruler merely affirming the succession of an heir to the post. The various chiefs subordinate to the ruler formed a judicial hierarchy, ruled their local areas, gathered tribute for the ruler, and called men to war.

The ruler was a member of a clan and had certain obligations to his kinsmen. However, in delegating authority to a prince who shared his ascribed status, the ruler opened the way to secession. Secession was the most common pattern of state foundation in pre–colonial Busoga. The stronger Soga states managed to avoid princely secession through the distribution of important offices to commoner rather than royal groups. Lower level offices might then be given to princes who could be watched by their commoner superiors. While a few states managed to retain vitality and unity through such delegation of office, most Soga states experienced fragmentation resulting from the delegation of substantial authority to members of the royal

---

[26] Fallers, pp. 126–8.   [27] ibid., p. 126.
[28] In Luganda, *Katikkiro*.

family. In Buganda, by comparison, this problem was less acute. There was no true royal patriclan—the Kabaka belonged to his mother's clan and the relatively smaller group of princes was excluded from important political office. Their fates were most often sealed during the usually tense interval between the death of a Kabaka and the installation of a successor. While the royal princes of Buganda were eliminated, the royal clan in the typical Soga state proliferated. If the ruler could not balance and control the status and dormant power of these royal kinsmen, the result could only be a proliferation of states. In earlier periods, a proliferation of state-foundation typically meant colonization. Princes would occasionally leave the state centre to establish new polities outside the area over which the central ruler had firm control. In later years, and particularly in the nineteenth century, proliferation did not mean colonization, but rather disintegration. A state, well defined and limited by external factors, fragmented as a result of princes seceding from the centre. This delegation of authority to commoners which limited the opportunities for princely secession falls within the context of Fallers's third organizational principle, the 'patron-client relationship'.

This relationship between royal patron and commoner client, so crucial to the maintenance of the state, involved more than the delegation of authority. Marriage appears to have been an important factor linking ruler and commoner. Because in each state there was only one royal clan, the ruler, in respecting the limits of exogamy which prohibited him from marrying women from his own royal clan, was obliged to marry women from clans of commoner status. The alliances established out of these marriages set the ruler and his allied in-laws in a certain balance against the proliferating group of princes.

However, competitive commoner clans, each pressing the claims of their princely son-in-law, were, in a number of cases, the inciters of royal succession wars in Busoga. A commoner clan gained tremendous status, wealth and power by being the 'mothers' or in-laws of a ruler. In a succession dispute, a princely candidate expected open support from his mother's clan. A clan occasionally initiated a candidacy if it found that a daughter of the clan had produced a prince. This situation, in which the commoner clan had an enormous role in the succession struggles, very much parallels the situation in Buganda, where the mother of a prince and the mother's clan would constitute a political pressure group at times of royal succession,

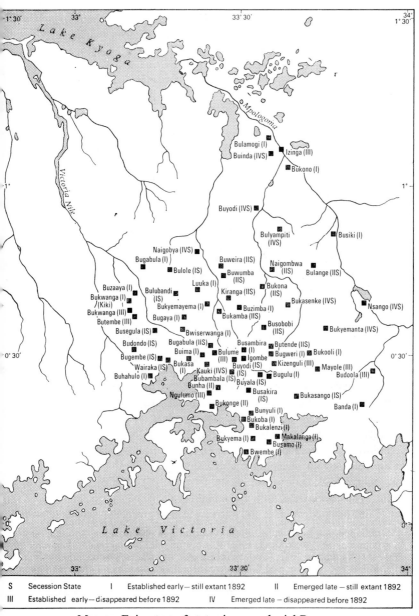

| S | Secession State | I | Established early – still extant 1892 | II | Emerged late – still extant 1892 |
| III | Established early – disappeared before 1892 | IV | Emerged late – disappeared before 1892 |

MAP II. Epicentres of states in pre-colonial Busoga

resorting to arms if the tension surrounding the succession dispute could not be resolved otherwise. This role of the mother's group is largely replicated in every Interlacustrine kingdom, particularly in respect to the important role played by the Queen-Mother in the royal court.[29]

The Control of Land

A critical point at which the institutions of state and clan intersected was in the assignment and control of land. There were several patterns of land control in pre–colonial Busoga. Every clan had at least one *butaka*, ancient clan land on which ancestors were buried. Typically, this was the site of an important clan shrine. This ancient *butaka* was often the place of primary settlement of a clan or family group in the Busoga area. The rights of the clan to that land were generally acknowledged by other groups, including ruling clans, who came into the area. If the clan group living on the *butaka* evidenced some fealty towards the ruler in whose sphere they found themselves, they were not deprived of their sacred place.

There was a second type of *butaka* which could become hereditary land, and this was an estate assigned by the ruler because of some great service to the court, or as a gift to a favourite in-law of the ruler. Such a *butaka* could not be taken away from the hereditary land-holders unless some great offence had been committed. The *butaka* lands of either origin were held by lineage groups and the *butaka* head [*omutaka*] status passed through the normal succession patterns of clan or lineage. The *butaka* land tenure system, though by no means the most common, was historically the most important pattern of land occupation because of the relative permanence of the holding. The *omutaka* could assign land within his estate and would do so after an acceptable applicant brought gifts. However, the *omutaka* took care to obtain the permission of the ruler or chief of the area before welcoming a stranger.

Another pattern of land control was more directly associated with

[29] Of the sixty-eight states which existed in Busoga before 1892, four general groups may be discerned: (1) states which were established early on, and which were still extant in 1892; (2) states which emerged relatively late, particularly in the nineteenth century, and which were still extant in 1892; (3) states which were independent polities from very early on, but which disappeared well before 1892; and (4) states which appeared at a relatively late date and which disappeared well before 1892. The locations of the sixty-eight states of pre–colonial Busoga may be identified by their epicentres, or points of initial emergence, and all the states may be classified according to the categories discussed above. See Map II.

the administrative organization of the state. The ruler, in a large sense, held his country as a *butaka*. He could distribute land and keep land as he wished. He could remove anyone from the land as he wished. In delegating political authority to princes and commoners, he distributed, in the same motion, the control of land. The distribution of land was one of the devices which the ruler manipulated in order to gain fealty from individuals and descent groups, thereby enhancing his power.

The appointment of princes would give them permanent rights to the land. Commoners, if appointed to territorial office, generally received administrative posts rather than permanent estates. These territorial chiefs were permitted to appoint underlings to assist in the administration, though often the sub-village [*kisoko*] chiefships came to constitute hereditary offices.[30] Their lineage held the office in virtual perpetuity, as long as fealty was paid to the higher administrative chiefs and to the ruler. The fact that a lineage held administrative control of a *kisoko* on a hereditary basis did not necessarily mean that they held the *kisoko* as a *butaka*. Non-kinsmen could settle in the *kisoko*, paying fealty and gifts to the *kisoko* chief. The *kisoko* chief had reason to press non-kinsmen to come to his village. Like the ruler of a state, he had the problem of dealing with his own kin group. By bringing non-kinsmen into his village, he could create a balance between his administrative responsibilities—collecting tax, gathering men for war, and so forth—and his responsibilities to his own kin living in his village. As in the case of the ruler, marriage could be a conduit for enticing a wife's kinsmen to settle in the *kisoko*; their special support, through the marriage link, enchanced the power of the *kisoko* chief. Other lineage groups could establish permanent rights to land in the *kisoko* so long as they respected the authority of the *kisoko* chief and gave him, and superior chiefs, occasional tribute. Both of these responsibilities could be fulfilled, as a matter of course, within the context of marriage.

Fallers has described how the prospective tenant sought his plot [*kibanja*] in the *kisoko*. He engaged a representative [*mukwenda*] to handle his dealings with the *kisoko* chief. The representative and the *kisoko* chief negotiated an allotment fee, which traditionally was symbolic, a hen or a barkcloth. The *kisoko* chief then sent his own

---

[30] Within a *mutala*, the rise of land between swamps, there were typically several *bisoko*. Each homestead in a *kisoko* was surrounded by its gardens and fallow land and the homesteads were spread out across the *kisoko*.

C

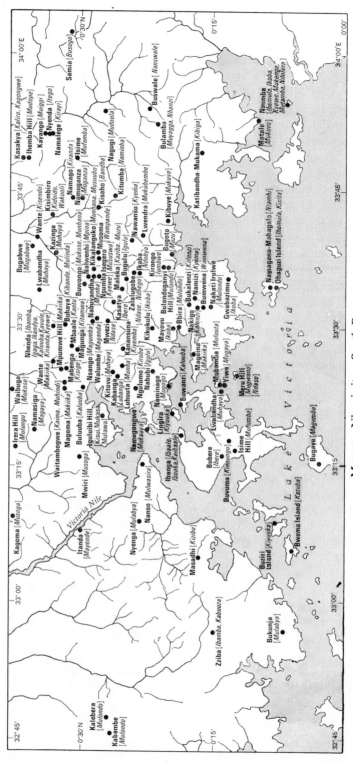

MAP III. Nkuni sites: South Busoga

representative [*mubaka*] to fix the boundaries of the assigned land. After the allotment fee had been paid, the tenant had rights to the *kibanja*[31] in perpetuity so long as he fulfilled his obligations within the traditional political system. The tenant or his successors forfeited the rights to the land if they did not maintain residence. If the tenant died and no heir was appointed by the lineage group, the tenant's lineage lost their rights in the land. Forfeited land went back to the *kisoko* chief for re-allocation. The tenant could not allot parts of his land to sub-tenants on a permanent basis.[32]

Permanent residence on the land gave a man the traditional status of *mutaka* ['man of the land'] no matter how the holding was obtained. The burial of ancestors on the land reinforced this permanent bond with the soil. But there was some difference between the ancient *butaka* and the assigned *kibanja* which could eventually achieve the status of *butaka*.

It was at the level of the *kisoko* or sub-village that the assignment of land was traditionally most common. The *kisoko* chief was, therefore, a vital link between the institutions of state and clan.

Traditional Religious Belief

In Busoga, when a man died, it was said that 'the spirit remained alive while the flesh rotted'.[33] These spirits [*mizimu*] of the dead were able to affect the lives of their descendants. They were usually malevolent. Every Musoga had to take proper care in the burial and remembrance of ancestors in order to placate their *mizimu*. Offerings were made when there were difficulties in the family which could be attributed to the malevolence of ancestors. The *mizimu* were respected only within the context of patrilineal kinship. They could not affect non-kinsmen. As well, distantly related ancestors were less likely to affect a living person than the ancestors of his lineage. Shrines were built and kept for the most important *mizimu* in each home.

Associated with the *mizimu* were the *nkuni*, typically the spirits of the first men of each clan arriving in Busoga. Nearly every clan had an *nkuni*, and the *nkuni* had a special dwelling place located where the clan first settled or first arrived in Busoga. In most clans, the

---

[31] This word is apparently of Nyoro derivation.
[32] Fallers, pp. 164–6.
[33] L. K. Bagimba, 'Emizimu, Emisambwa, Enkuuni, Ebisweezi, Balubaale', manuscript, CTBTH.

MAP IV. Nkuni sites: North-East Busoga

nkuni was worshipped as the creator of the clan. Clansmen went to the *nkuni* to make offerings at times of war and at times of need. The *nkuni* were generally beneficent. The *nkuni* might travel with clan segments as they dispersed to secondary settlement places within Busoga, but the primary *nkuni* site in Busoga was remembered as such.[34]

There were also the spirits of deceased rulers, the royal *mizimu*. Shrines were usually built to them. They were worshipped and consulted as state figures, and it was assumed that they had a deep concern for the preservation of the state. They were acknowledged by all the people living within the state, though particularly by the rulers.

There were also spirits called *misambwa*. A number of these spirits were of the dead, but of people more important to the country at large than were the *mizimu* or *nkuni*. They were thought to be the spirits of people who had lived on the Earth and who had displayed supernatural prowess. These *misambwa* had more power than the *mizimu* and were often associated with such important forces as fertility and death, and such important events as birth and marriage. The two most prominent *misambwa* were Kintu and Mukama, and sacrifices were taken to their shrines, found all over Busoga, at critical moments in one's life. In Busoga, whenever one settles in a new place, and before the erection of a house, a tree, the *omugaire-gaire gwa Kintu*, is planted as a dedication to Kintu. Any blemish or deformity associated with a new-born child is associated with the Mukama spirit. A third *musambwa*, Walumbe, is specifically associated with death.

There were, as well, 'older *misambwa*' which were not anthropomorphic but rather were the spirits found in stones, trees, wells, rivers, and hills. Some of these spirits were stationary, but others moved along rivers with reptiles. These spirits were consulted by local people in times of difficulty.

In Busoga, there were several means whereby a person could reach and communicate with the spirits. He could be possessed by ancestral spirits without the aid of a medium. For more important spirits, one required the services of a *musamize*, a medium. The *musamize* had

---

[34] The *nkuni* [*kunu*] was also significant among the Nilotic-speaking Padhola located to the east of Busoga. B. A. Ogot, *History of the Southern Luo*, p. 79. For location of clan *nkuni* sites in the Busoga area, see Maps III, IV, and V. The use of the *nkuni* data as historical evidence is discussed below, Chapter II, pp. 44–5.

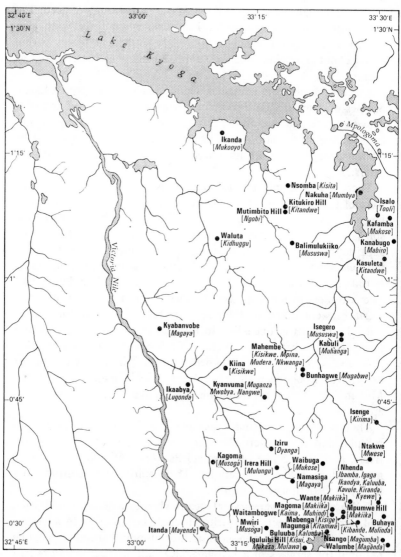

MAP V. Nkuni sites: North-West Busoga

no special skills, but it was generally acknowledged that he could be possessed by a neighbourhood or lineage spirit. A somewhat more professional medium was the *mulaguzi*, who was not only a medium but could diagnose the specific troubles at hand and could suggest a remedy to placate the particular bothersome spirit.

These *balaguzi* were the skilled practitioners of divination. Those people who were possessed by important spirits were called *basweezi*, and when it was learned that someone had become *musweezi*, the *balaguzi* went to him and taught him the skills of divination and mediumship. These *basweezi*, very likely related to the *Bachwezi* cult groups found in the western part of the Interlacustrine region, formed something of a corporate group. This was particularly so when a *musweezi* died and they came together to bury the deceased. They did not, however, constitute a formal cult such as that which emerged in western Uganda.

There was also the almighty god called *Kibumba* or *Gasani*. He played no role in the day-to-day earthly affairs of man. He was remembered as the Creator who set the most important figures upon the Earth.

Many of the important spirits worshipped in Busoga were referred to by the same names as deities worshipped in the Ssese Islands of Lake Victoria, in Buganda, Bunyoro, and in other parts of the Interlacustrine region.

Sorcerers [*balogo*] and herbalists [*basawo*] were also consulted in times of personal difficulty.

The Lusoga Language

Linguistically, the Basoga today are part of the Bantu-speaking world. Guthrie has placed Lusoga in Zone E of his classification of Bantu languages.[35] Zone E includes the Bantu languages spoken in the north-eastern part of the Bantu world—around Lake Victoria, central Kenya, north-eastern Tanzania, and along the Kenya coast. Guthrie places Lusoga within Group 10 of Zone E. Group 10 includes the languages spoken around the northern coast of Lake Victoria.

Busoga itself should be divided into two dialect zones. Across the northern part of Busoga, a dialect known as *Lupakooyo* was traditionally spoken. Lupakooyo perhaps resembled Lunyoro. It is probable that there was a belt of Lunyoro-associated dialects running east from

[35] Malcolm Guthrie, *The Classification of the Bantu Languages* (London, 1948 and 1967), pp. 42–6.

Bunyoro, across the northern region of present-day Buganda, across northern Busoga, and through Bugwere east of Busoga.

In the southern part of Busoga the dialect known as *Lutenga* was traditionally spoken. Related dialects were spoken in the Ssese Islands, Buvuma Islands, and eastern Buganda. All these dialects were apparently closely related to Luganda.

Both Lusoga dialects and the intermediate dialect spoken in the marginal area between them were characterized by prominent lisps. Robertson has attributed this lisp to the Soga practice of evulsing the four front teeth of the lower jaw, 'which gave their speech a curious lisping sound as if the tongue was swollen and filling the front of the mouth'.[36]

The Demography of Busoga

The colonial era in Busoga was marked by tremendous demographic upheavals. The recent population movements, evidently far more significant than movements before the colonial era, cannot be ignored, even in a study of pre–colonial history. In many cases, people have left their traditional lands. Some state structures have entirely disappeared. A number of clans and states have been decimated. Peoples have migrated into Busoga in large numbers in this century, carrying with them the traditions and cultures of other lands.

The most important causes of these movements have been the famines and epidemics which have occurred in Busoga and the surrounding areas in the past seventy-five years. A secondary cause, the development of commerce and industry, has stimulated a flow of population towards the towns and peri-urban areas.

In the late nineteenth century, one of the principal routes along which Europeans travelled from the Coast to Buganda passed through the southern part of Busoga. Sir Gerald Portal,[37] F. D. Lugard,[38] J. R. Macdonald,[39] and Bishop Tucker [40] all noted that the

---

[36] D. W. Robertson, *The Historical Considerations Contributing to the Soga System of Land Tenure* (Entebbe, Uganda, 1940), p. 2.

[37] Sir Gerald Portal, *The British Mission to Uganda* (London, 1894), p. 132.

[38] F. D. Lugard, *The Rise of Our East African Empire* (London, 1893), i. 366.

[39] J. R. Macdonald, *Soldiering and Surveying in British East Africa* (London, 1897), p. 133.

[40] A. R. Tucker, *Eighteen Years in Uganda and East Africa* (London, 1908), p. 209.

country was plentifully supplied with food and densely settled with people. Sir Harry Johnston described this southern area as the most densely populated part of Busoga.[41] However, in 1900–1, the first indications of Sleeping Sickness were reported from this southern region of Busoga. In 1906, orders were issued to evacuate the region. Despite the attempts to clear the area, the epidemic continued in force until 1910. As a result, the most densely populated part of Busoga, the homeland of perhaps 200,000 persons in the late nineteenth century, was totally cleared of population in ten years. South Busoga constituted about one-third of the land area of Busoga, and, in 1910, South Busoga was vacant. In the 1920s and 1930s, some of those evacuees who survived the epidemic began to return to their original lands. However, in 1940 a new outbreak of Sleeping Sickness struck the area, and it was only in 1956 that resettlement, this time promoted by the government, began again; but few Basoga returned to their traditional lands.[42]

The consequence of this catastrophe is that the southern part of Busoga, the area roughly corresponding to what Johnston delimited as the most densely populated area, is now virtually uninhabited. Other areas originally affected by Sleeping Sickness, including the eastern margins of Bukooli and Busiki Counties, have evidently been depopulated too.

Famines, too, have resulted in substantial population movements. Several areas in north-east Busoga and in the adjacent Bukedi district across the Mpologoma River were repeatedly struck by famines —1898–1900, 1907, 1908, 1917–18, and 1944—and the population in these affected areas has been reduced, many falling victim to the famines, others moving to areas considered safe.

One of the effects of these recent movements of population has been the apparent growth in population density in the central area of Busoga and in the urban and peri-urban areas of Busoga. As well, there has been a substantial influx of peoples whose antecedents were living east of Busoga before 1892. Basoga have left Busoga in the same colonial period, settling in other districts. The demographic profile of Busoga today is, as a consequence of all these developments, quite different from that of 1892.

[41] Sir Harry Johnston, *The Uganda Protectorate* (London: 1902), i. 248.

[42] A discussion of the problems and progress of resettlement schemes in southern Busoga can be found in: Susan J. Watts, 'The South Busoga Resettlement Scheme', *Occasional Paper No. 17, The Program of Eastern African Studies* (Syracuse, N. Y., April 1966).

The Memory of the Past

A prominent feature of Busoga and a determinative feature of the Busoga historical tradition was the complete absence of traditional officials or groups with the specialized functions of preserving and transmitting traditions, whether of state, clan, or lineage. While there were persons in a good position to observe and record particular events and in positions favourable to the transmission of the traditions to succeeding generations, this was in no way formalized nor did there exist any official obligation or directive to pass on the tradition to the next generation; rather, every man was the keeper and transmitter of traditions germane to his own community, family and self. Lines of transmission were sometimes regularized, with traditions uttered at special occasions—births, marriages, funerals, and investitures—and sometimes not, with traditions told and transmitted in casual conversation over camp fires and beer pots, from neighbour to neighbour, from kin to kin, and from stranger to stranger. Every home and every village, every family, lineage, and clan, every state and every office had its own body of tradition, and every person had his own body of knowledge of things past.

The historical tradition of Busoga thus seems a diffuse and amorphous lot: families, lineages, and clans, each with their own heritage; and sixty-eight states within the Busoga region, each with a recollected tradition of independent existence and action. Yet, in larger perspective, the historical tradition of Busoga parallels the historical experiences of the diverse groups which, in a myriad of integrative events, contributed ultimately to the building of a relatively distinct Soga culture and to the emergence of a unique Soga ethos. The building and preservation of an historical tradition in a society may parallel the streams of its social, religious, political, and intellectual development. Tradition, in Busoga, was not the flower of historical experience; rather, it was the necessary and ever-functional intelligence which defined one's place in ever-changing social currents.

The historian working in any field must take as a given the inequality of the content of a source and the thing described. The source only approaches a replication of the event; it cannot mirror the event in its entirety. The historical statement not only will reflect the observation or the interpretation which generates the source, but also will reflect the broader experience—the social, political, intellectual, and ideological milieu—of that observer or interpreter. Tradition, too, will at the same time reflect an image of the event and the milieu of the observer and the communicator. Of course, we probably know less about the initiator of a particular oral tradition relating an event some eight generations back than we do about the English diarist recording in ink his observations on an event of 1750. The page in the diarist's notebook survives not so much as a result of his wisdom, but rather as a consequence of the favourable physical composition of the paper on which he recorded his observations. Similarly, the oral tradition may have within it a substance—a meaning, a value, a purpose—which causes it to be preserved and transmitted from generation to generation. The tradition may record a marriage, or deed, or testament, or contribution of a family to some event of importance, or religious duty, or political obligation. These are vital facts. It is from such tradition that man comes to reckon his place in his family, in his community, in his society: his rights, his responsibilities, his laws, his debts, his assets. They are vital, and no important detail can be forgotten. If he attempts to discard some detail of importance, his neighbour, his brother, his client, or his patron may not forget it. One old man in the centre of Busoga has remarked, 'When an old person speaks a word, it becomes like a stone and is not forgotten.'[43]

The remembrance of the indispensable and the obliteration or decay of the obsolete are perhaps the most important of the determinants of a developing historical tradition. The historical tradition develops in parallel to the historical experience of the emerging society. This incapsulated historical tradition, fulfilling the needs of both the individual or family and the society at a particular moment, is forever prey to excision and revision to conform to the constant ferment and change. Yet the excision and revision may replicate the very alterations in the society; the circumstances of social change and upheaval may provide an indication of alterations in tradition, and the changes in the record of tradition may themselves reflect the changes in society.

[43] STBTH, i. p. 100.

CHAPTER II

Reconstructing the History of Busoga

THE diffuse and unwritten character of Soga tradition places an enormous distance between the evidence which the historian of Busoga has at hand and the conclusions which he may ultimately draw. In African history, conclusions are certainly no less important than in other fields of history. But the African historian's methodology—how he bridges the enormous gap between the available evidence and significant historical reconstruction—may be particularly crucial. Often the Africanist works in areas where there is little available material in which to find a foothold. More likely than not, his work will involve a good deal of primary research for oral tradition, sociological data, place-names, historical sites, and information of a similar nature. The very manner of his approach to this primary research may affect the quality of the information received.

At this stage in the development of the field of African history, the reader may not be able to find grand contexts in which to place the individual Africanist's narrow contribution and by which to judge the value of that contribution. It may be the methodology alone that can suggest to the critical reader the possible ultimate value of a pioneering contribution in an area where our understanding is still very fragmentary. For the problems of doing scholarly study in a very different culture from one's own are acute. A full disclosure of one's procedures and methodology should indicate how these problems were handled. Under these conditions, the historian must necessarily acknowledge that his methodology is critical at every stage of his study, from the primary search for materials to the subsequent analysis of the collected data.

If one can note a single advance over the earlier approaches to primary research in the field of African history, it is the present emphasis on strictly distinguishing between the process of collection and the process of analysis of primary evidence. The earlier recorders of African tradition, for example, failed to note the names of their sources or the character of their interviews or describe their general methodology, much less record the verbatim text of the testimony.

The collection of 'facts' was intertwined with the writing of history. In contrast, the African historian today finds himself an archive builder as much as an archive user. He is compelled by the present standards of his discipline not only to distinguish between the source and the interpretation, but also to leave behind him an accessible record of his research, hopefully in the form of annotated and edited transcripts or original sound recordings.

These two tasks—the collection of tradition and the analysis of evidence—correspond to the two distinct stages of involvement in this work of reconstructing the history of Busoga.

The Collection of Tradition

In terms of methodology, the collection of oral tradition in the field was the more critical of the two tasks. A comprehensive project of traditional history research is difficult to repeat[1] and therefore must be sound in the first instance. The very character of the informants and their testimony may be affected by an extensive research project. Informants may refuse to be interviewed on the grounds that research has been done before. In this, the problems of oral history parallel those of archaeology; the researcher contaminates and destroys as he attempts to uncover, recover, and salvage the remains of the past. The researcher, therefore, must be exceptionally careful and skilful in approaching the research project. Once the testimonies are collected, and an understanding of how they were collected is communicated, numerous attempts can be made to interpret and reinterpret the data, to build constructs, and to write histories. But it is unlikely that the actual comprehensive collection of historical tradition could be repeated.

In designing the research project, I was initially more concerned with the delimitation of an area of primary research than in constructing specific historical hypotheses for examination. A research area conforming closely to the political boundaries of present-day Busoga was established, yet I recognized that the history of Busoga was not exclusive, but that it would have to be seen against the backdrop of broader historical developments and upheavals in the Lake Victoria

---

[1] Of course, there have been previous research efforts in Busoga. But these were not comprehensive. Perhaps it should be said that 'a comprehensive project of traditional history research cannot be profitably undertaken twice in a single generation'. For a discussion of the existing material on Busoga history, see Bibliographical Note', below, pp. 204–6.

region. A period was designated stretching forward from the early Iron Age in the first millennium A.D. to 1892, the year of the opening of serious European involvement in the affairs of the Busoga states. While I avoided drafting specific hypotheses, several general areas for investigation were recognized. The first was the problem of the origins of the peoples of Busoga, their migrations, their first settlements, and their dispersals across Busoga. A second was the problem of the emergence and development of the political institutions of Busoga society, the origins and migrations of the royal families, the emergence and development of the Soga states. A third problem was how historical activity in Busoga was related to developments in the wider region. A fourth was how Busoga evolved, if it indeed evolved at all, into a distinct cultural area.

When I first reached the field, I soon learned that there would be few 'fixed texts' to collect in Busoga. Rather, the oral testimony would comprise loose collections of data and unstylized narrative. I found that there were no traditional officials or specialists responsible for the preservation and transmission of oral tradition. While Vansina had found such specialists in Rwanda to the west, in Busoga every person knew some material of historical interest. It became clear that if the traditional history of Busoga could be reconstructed, it would have to be built up from a large number of small pieces rather than from a small number of large pieces.

Fortunately, I found that there was little problem of contamination of the traditional sources by already published local histories. Of the people whom I interviewed, only one mentioned that Lubogo's book existed, another person having read him one chapter. Even generally well informed people had not heard that the book was published. The fact that it was published only in English and that its sale was unadvertized perhaps explains why the book is virtually unknown. Few people had heard of it, much less seen it, and I had the fortune of being able to consult it as a source yet was spared the anguish of dealing with it as a contaminator.

Whatever pretensions I might have had about my abilities to speak the local language, Lusoga, which is akin to Luganda, I still felt it absolutely necessary to have an interpreter to assist me in the field research, and finally found a junior secondary school teacher whose English and feel for translation were both good. We were able to criticize one another without destroying our working relationship; he

corrected my slips and apparently did not equate the alien researcher's difficulty with the language with any general deficiency in his
approach to the research project. Just under forty and looking and
acting much older, he was well able to bridge the gap in age between
the elderly informants and myself.

Once realizing that the sources in Busoga were myriad, I was confronted by the problem of selecting sources. I was, from the beginning, wary of the dangers of random or statistical samples and consensus in mass interviewing. Clearly, testimonies cannot be of equal
weight or veracity. During my first week in Uganda, I had the good
fortune to meet a carpentry teacher, L. K. Bagimba, who had broad-
cast about Busoga in Lusoga on Radio Uganda. He had taken an
interest in the origins and customs of the numerous clans of Busoga,
and he had attempted to build up a list of clans and their totems in a
series of radio programmes. Much of the material which he presented
on the air was inaccurate, and, as a result, he was bombarded with
letters containing corrections of his presentations and corrections of
his omissions. He lent me these letters, and from them I was able to
build a list of clans and totems, a list of clan elders and leaders, and a
list of the letter writers, all of whom by their interest in the pro-
gramme appeared to be potential sources for interview. The first list
of possible informants comprised about 100 names.

I decided that the most economical way to do the research was
county by county, of which there were eight in Busoga. I began in the
very easternmost county, Bukooli, and worked westwards. As I
worked in each county, I added more names to the list of possible
informants, both within the county being worked and in the other
counties. I moved on to a new county when the list for the previous
county was exhausted or when the possible informants left uninter-
viewed were so dispersed around the county that it was uneconomical
at this stage to attempt to reach them. As I worked in each successive
county, I obtained names of possible sources in the counties already
researched. I saved these names for later consideration. For the most
part, I went through all eight counties in this way, though occasionally I did work very intensively in a selected small area interviewing a
number of people more or less at random. With this approach, a good
number of interviews could be conducted in a single day as explanations of the research could be more or less omitted after the first
few interviews. People were generally extremely co-operative and
many sources came forward to ask to be interviewed. But there were

few places where this intensive approach seemed really worthwhile. The quality of these rather random sources, while on occasion surprisingly good, was not as high as that of the pre-considered informants. Nevertheless, this second approach did bring more clans into view than otherwise might have been found.

As the research progressed, I felt more able to be discriminating in the selection of informants. Certain regularities emerged. It became clear that the clan head and other clan officials had no better grasp of clan tradition than their fellow clansmen. Clan heads were often chosen because of their wealth. Occasionally, the clan head was 'elected' because he held a government post. Generally, the clan head was a man with a large home accessible to most of the people of his clan. The clan head, while typically not an expert on his clan's history, was usually able to supply data on the extent of, and changes in, clan organization in this century.

Although no specialists or officials responsible for the preservation and transmission of tradition were found, ideal types of informants on clan and royal history were perceived. The ideal informant on clan tradition usually lived where his forefathers had lived. He may have written down some of the details which his fathers had told him concerning the clan's heritage. He was old enough for the elders of his generation, or those of his father's generation, to have been adults in the pre–colonial period. An ideal informant on royal tradition was the son, or descendant of a son, of a ruler's favourite daughter who lived at the side of the ruler and moved about in and around the capital. He may have recognized no special responsibility to the royal clan at large concerning the traditions which he heard in court. In the context of Soga kinship practice, the daughter's son is an important figure and will be omitted from no deliberations. But he retains an extensive freedom of action and expression in respect to his mother's clan of birth. He may have taken a considerable interest in the history and activities of the ruler and the royal clan just because he was so close and yet not a member.

When I had completed interviewing all the names on the list in the eighth and last county, I returned to the first counties, doing second interviews of fruitful informants, catching possible sources that were missed the first time or were added to the list at a later date. In this way, each of the eight counties was visited a second time.

The first problem in the interview session was to dispel any suspicions about myself and the research, to convince the prospective informant that it was worthwhile to contribute as much as he knew, and to explain the general format of the interview and the intended use of a tape recorder.

I had made my base in Busoga at a well known girls' junior secondary boarding school where my wife had secured a teaching position. Many of the informants' young relatives attended the school, and this connection with the district proved to be helpful in breaking down suspicions about my work. I found that many Basoga were interested in history, that they appreciated the complexity of Soga history, and were satisfied, if not pleased, that an attempt was being made to clear up the 'confusion' about the many clans and states in their country. I felt well received, and, usually, little convincing was required. When a prospective informant would refuse to speak at a first meeting and requested an interview at a later date, he would generally prove to be a dry source or would not appear at the appointed time and place. Eventually, I decided to avoid deferment of the first interview, even if it meant abandoning a possible source after some contact had been made. If the informant were not willing to present some testimony at the first meeting, his name was removed from the list of possible informants. Appointments for second or third interviews were made with initially productive informants, and these invariably were kept and usually proved fruitful.

I was surprised that the tape recorder was so easily accepted. Little explanation was required. It was usually only a matter of switching on the machine after a brief remark and acknowledgement. Some informants were enthusiastic about the recorder when it was explained that no mistake would be made with their testimony; it would record their words without misquoting. I considered from the beginning that the verbatim recording of interviews was important in spite of the loose character of the testimony. Approximately 200 interviews were recorded on tape. The exceptions[2] were a few complete interviews and sections of a few other interviews where there were technical difficulties with the recorder: end of tape, too much extraneous noise, or dead batteries. Occasionally, the infirmity of an informant made it necessary (or more simple) to record the interview word by word on paper. My assistant and I always took notes during the interview, and these were referred to as the interview progressed.

After encouraging the prospective informant to tell as much as he

---

[2] Besides the questionnaires, which are discussed below, pp. 35–6.

D

was able, my assistant or I explained the general range of data in which we were interested. We explained that it would be preferable if the informant spoke freely at first, with questions saved for the end. From this point, the interview began, the informant usually beginning with his name, the name of his clan, the clan totem, migrational history, and genealogical data. These narratives sometimes ran for a minute or less, occasionally for as long as an hour, and once for two hours. No narrative form or style was discernible. When the informant stopped or wandered too far from the point of the interview, a general question was posed which might recommence the narrative. When he appeared unable or unwilling to carry on without questions, the question and answer part of the session began. A large body of questions was developed in the course of the research, and my assistant and I tried constantly to improve the phrasing of these questions so as to avoid leading or confusing the informant. Some of these questions were intended to elicit information left untouched in the narrative testimony: perhaps the explanation of a clan drumbeat slogan, information about the rulers of the area, data on traditional iron-working or other crafts, the procurement of salt, and trade. Some were intended to clarify or enlarge points made in the narrative. The most significant of these concerned movements of clans and families, movements often described only in vague terms in the narrative. Another problem requiring clarification concerned the presentation of genealogies. These were sometimes presented with apparent contradiction, or they were only presented to a very shallow depth. Genealogies were usually clarified in the questioning, though sometimes they became more confused.

The interview was concluded with questions about other possible sources in the informant's clan or neighbourhood. A few questions were usually asked which would elicit information on the extent of clan organization and clan corporateness at the time of the interview. Biographical data concerning the informant and his family were recorded. The date and place and any unusual circumstances of the interview were noted.

I made it a point not to pay informants. Putting the research on a commercial basis where such was not necessary would have damaged the project. The credibility of all paid informants would have been in doubt. Fabrication would have been rife. Only two possible sources demanded payment and they, accordingly, were not interviewed. I did leave gifts of tea and sugar in conformance with the local etiquette of visiting. I also took photographs of the informant at the conclusion of the interview and gave prints if and when I returned for a second or third time.

In Busoga, I made a methodological decision against group interviewing.[3] In Busoga, a group interview, at best, could only be a session in which various people come together and prepare, among themselves, a consensus text to present to the interviewer. The effect of this procedure would have been to leave in the hands of the informants the task of evaluating the tradition against other versions of the tradition. It is the historian's task and not the informant's to weigh and compare variants of a tradition and to consider the tradition against what he knows about the individual informant.

In Busoga, I faced the problems of an organized group interview of one royal clan, and when this ordeal concluded I decided to avoid the group interview and interviewed two people together only when they were very close agnates. Of the more than 900 interviews and questionnaires, all but about eight were of single informants.

I was concerned about the possibility of not getting data on some of the dispersed clans in Busoga. There was no existing comprehensive list of Soga clans. For some young boys, it has been something of a game to compile a list of 'all the Soga clans'. Most such lists comprised between 120 and 160 clans. As there was no way of constructing an authoritative list without involving the local government in the research, I decided to use a questionnaire. I did not attempt this until I was completely satisfied with the questions used in the tape-recorded interviews. The questionnaire included some forty-six questions.[4] The questions were translated into Lusoga, and the questionnaire was reproduced. Three assistants were hired, one working full-time and the other two working part-time. They were instructed on the use of the questionnaire and on the desirable approach to the prospective informants. In their introductions to each informant, they explained the purposes of the questionnaire project, emphasizing the non-governmental and non-commercial character of the work.

Four different areas of Busoga were fairly intensively covered with some 700 questionnaires. One area selected was the Budondo-Lubanhi part of Butembe-Bunya County. This area had been densely

---

[3] In some parts of Africa, a tradition may properly belong to a group in the sense that the tradition was passed to the group as a collective entity, and, in this case, the group interview would seem to be a viable proposition.

[4] See Appendix A, pp. 197–9.

re-populated over the previous fifty years and appeared to be the most heterogeneous, in terms of clans, of any area in Busoga.

The second area was the Naminage part of Bugabula County, the most densely settled area of Busoga apart from towns and peri-urban areas.

The third area selected for the questionnaire work was Bulamogi County where my own interviewing was made difficult by the widespread view that I should collect a single historical text from a large meeting headed by the traditional ruler of the Bulamogi state.

The fourth area selected was Busiki County. Busiki is located in north-east Busoga along the Mpologoma River, which marks the frontier between Busoga and Bukedi districts. There has been a substantial movement of people from the east to Busiki over the past 100 years, and a study of clans in Busiki today would include a large number of clans from the areas to the east of Busoga where I did not do research. Also, many clans in Busiki today are represented in Bulamogi as well.

When I undertook the second round of visits to each of the eight counties, I checked a number of the interviews carried out by the assistants using the questionnaire forms, and several of the questionnaires led to more thorough interviews. These questionnaires not only produced a considerable volume of data on clans missed during the first round of research, but also provided further data on clans otherwise researched.

Some investigation was incidental to the main task of interviewing. Landmarks were visited. These included places where royal families had arrived in Busoga, capital sites, *nkuni* shrines,[5] and clan and royal graves which were infrequently marked. I attempted to obtain a testimony in conjunction with a visit to a site of significance. Usually, the only way to find such sites was from spoken testimony; the climate leaves few visible remains of the past. A rider in the automobile might point out a stone or a battlefield of significance. Chance meetings such as these often evolved into important interview sessions. I also learned of many local variations in culture by asking questions constantly of my assistants and of people whom I met casually in the course of the work.

In the course of the interviewing work, I came across a considerable volume of material of a written nature. Notes had been penned

[5] These usually mark the site of first settlement of a clan in the Busoga area. See above, pp. 19–20, and below, pp. 44–5.

on the histories of various clans. One 'History of Busoga' was found in notebook form,[6] and I was able to photograph this work and to learn how it had been written. There were also a number of 'clan books'. These were often referred to in the interviews: 'You should see so-and-so. He has the clan book.' In many cases, this referred to the person who had brought a notebook to a clan meeting and had put a few words into it. Chasing down these clan books was often exasperating and discouraging. However, I did find a few very impressive handwritten volumes on particular clans. One constituted the product of a research effort which a petty government chief had made in the first two decades of this century.[7] This man, Y. K. Kabali, traced the lineages of his clan, not a small one, back some ten to fifteen generations. His two volumes appear to deserve the claim that they contain the name and genealogical position of every male clansman who lived during more than ten generations and who produced male offspring (and a good number who produced no offspring). A number of other notebooks which I saw purport to do the same thing but not to the scale and to the thoroughness of the Kabali book. I photographed many of these clan books, or sections of them, when allowed to do so, and they together form about 500 pages of text.

For researchers of primary data in whatever field, the decision when to stop research is an important and difficult one to make. Originally, I had projected working right through most of 1967, but by the end of 1966, I began to feel that the research was at the point of diminishing returns. I had finished the second visits to each county and had been around a third time to a number of areas of Busoga. The possible informants remaining on the list became fewer and fewer. More and more, I found that 'possibles' suggested by informants had already been interviewed. Those remaining on the list of possibles were so dispersed as to make it uneconomical to reach them. More and more testimony was becoming repetitive in content. The questionnaires appeared to have elicited much more useful data than had previously been expected. All these factors fell together, and the decision was made to halt research in January 1967.

In all, I had recorded some 150 to 200 hours of testimony. I had

[6] Daudi Waiswa, 'History of Busoga', manuscript kept by author at Kabira, Nabitende, Kigulu County, Busoga; translation by present writer may be found in CTBTH.

[7] Y. K. Kabali, 'Book of the abaiseMusuubo', volumes kept by author at Nawandio, Bugabula County, Busoga.

hired one full-time assistant to do nothing but transcription. He worked concurrently with the interviewing. On the average, it required five hours to transcribe one hour of tape recording. I checked over each transcription both against the tape and against the notes taken during the interviews. I then typed the transcriptions. Usually the transcriptions were through the typing stage within ten days of the interview. The next stage was that of translation, which either my interpreter-assistant or I worked on during spare time. The work of translation fell far behind the rest of the work, and so a secondary school student was hired for one month towards the end of the research period to work on nothing but translations. I checked over each translation, and this was later typed. The questionnaires were also translated and typed.

This collection of translated texts was then annotated. Place-names were given precise references. Individuals in the texts were identified. Lusoga proverbs and drumbeat slogans were explained. Significant points were cross-referenced where possible. The resultant annotated collection constitutes 'Collected Texts, Busoga Traditional History', the major archive for the reconstruction of the history of the Busoga region in pre–colonial times.[8]

The Interpretation and Analysis of the Traditional Texts

Basic to any interpretation or analysis of the traditional texts is a general understanding of the character of the traditional material and the patterns of transmission of these records from the past into the present. Two determinative features stand out. First, there were, in Busoga, no traditional officials or groups with the specialized functions of preserving and transmitting traditions, whether of clan or of state. There were figures who were obviously in a good position to record or generate particular traditions and who were in a position

---

[8] Preparation of three volumes of these collected texts, entitled 'Selected Texts: Busoga Traditional History' [STBTH], has been completed. The selections include the more important testimonies together constituting approximately one quarter of the whole archive. These volumes have been deposited in the library of Indiana University, the library of the School of Oriental and African Studies, London University, and the Makerere University Library, Kampala, Uganda. Microfilms of these volumes are available from the CAMP Project Center for Research Libraries, 5721 Cottage Grove Avenue, Chicago, Illinois, 60637, U.S.A.

A selection of the Soga texts is to be published by the Clarendon Press under the title *Historical Texts of Busoga, Uganda.* The whole archive—'Collected Texts: Busoga Traditional History' [CTBTH]—will eventually be made available in microfilm.

favourable to the passing on of the tradition to the next generation. But this was in no way formalized nor did there exist any official obligation or directive to pass on the tradition to the next generation.

The second feature of Soga traditions is that they are, with few exceptions, in free, or unfixed, form. The exceptions are proverbs, songs, riddles, and drumbeat slogans, all of which are structured in a way that form reinforces content. However, most of the texts are loose narratives or collections of assorted data. The testimonies which make up 'Collected Texts, Busoga Traditional History' are not formally structured, nor, for that matter, do they contain well-structured forms of narrative. Accordingly, for the work of evaluation and analysis, it is not the structural, literary, or fixed aspects of the material that must be emphasized, but the informational content of the testimonies.

It is possible to distinguish, in terms of informational content, a number of types of data, and it is useful to assess the significance of each type of data in respect to the reconstruction of Busoga history. Three classes of data types emerge. The first class comprises explicit types of data, overtly historical, immediately relevant to historical reconstruction. The second class comprises inexplicit types of data, the relevance of which to historical reconstruction is much less clear, requiring deeper analysis and examination in the light of other data. The third class comprises types of data which may be explicit or inexplicit.

Explicit types of data

1. Activities of clan figures. Most texts include some explicit data on the activities of antecedents of the informant. Often, memorable deeds of a particular clan are attributed to the clan founder. He is sometimes described as the leader of a major migration. The clan founder is always greatly respected and is usually the most important ancestor spirit worshipped by the members of a particular clan. Usually, information on the activities of a clan figure will bring him into relationship with other figures, other groups, or particular rulers. Such correlations are indispensable in the formulation of historical constructs.

2. Migrational routes. Information on the migrational routes of families, individuals, royal groups, and clans can be extremely significant. Besides pointing to 'origins', such data can relate migrating groups to other settlements and migrations, may suggest the penetration of new cultural elements, and may point to combined or differentiated migrations. The migrational route is usually recalled in terms of a list of place-names. These toponyms may not be close enough together geographically to allow for a precise reconstruction of a particular route, but, at a minimum, they may suggest a general route or direction. A close study of the purported routes through Busoga of Mukama, a Busoga folk hero and alleged king of Bunyoro, suggests that there was more than one Busoga journey of 'Mukama'. It also suggests that certain families which claim to have travelled with Mukama did not do so, and that certain groups making no such claim may very well have done so. Moreover, by subjecting the purported routes to a thorough analysis, a predominant route *does* emerge and is apparently the general route which a Mukama followed through Busoga. One must be somewhat wary of the toponymic points of reference on a route of migration. Many migrations obviously passed through 'uncharted' regions. Presumably, a toponym could be carried forth if some earlier group were resident there and had a name for the particular place which the migrants picked up, or if the migrants themselves settled there for a time and gave the place a name which may have gained general usage in the neighbourhood.

3. Manner of clan dispersal. Every clan in Busoga underwent some dispersal before the colonial period. Encompassed in these dispersals were many individual or group migrations. With rare exceptions, migration effectively meant dispersal. Such data often include references to conflicts which developed within the clan, or problems in a particular neighbourhood, perhaps causing dispersal. Dispersal data often include the names of the principal figures involved in the migration, the route taken, the place of secondary settlement, and the name of the chief ruling at the place of secondary settlement. Such data can also suggest whether an informant has learned information from a clan meeting. When a clan has had no general meetings, or when the informant has not attended or received information from the clan meeting, the informant would know only about the dispersal of his own clan segment and would know nothing about the dispersals of other segments dispersed around Busoga.

4. Activities of clan in relation to rulers. This is one of the more important categories of explicit data. A particular clan may have had special functions in relation to the rulers of a particular state. A clan may have filled special offices in the state structure or may have worked at a special craft. A clan may have supplied a girl to be the wife of a ruler, she perhaps later producing the successor. A clan may have gone to war in support of the ruler or in support of a pretender. Such data may relate a particular clansman to a particular chief, and this link may then be significant in the testing of other data and in the construction of a chronology. Often, such evidence may be helpful in explaining how a particular family obtained political control of the people resident in an area. Frequently, this type of evidence illuminates the traditional structures of state.

5. *Activities of state rulers.* The value of this type of data is self-evident. Information on the activities of state rulers may be related by a member of the royal clan, including the traditional ruler himself, or by a commoner. As told by the ruler or royal family, such information typically constitutes a charter of political power, and a good deal of falsification can be expected. Information on state rulers recorded from commoners may present a somewhat different picture, though all interested parties may agree on such details as where the rulers resided, where they were buried, whom they married, who their children were, and who their important functionaries were.

6. *Wars in Busoga.* There were numerous wars—inter-state and civil—in Busoga. They are important for historical reconstruction not merely because war *is* significant in any society's history, but also because it is the principal key one has for correlating the ruler of one state with the ruler of another, such linkage being crucial to the construction of a chronology. The best remembered details of any war tradition tend to be the names of the rulers involved in the conflict. Subsidiarily, the places of battle, individual outstanding warriors, the outcome of the battle, and the reasons for the battle are sometimes recalled.

7. *Activities of the Baganda in Busoga.* Explicit detail on Ganda activities in Busoga emerges from the traditional material from both Buganda and Busoga. During the nineteenth century, parties of Baganda pillaged Busoga, often for the sake of cattle and slaves, sometimes to replace an undesirable ruler of a Soga state. This type of data is particularly useful, not only suggesting the moments of political turmoil and weakness within particular Soga states, but also relating individual rulers in Busoga to contemporaneous rulers of Buganda. This is essential in the construction of a chronology for Busoga.

Inexplicit types of data

1. Totem. In Busoga, every clan has a *muziro*, a forbiddance, a totem. Many clans have a secondary totem [*kaibiro*] as well. The totem functions as a secondary feature in differentiating one clan from another. The primary differentiating feature is the clan name.

In Busoga, there is some information which each grown person is expected to know about his heritage. The totem is one element of this heritage. The totem, where it has not undergone change, may be one of the oldest marks of identification of an ethnic or kinship group. In the Busoga case, with some exceptions the totem appears to be older than the particular name by which the clan is known today. In some cases, the totem may immediately suggest relationships with groups outside Busoga. For example, the abaiseNdhego (a Soga clan) recognize the Civet Cat as their totem. In Buganda, there is a Civet Cat clan, clans in Buganda being known by their totems and not by their eponyms, as in Busoga. If one accepts that the totem is a fairly unchanging feature of a clan's heritage, a relationship is suggested. Coupled with other types of evidence, this suggestion of relationship between the abaiseNdhego of Busoga and the Civet Cat clan of Buganda may be confirmed.

There are a number of Bushbuck clans in Busoga, and the Bushbuck is the most common totem of the Nilotic Lwo groups that migrated south from the Sudan and which penetrated the Interlacustrine region. Again, considering other data, a relationship seems clear between the Bushbuck clans in Busoga and the Nilotic Lwo.

There are some indications that certain clans changed their totems. Occasionally, one finds evidence that a particular clan underwent fission and produced two effectively autonomous segments having different totems. There is the case of the abaiseMukuve-Isanga. This clan split into two parts with different totems, the abaiseMukuve with the Egret totem and the abaiseIsanga with the Guinea Fowl totem. From other evidence, the Egret would appear to be the parent totem, though the two may have been separate still earlier.

There are some examples of a clan not being in total agreement about its totem. Usually, the apparent cause of this is that a clan segment changed its totem for one reason or another and then, in this century, when the clan searched out its dispersed elements, the conflict over totem became known to the clan at large. A second cause of this seems to have been when a clan absorbed another kinship group, usually a runaway family. This occurred in several cases during the

upheavals in Buganda—over the two centuries before colonial rule—
when many families ran away to neighbouring countries. When this
absorbed family was of a totem different from its hosts, the two
totems might survive, both of them outlasting the tradition of absorption.

Difficulties over the clan totem may arise from simple confusion
over the meaning of the totem name. The clan members may not be
in agreement about just what species of animal or plant a name refers
to. From this point, the confusion may pass to the name itself.

The Civet Cat totem of the abaiseNdhego of Busoga has suggested
a relationship with the Civet Cat clan of Buganda. Within Busoga,
there are a number of clans with the Reedbuck totem. Does this suggest relationship? One could generalize from the evidence of totem
alone and assert: 'These twenty units are essentially independent sub-
clans of a major clan of the region.' But this assertion does not consider the possibility of altered totem; nor does it consider the historically significant questions of where and when and how the supposed
major clan became articulated. The totem, though significant, is only
one particle of the mass of data necessary for answering such questions or testing such hypotheses. The totem can suggest, but it cannot
provide the ultimate proof alone.

2. *Clan name.* The name of the clan in Busoga is its chief distinguishing feature, and the clan name is typically the name of the
founder of the clan. There are several cases in Busoga of different
clans having the same name, but this is probably due to coincidence
rather than to common ancestry. The problems which arise in working with the clan name are generally similar to those which arise with
the totem. The clan name may change, and this may occur when the
name of a prominent clansman displaces the older eponym. This may
or may not mean a change in the actual composition of the clan.
Older dispersed segments may not recognize the new name; however,
they may not recognize the newly named group as a kin group any-
way.

There are several examples of a clan submerging itself within
another clan to avoid extermination by a ruler. The original clan
name was not necessarily lost in such a case, although the name of the
protector clan was used during the period of crisis. In the colonial
period, the protected group may have re-emerged under the older
name. One example is the abaiseMususwa. This clan 'hid' among the
abaiseMusobya during a period of conflict in Bukooli following the

alleged murder of a ruler by a mwiseMususwa. In this century, the clan confidently emerged from 'hiding' and re-affirmed that they were abaiseMususwa and not abaiseMusobya.

The 'purity' of a clan's composition may be altered by the permanent absorption and assimilation of alien groups. This may not have been a common phenomenon. In some cases, such an occurrence is suggested by other evidence, and the fact of the absorption can be unveiled. In other cases, however, the absorption is suggested, but the manner of absorption cannot be established. The clan name, while it may differentiate functional kinship units, does not necessarily define true, genetic units. The clan name cannot be taken alone as historically absolute. It must be considered along with other data available for historical analysis. One must be particularly careful to assess whether a clan eponym corresponds to the name of the founder of the kinship group or whether the name may have been changed at some later date, with the concomitant repercussions on the clan composition that such a change in name could involve.

3. *Nkuni shrine*. The *nkuni* are the spirits of the first men of each clan which arrived in the Busoga area. Nearly every person remembers his clan's *nkuni*. The *nkuni* had, and in some cases still have, a special dwelling place, marked by a shrine, where the clan or *nkuni* first arrived in the area. Offerings were frequently brought to these shrines. The first settlement shrine is closely involved with the early land-holding patterns. The presence of an *nkuni* shrine gave a clan 'permanent' rights over the surrounding lands.

The *nkuni* shrine data are of tremendous value in historical reconstruction. They indicate the place of first settlement of the clan in the Busoga area. The *nkuni* is often the very name of the leader who settled at that place where the shrine was later established. An example is Bunalwenhi in Bugweri County. At Bunalwenhi is the *nkuni* Nalwenhi of the abaiseMpina. The shrine there is not kept up diligently because the area became depopulated as a result of Sleeping Sickness. However, it is still well remembered.

Where there are differences in *nkuni* shrine sites for a particular clan, differentiation of the clan or absorption of alien groups may be suggested. Clans often have secondary *nkuni* shrines but recognize these as secondary.[9] These shrines were established after a dispersed

---

[9] The typical Busoga area *nkuni* shrine may be merely one of a succession of ancestral settlement shrines stretching back into the far and indiscernible past, and the use of 'primary' and 'secondary' to identify those considered here is arbi-

segment settled in a new area and could not visit the original, primary *nkuni*.

In a few instances, several clans may recognize the same *nkuni*. At Kyanvuma, in Luuka County, is found the *nkuni* shrine of the abaise-Muganza, the abaiseMwebya, and a secondary *nkuni* of the abaise-Nangwe. Likewise, two or three clans may recognize similarly named *nkuni* spirits, while the shrines are located in different places. This may suggest an earlier association which can be tested with other data. Occasionally, a source asserts that his clan's *nkuni* is the husband or wife of another *nkuni*. This may suggest an earlier preferred marriage relationship, or actual marriage between the two groups.

The concept of *nkuni* exists outside Busoga. Ogot found the *kuni* as significant among the Padhola of eastern Uganda.[10] The origins of the *nkuni* concept are unclear, though it is an important type of evidence in the reconstruction of migrations and settlements.

4. Alignment of graves. Throughout most of Busoga, the alignment of the grave of a deceased person indicates the direction from which his clan came. For example, the grave of a mwiseIumbwe in Busoga faces Mukobe Hill in Butembe-Bunya County. The grave is dug so that one end points to Mukobe Hill. The corpse is placed in the grave with the head pointing towards Mukobe. The grave is filled, and a small mound is built up, with the head indicated by stones or by a raised level of earth.[11] At Mukobe Hill itself, the grave of a mwise-Iumbwe is aligned towards the east. Other evidence relates that the abaiseIumbwe came from the east and arrived in the area of Mukobe Hill from where they later dispersed. The usual explanation of this practice of grave alignment is that the spirit of the deceased must be directed back to the lands of his ancestors.

In Bulamogi County, commoner graves point in the same direction as the royal graves. This seems very much a part of an identifiable sub-culture which emerged around the Bulamogi rulers. In the Bulamogi case, the evidence of grave alignment is not, therefore, significant as evidence for the reconstruction of migrations and dispersals.

5. Canoe name. In some traditions, migrant groups are said to have passed across Lake Victoria by canoe. The names of the canoes are

---

trary. By 'primary', I refer to the earliest recollected shrine of each clan, which in most cases happens to be in Busoga or the near-surrounding areas. See Maps III, IV, and V.

[10] B. A. Ogot, *History of the Southern Luo*, pp. 79, 88.

[11] The commoner grave is generally left to deteriorate and within a few years it becomes unmarked.

often remembered. It appears that the canoe name is taken from the name of the tree from which the canoe, or its main keel, was shaped. Many trees are, and were, known by the names of spirits associated with them. The tree spirit became the spirit which accompanied and protected the canoe-borne travellers. A stereotypic story is common, a story relating that when the important canoe journey was completed a tree sprung up where the canoe was left to rot. The spirit that protected the travellers then became associated with the new tree, which was henceforth known by the spirit's name. There are some twenty-five different canoe names mentioned in the collected texts.

The canoe name may indicate the places where a particular journey commenced and ended, particularly the very place where the migrant group landed in the Busoga area. It may also associate groups which claim to have taken the same canoe. For example, there is a tradition that the abaiseKisige travelled from Buvuma Island in Lake Victoria to Buluuba in Butembe-Bunya County in a canoe called Mabenga.[12] Some abaiseKaluuba claim to have travelled in this canoe.[13] Another testimony records that the abaiseKisige came together with the abaise Kaluuba in the Mabenga canoe.[14] There is still another tradition that the abaiseKisige travelled in the Kasota canoe with the abaiseMuyobo.[15] And there is still another tradition that the abaiseKisige came in the Mabenga canoe, accompanying the abaiseKaluuba travelling in the Wambete canoe.[16] The unravelling of these differing traditions is dependent on an examination of other types of data—migrational routes and shrine sites—along with the canoe evidence.

In some instances, a number of clans all claim to have travelled in a single migrational group. Six different clans are associated with the canoe called Walukiriri, and some ten clans are associated with the Waiswa canoe. Does this mean that these clans travelled together? Groups may have travelled at different times in the same canoe. The life of a canoe was unlikely to be longer than 100 years, but the name of a particular canoe may have been revived at a later date. In attempting to group clans claiming to have migrated together in one canoe, one must also examine the routes taken and the explicit traditions of common travel. One must also be aware of the possibility that different clans claiming to have travelled together in the same canoe may have been one clan when the journey was actually made.

6. *Personal names.* Certain names or nicknames are often sugges-

---

[12] CTBTH, Texts, 162, 227.   [13] CTBTH, Text 164.
[14] CTBTH, Text 229.   [15] STBTH, i. 80.   [16] CTBTH, Text 162.

tive of personality, of an event in a particular person's life, or in the lifetimes of a person's parents. Names may, as well, suggest associations with other linguistic groups. Care, of course, must be taken that the name of a particular person considered is not merely recollective of the name of an earlier figure. It is useful to have some commentary which indicates the aptness and explains the meaning of a particular name. One ruler of the Bugweri state was called *Menha ow'eKibedi* or Menha Kibedi because he was so fat and physically helpless that a litter [*kibedi*] was required to carry him about.[17] The name *Banamwita* indicates that a child's father was killed. The name *Batabaire* indicates that a war was fought, usually just before the birth of the child who received the name. But if someone named Batabaire became very famous, the name would be passed down from generation to generation with the inspiration of the name becoming meaningless in respect to the later figures bearing the name. Such a case is that of Musuubo, a ruler who was known for his 'playing and swinging' [*Musuubo* = one who swings], and who purportedly lost his kingdom because he was inattentive to the tasks of chiefship.[18] The name has been passed down to various children right up to the present day.[19]

A name may suggest or indicate a relationship with a different ethnic or linguistic group. *Okali* is the recollected name of one of the early rulers of Bukooli. *Okali* is a Nilotic Lwo praise-name, and the possibility is thus raised that the Okali of Bukooli tradition was of Nilotic Lwo derivation. Other evidence supports this hypothesis.

Another important aspect of this problem of the application of personal names is the question of the names given by persons of a clan to their *baiwa*, the children of the daughters of the clan. For instance, every mwiseMutamba calls every son of a fellow clanswoman *Kagolo* and every daughter of a fellow clanswoman *Nakagolo*. *Baiwa* names may go back to the earliest times, perhaps earlier than most traditional evidence, as indicated by the fact that the same names are used by dispersed abaiseMutamba everywhere. Other evidence suggests that the abaiseMutamba were formerly called abaiseKagolo. It is common for the *baiwa* names to be similar to the names of very ancient clan figures. Occasionally, the *baiwa* names of a particular clan are similar to those of another clan, suggesting a possible early relationship between the two.

[17] STBTH, i. 131.   [18] STBTH, i. 125–6.

[19] And there was the late heir to the traditional office of Menha of Bugweri. His name was Kibedi, after his ancestor, but he was neither fat nor physically helpless.

7. Place-names. As with personal names, place-names can best be understood with an accompanying explanation. Some place-names are reminiscent of places occupied in the more distant past. Many of the place-names in Busoga come from the names of famed village headmen of the past. For example, Bunaibani in Busiki County comes from Naibani, the name of a village chief there. Some places are known by the names of *nkuni* spirits whose shrines are located there. Other names may be associated with an event which occurred there, or with everyday events in the neighbourhood. Namunhagwe in Busiki County is named after the pillaging of travellers which was apparently an everyday event there.[20]

Many place-names appear to be associated with proverbs or stories. Most of these are today apparently lost. The meanings or derivations of such names as *Bugwang'oma* ['where the drum fell'] cannot be explained by many people living near that place today. Explanatory commentaries on place-names are difficult to obtain.

8. Genealogical data. Genealogical data becomes basic to the construction of a chronology and the placing of events and persons in a chronological framework. There are really two categories of genealogies in Busoga: the royal or dynastic genealogies consisting of the names of rulers of states; and commoner genealogies consisting of the names of people in non-royal clans, as well as non-ruling lineages within ruling clans. More people than those directly involved are interested in the preservation of the genealogies of rulers, and complete genealogies can be ascertained and cross-referenced with other genealogies and other data. With commoner genealogies, only the descendants of those mentioned in the genealogy have any interest in the preservation of the genealogy. The conditions ensuring preservation are, then, partially absent in the case of the commoner genealogy. The problem of genealogy is complicated by the dual succession-inheritance system in Busoga and a fraternal and collateral succession pattern in many families.[21]

Genealogical evidence is typically presented in simple lineage form, the informant beginning with the founder of the lineage or clan and then naming his son and the son of his sons and so forth; or, the informant may begin with himself and name his father and then his father's father and so on.

When comparing associated genealogies, one must look for intro-

[20] From *kunhaga* = to pillage.
[21] For a discussion of this dual system, see above, pp. 10–12.

duced and reminiscent names. Where a name is present in one genealogy and absent in an associated genealogy, it is suggested that the particular name was introduced after one lineage had become separate from another. Where reminiscent names appear in two associated genealogies, it is suggested that they may have once been a united lineage. Where no names are similar between two possibly associated genealogies, it is suggested that either or both genealogies are inaccurate or that there is, and was, possibly no real association between the two lineages.

An important task in the construction of a chronology involves relating a person named in one genealogy through some event to a contemporaneous person named in another related, or unrelated, genealogy. A war or marriage or some other event may establish that two persons were contemporaries. This linkage is useful in both assessing the credibility of genealogies and constructing a chronology for Busoga history.[22]

9. Marriages. Another type of inexplicit data is information on the marriages of important figures. In many testimonies, the name, or at least the clan, of the wife of an early clan figure is indicated. In some cases, the marriage which is recalled is between the clan's *nkuni* figure and the *nkuni* figure of another clan. Royal marriages are recalled by the descendants of both parties to the marriage, particularly when the offspring of the marriage was a royal successor. In commoner marriages, the descendants of the husband are the ones who typically recall the details of the marriage.

Such data are important for the reconstruction of Busoga history for they can indicate when two clans have been in contact. Marriages were probably not contracted over great distances; therefore, it can be assumed that if two clans were parties to a marriage, they most likely lived in close proximity to one another. As well, marriage traditionally had an alliance function, and the details of marriage may suggest alliances among clans.

10. Trade. Trade was extensive in Busoga, particularly in the southern reaches, and along, around, and through Lake Victoria. There were specialized producers of goods, specialized areas of production, and a number of markets where goods were traded. Such data may suggest regular patterns of movement of groups, as well as relationships between groups. Important areas of production, or

---

[22] The problems of constructing a Busoga chronology are discussed below, pp. 62–8.

E

groups involved in production, may be suggested or indicated. Early centres of power may be indicated. General values in terms of foods and goods, as well as shortages and surpluses, may be indicated, permitting the construction of hypotheses on early subsistence patterns.

11. Deities. There is a considerable body of data on the deities respected or worshipped in Busoga. This type of data generally includes information on the shrine of the particular deity: who or what clan is (or was) responsible for keeping the shrine, where the shrine is located, the spiritual function with which the particular deity is associated, the earthly activities of the deity figure, and the relationship of the deity to other deities. Such evidence not only helps one to develop a comparative picture of traditional religion in the region, but may also help one to assess the possible historicity of a particular deity. A deity may have been a great earthly figure in former times. Information about such a figure could suggest, and possibly define, early dominant groups and political realms, ethnic group centres, and important migrations.

12. Birth and death customs. In Busoga, there appear to be certain variations from clan to clan and from area to area in birth and death customs. These variations may suggest different alien influences and diverse lines of development. It is difficult, in such a minute and heterogeneous area, to build any clear ethnological constructs with such data, but these crucial customs of birth and death may very well be part of the preserved heritage of the clan. One important variation is whether or not fish is prepared for the birth ceremonies, and if so, which kind of fish is prepared. Another variation is whether infants are bathed in milk at birth. Still another is whether a corpse is smeared with butter at the time of burial. Another is whether the important ceremony for a new-born child is held at any time, or is delayed until after the millet-growing season. Still another is how the placenta of an infant is buried. Some of these customs may be survivals from unique economic situations and from different environments and thereby may suggest the possible 'origins' of particular clans.

13. Material culture. Differentiated cultural effects and styles can be of significance for historical analysis, though only in the most general way. For instance, the *kinakyeri* is a drum found in the north-eastern Soga states and in the adjacent areas east of Busoga. This may suggest common or mutual influences in the area, influences that were largely absent from the rest of Busoga.

Differences in hoe or pottery types suggest that there was a northern Busoga cultural area and a southern Busoga cultural area, at least in terms of these items. This hypothesis is supported by other evidence, including the significant variations in origins of the ruling houses in the North and in the South.

In some cases, identities can be discerned in names and styles of certain items of regalia between one state and another, suggesting the possibility of common origins or common influences.

This type of data is less significant for intensive historical reconstruction than most other data types, both because it is often general in reference and because it is difficult to assess the extent of cultural diffusion in such a small area.

14. Ornamentation. Across nearly the whole of Busoga, two or four lower incisors were traditionally extracted from all boys and girls at puberty. Lines were scarified on the stomachs of all girls. These practices of evulsion and scarification suggest some common experience between the peoples of Busoga and the peoples living to the east and north of Busoga, and with the people of Bunyoro, all of whom evulsed and scarified according to one pattern or another. As with material culture, this type of general cultural evidence is of minor significance for intensive historical analysis in a limited area.

An interesting, and perhaps suggestive, contrast appears between the practice throughout most of Busoga and that among the people of Busiki, in north-east Busoga, who, like most of the people of Buganda,[23] did not traditionally evulse.

Explicit or inexplicit types of data

1. Clan drumbeat. Every clan has at least one drumbeat with an associated slogan; the drum is beaten in rhythm with the intonation of the words of the slogan. This is a fixed form of tradition, the words fixed by the drumbeat. The drumbeat was traditionally used, and for some purposes is still used, to collect clansmen for meetings, for warfare, and at times of birth and death. As well, rulers used drumbeats to rally their subjects. Dispersed clan segments often have different drumbeats.

Some of the drumbeat slogans are inexplicit and some explicit. The

---

[23] One incisor of the Gabunga, the admiral of the fleet of Buganda, was removed some time after burial, suggesting that evulsion may have been common in Buganda at an earlier time, or in the Lungfish clan of Gabunga before they reached Buganda.

drumbeat slogan of the abaiseKiyuuka is, 'He came from Buziri with spears.'[24] This slogan refers to the travels of the leader of the most important expedition of the abaiseKiyuuka. This expedition came under arms from Buziri Island in Lake Victoria to Lingira Island, which became a dispersal point for the clan. The slogan reinforces other data both explicit and inexplicit.

Another drumbeat slogan, 'Kinhama, you killed the cow,'[25] is less explicit than the above example. This drumbeat slogan of the abaise-Kinhama is explained by an accompanying commentary: 'Kinhama was given a cow and when he reached Nakyandiba [a river in the southern part of Busoga], he killed it and went into the water to catch fish.' This drumbeat slogan, while less explicit than the first, is clearly of historical significance.

A third example—this one inexplicit—is the drumbeat slogan of the abaiseIrombe: 'What is returned is not sacrificed.'[26] While the meaning of the slogan is apparent, there is no historical significance, and there is no accompanying commentary which provides an historical context.

Occasionally, two or more clans have the same or similar drumbeat slogans. This may suggest some association. In the most prominent case, several clans have the same drumbeat slogan, and all of these clans dispersed from the area of the Bukoba state in the southern part of Busoga. The royal clan of Bukoba, the abaiseIkoba, have the same drumbeat slogan, and it appears that the other clans adopted this royal drumbeat slogan as their own.

It is possible that quite different drumbeat slogans may be associated with a single drumbeat and thereby suggest a possible association which might be checked with other data. This analysis would be difficult; within 'Collected Texts' alone, there are more than 500 different drumbeat slogans recorded.

2. Proverbs and sayings. Proverbs and sayings[27] may also be fixed forms of tradition. They are frequently uttered and therefore are perhaps more enduring than many other types of data. They may be based on well-known historical events. Occasionally, a name or word in the proverb or saying may suggest some commentary having historical content. One example is, 'The sun [*kiyuba*] is pleasant in the

[24] '*Nava Buziri n'enkabi*', CTBTH, Texts 263, 265–7, 270.
[25] '*Kinhama wattente*', contraction of 'Kinhama watta nte,' CTBTH, Texts 199, 200.
[26] '*Ekidda kitambirwanga*', CTBTH, Texts, 116, 117.
[27] The Lusoga word *olugero* (singular) encompasses both proverbs and sayings.

morning, but a cloud [*kireri*] covers the sun.' In the second half of the nineteenth century, Menha Kirunda of Bugweri fought and defeated a dissident prince in battle. After the battle, Menha Kirunda is reputed to have said, 'The sun is pleasant in the morning and everyone likes it, but come noon, the sun is fierce and all fear it.'[28] Menha Kirunda was given, or took, the nickname *Kiyuba* [Sun] because of his fierceness. But in a later battle, this Kirunda Kiyuba was defeated by Kakaire Nandigobe, another dissident prince. Kakaire Nandigobe took the nickname *Kireri* [Cloud], because he defeated Kiyuba and 'covered the sun'.[29] Thus, the proverb parallels the event; through a commentary on the proverb, the historical experience is revealed.[30]

3. Songs. Only a few songs constitute explicit historical texts. Most reflect common social values, yet a few may, through commentary on the meaning of the song, suggest some historical event or personality. One goes,

> He who was my trusted friend died,
> Let me cry for myself, no one will cry for me,
> Let me cry for myself, no one will cry for me,
> I have no son that will come crying,
> Death has taken all the people.
> We were many but I am now alone.
> Among many children there must be one who needs,
> Among many children there must be one who is needy,
> Among many children there must be one very poor.[31]

There are quite a few praise songs. One sung to Kaunhe, nineteenth-century ruler of Bukooli, goes,

> You are handsome but you cannot see yourself.
> You are brown [light] but invisible.[32]

There are a number of war songs, but few relate to a specific battle. One song, sung by warriors as a vow before setting off to do battle for Wakooli Kaunhe, goes,

---

[28] This suggests an even deeper historical context. A stereotypic tradition, quoted by Crazzolara, *The Lwoo*, pp. 373–5, describing the break-up of the Padzulu group of the southern Madi, is parallel to this particular metaphor from Busoga, the arcing of the sun across the sky representing the turning of the tide.

[29] It is possible that an eclipse was Nandigobe's cloud; however, there is no other evidence supporting such a hypothesis.

[30] The proverb and commentary are quoted from STBTH, i. 138–9.

[31] ibid., i. 16.   [32] ibid.

I am a little male goat,
I am a little male goat,
Whatever I eat is my only share.
I am a male goat,
I am a male goat which they say will be killed.
A warrior eats his share.
A warrior eats his share.[33]

The ballad is still a popular carrier of news and opinion. However, the ballad seems to have been, and to be, a rather transitory form of tradition. Ballads would be an ideal and explicit source of information about events in the past if they had been transmitted down to the present; but few ballads were transmitted and preserved.

4. Titles. The titles of the rulers of many states in Busoga are recollective of some stories of historical interest. Ngobi Mau, the first ruler of Buzaaya, was nicknamed *Muzaaya*, 'the one who disappeared', because he was left in a country full of hardship and nearly empty of people. The Muzaaya name became the title of all the successive rulers of Buzaaya. Nabwana Inhensiko of Luuka was nicknamed *Tabingwa*, 'the undefeated', because he did not lose a battle. This name became the title of subsequent rulers of Luuka. The title *Waguma* of the chiefs of Buhahulo, in Butembe-Bunya County, was also an applied nickname; it too is of historical interest. One version has it that the chief was nicknamed *Waguma* because he stuck it out [*kuguma* = to be firm] in a difficult country. An alternative explanation has it that the nickname came from the sharp wooden stakes [*miguma*] which they used in combat. From other evidence, and by considering the circumstances of the transmission of the two traditions, one can be fairly certain that the first version is correct. But this does not necessarily mean that the Waguma group did not fight with the sharp wooden stakes. In fact, from other evidence, this is confirmed. So, what are left are two different explanations, both possibly valid, both very likely based on historical realities. While the etymology of the title may be of interest, and while an attempt may be made to settle on the soundest etymology, the very title may recall stories of historical interest which are not directly involved with the 'sound etymology'.

Wars and armies also have titles, and these titles may also bring to mind other information. One example is the name of a battle fought during a civil war in Bugweri in the last century. This battle was

---

[33] ibid.

called 'Hornbill'.[34] The army of Menha Kirunda Kiyuba was sent to cut down a sacred tree of the recalcitrant prince of Bukasenke. When this task was completed, the Bukasenke prince retaliated, sending an army to fight Menha Kirunda. Each Bukasenke warrior put a dressing on his face, and their appearance was that of an army in which every warrior had lost his nose. Menha Kirunda's people laughed at the army when it attacked, calling it the 'hornbill army'. But the Hornbill army was victorious, and they cut off the noses of the people they could catch on Kirunda's side.[35] There are many other examples of titles of armies and names of battles which are evocative of substantial traditions.

5. *Commentaries and explanations.* The nature of a particular tradition may evoke a commentary or explanation. Often, the tradition and the commentary are combined in a somewhat fixed form. In the case of certain drumbeat slogans, the slogan beaten out on the drum may be only the first part of an expression which, when heard in its entirety, explains the slogan itself. Where the explanation or commentary is not in fixed combination with the particular item, the explanation or commentary may be open to distortion or fabrication. For the informant, it may be a matter of pride to explain a song or proverb even when such an explanation is not called for. This pride may lead to distortion. A narrative given as an explanation of some song or proverb must then be understood *as an explanation*, and must as with other information be assessed against the weight of other data. The commentary or explanation may or may not contain data of historical interest.

6. *Stories about the introduction of food crops.* These are relatively common. In certain cases, they are told as part of narratives on the activities of clan figures or culture heroes. One example is the tradition of Mugogo, a mwiseMugogo, who was fishing and caught a banana shoot in his fishing trap. He planted it and introduced banana cultivation to the Buvuma Islands. The story may be merely symbolic of the general introduction of banana cultivation in the region; still, the name of the figure involved—*Mugogo*, 'the banana shoot man',—and the name of the clan—abaiseMugogo—suggest that there was some significant relationship between the man and the banana shoot. But without extensive correlative evidence, it is difficult to reach any conclusions on the historical role of Mugogo.

There are a number of statements which allege that the banana

[34] *King'ang'a.*   [35] STBTH, i. 139–40.

diffused throughout the region from one particular place in Busoga, Bukyemanta, located in Bukooli County. If there were a number of different epicentres of banana diffusion pointed to in Busoga, one could reject outright the story and suggest instead that the epicentric account is merely stereotypic. But as all the various statements point to Bukyemanta, one must look for further data with which to assess the substantiality of the tradition. But little correlative data from Busoga exists on this point. One must consider that it may be a diffused story as much as a diffused banana.

A good many food-crop origins stories are related in very general terms without any specific reference to place, person, or time. Many are apparently stereotypic, and with most, the entertainment value seems more important than the instructive value.

7. *Stories about Mukama and Kintu.* Mukama and Kintu are the two most prominent folk heroes of the Basoga. Stories about them have evidently undergone considerable distortion, making each tradition much more difficult to handle. Some stories about them have very likely been entirely fabricated. Others have undergone contamination from published sources. There has been some diffusion of the stories, and certain clans have evidently made spurious claims of original attachment to one or the other of the two figures. To some extent, the stories have undergone intermixture, the deeds assigned to Mukama transferred to Kintu, those of Kintu assigned to Mukama, and in some variant traditions, the two have merged, Mukama and Kintu becoming one figure. Some of the stories are political in purpose and others largely religious. The whole problem is complicated by the fact that Mukama and Kintu emerge as Adamic figures, placed between this world and the spirit world, the originators of society and culture. To some extent, traditional history begins with them—they are the springboards of history.

Out of this muddle of tradition, the fundamental traditions must be found and examined. Requiring the interpretation and analysis of every variant of the traditions and requiring correlation with all the other data available—on migrations, clan activities, royal custom, religious figures and custom, shrine sites, and so forth—the reconstruction of the presence of the Mukama and Kintu figures is basic to the reconstruction of Busoga history.

The period of interest of the present study has, for the most part, excluded the possibility that events would lie within the memories of surviving participants. The question of how traditions were transmitted from the past to the present thus becomes important. There were no officials charged with the responsibility of preserving and transmitting tradition, and there is only a rare reference in the 'Collected Texts' to a pattern of transmission of a particular tradition. Often transmission was diffuse, random, passing from neighbour to neighbour, state to state, down roadways and pathways, through neighbourhood gatherings, and from the transient tongues of minstrels. Yet some patterns are better defined. There were certain moments when traditions were uttered and thus transmitted to those hearing them. One time was at the naming ceremony of a child. Another was at the time of marriage, when the parties concerned were obliged to consider the possibilities of a marriage prohibition existing. Another moment was at the funeral of a clansman, a time when the heroic events and personalities of clan and lineage were mentioned. Royal or state traditions were voiced in councils, at the times of death and installation of rulers, and in the consideration of precedents during judicial cases. In times of hardship, traditions were voiced and discussed. When offerings were taken to a shrine, traditions were uttered. All these were, and still are in many cases, times when traditions could be transmitted from the speaker to the rest of the people present.

There were apparently two relatively well defined patterns of transmission of royal tradition. There is, of course, the tradition preserved and transmitted down the royal line; this is the official tradition. The ruler's mother's clan is the second agency of transmission of royal tradition. The ruler's mother had an important role in traditional society. The ruler's mother's clan preserved the tradition dealing with their 'son' specifically and, to a lesser extent, the tradition relating to that son's father and their son's children. The royal tradition can be seen here as a chain of links, each preserved by each ruler's mother's clan. The sum of these links is often a more substantial body of tradition than that preserved and transmitted through members of the royal family. While the royal family, with its ascribed status, may be careless in the preservation of its tradition, the status of a commoner clan may be affirmed only by a detailed tradition of its role in the state structure. These commoner traditions form an interlocking chain, and these interlocking pieces serve as a control over the accuracy of each link. No clan can put itself forward as the 'mother clan' of a particular ruler unless it is so, for not only will the true 'mother clan' tradition contradict it, but so will the links of tradition relating to the particular ruler's father and son, or predecessor and successor.

Because there has evidently been a large measure of randomness in the transmission of tradition, it is difficult, in most cases, to assess the worth of a particular text on the basis of the manner of transmission. Only in the case of the transmission of royal tradition, discussed above, and in the case of the transmission of fixed texts, is it possible to point to mechanisms controlling the transmission. However, it is sometimes possible, and useful, to make a rough estimate of whether the chains of clan tradition—the involved lineages and sub-lineages functioning as chains—are closely related or whether they are distantly related. Two men descendant from the same grandfather may each relate a tradition about the beginnings of the clan. If the traditions recorded are similar, it is likely that the grandfather of the two informants relayed a tradition heard from his antecedents to his two grandsons. It would be considerably more significant if the informants relating a common story were more distantly related than this, suggesting greater depth of differentiation of the lines of transmission of the one tradition. As well, a testimony recorded on one side of Busoga can be a control for a testimony recorded on the other side of Busoga relating certain common details or concerned with a common theme. Of course, one must be aware of the possibilities of cross-contamination of such tradition, particularly as a result of cross-transmission of lineage or family traditions during clan meetings in this century. And, while one must accept that much of the transmission is random and diffuse, it is possible to estimate the distortion in the last link in the chain of transmission; that is, between the informant and the researcher. The special interests of the individual informant, comments from aside and to aside—these and other factors can be weighed by the historian estimating the extent of purposeful distortion in the last link of transmission.

But any analysis of the modes of transmission of Soga tradition is necessarily a less critical and less comprehensive means of interpreting and analysing tradition than is the evaluation of the data itself. Having rejected data on the grounds of historical irrelevance and obvious fabrication on the part of the informant, and aware of the problems of transmission, I found myself facing a mass of data of quite diverse character. The data are complex, and the typical item of evidence refers to small units of historical activity such as the family, lineage, or clan, rather than to broader complexes. In such circumstances, the task of the historian is to reconstruct the broader and more significant complexes from the minute data. This mass of evidence was initially approached in three ways: (1) evaluating the basic data; (2) reconstructing basic histories; and (3) constructing a chronology.

The first step in evaluating the basic data was to discern obvious identities in evidence, interconnections between essentially different pieces of evidence, and contradictions in the evidence. This involved the testing of individual items of evidence against the whole body of data. Every substantial piece of historical evidence is composed of at least one of three focal elements: person, place, and time.[36] The focal point of person involves the name of an individual mentioned in the specific piece of evidence. For instance, 'But trouble arose when Wakooli Kibubuka wanted to marry a girl from our clan.'[37] The focal point for comparison with other items is Wakooli Kibubuka. The focal point of place involves some place name mentioned in the item of evidence. For example, 'We were at the place called Isegero.'[38] Isegero is the focal point for comparison with other items.

A card was made for each person or place mentioned in the 'Collected Texts'. The items of evidence relevant to the name of person or place mentioned were noted on each card. For example, in Text 494, there is the statement: 'My forefather Gonakona came from Kibuye in the corner of Bukooli with his grandsons.' On the card entitled 'Kibuye', I wrote: 'abaiseMukuve under Gonakona came from here.' On the card titled 'Gonakona', I wrote: 'came from Kibuye with grandsons.' Each note entered on a card was accompanied by a reference to the text from which it was drawn. All information in the 'Collected Texts' was organized in this manner. The result was a set of 'person cards' numbering about 3,000, including some 9,000 individual items of evidence, and a set of 'place cards' numbering about 2,000, including some 13,000 individual items of evidence.

For each person mentioned, I attempted to establish some clear

---

[36] Handling the time focus promised to be extremely difficult; therefore, I decided to wait until a comprehensive chronology was constructed before using this focal point as a critical factor in the evaluation of evidence. I did, however, at this early stage, consider the rough chronological import of each item of evidence. The credibility of each item was roughly assessed on chronological grounds, but at this stage, person and place were the significant focal points for the critical evaluation of the evidence.

[37] CTBTH, Text 610.   [38] CTBTH, Text 610.

identification from the evidence on the card, or from some external source such as Ganda tradition; and for each place name, the geographical reference was noted. Some material was screened in the process of establishing these identifications.

On the cards, certain identities in evidence were discerned. For example, Text 415 reports that 'Lwabandha led the abaiseMuhaya from the Lake to Malongo.' Text 417 reports that 'Lwabandha led the abaiseMuhaya to Malongo.' Text 419 reports that 'Lwabandha gave Nanhumba thirty cows, and Nanhumba gave Lwabandha Malongo.' These three references, coming from informants not in contact with one another, suggest, at the minimum, a relationship between Lwabandha, the person, and Malongo, the place. Such identities can be accepted as reasonable certainties where there are no contradictions, and where the lines of tradition involved appear to be distantly, rather than closely, related.

Also indicated by the data on the cards were interconnections between essentially different items of evidence. For example, Text 457 reports that when the abaiseMukose reached Buwongo Hill, they found, among other clans, the abaiseMusuubo. Text 614 reports that 'Musuubo left Buwongo for Kalalu.' This suggests an interconnection between the abaiseMusuubo and the abaiseMukose at Buwongo. Such interconnections are useful for they may suggest broader historical complexes.

In organizing the material on the person and place cards, contradictions in evidence were revealed. What became clear was that there were two types of contradiction within the collected material: substantial and apparent. Most of the substantial contradictions occurred in the genealogical material related in the texts. These were apparently caused by failures in memory and transmission. Such contradictions were difficult to handle, though it was often possible to identify one statement seemingly more valid than others on the basis of the judged integrity of the informant and through consideration of the interconnections with other evidence.

Examination of the data occasionally revealed contradictions which were not substantial, but only apparent. One example is in the migrational routes related by abaiseMukose informants in Busiki County. Several informants related that all abaiseMukose came from Buwongo Hill in Bugweri County, and those reaching Busiki travelled directly from there. Other abaiseMukose informants in Busiki asserted that all abaiseMukose came from Waibuga in Luuka, some travelling from there directly to Busiki. Superficially, there appeared to be a contradiction between the two statements. But looking deeper, and considering other evidence, it became apparent that there were two dispersal points for the abaiseMukose in Busoga, and that somewhere in the unrecollected past there was, perhaps, one parent group and one primary dispersal point. These apparent contradictions were usually resolved by examining other data.

The full collection was searched in this way for identities, interconnections, and contradictions, and the evidence was partially screened in the course of this sifting. With this completed, I moved on to the second approach, attempting to reconstruct the individual histories of the identified effective units of historical activity. The state, clan, lineage, and sub-lineage were the effective units of historical activity. Individual state, lineage, and clan histories were reconstructed in outline form from the data immediately relevant to each unit. These were basic, relatively isolated histories, collated from the various items of evidence collected, organized, and screened.

A first step in this basic reconstruction was the grouping together of evidence relevant to each described unit. I then looked for identities and contradictions in the assembled data. The credibility of each piece of evidence was estimated on the basis of the conduct of the original interview, of the particular situation of the informant, and according to the other criteria already discussed. The significance of each item of evidence was assessed. From this, an isolated history was collated from the collected data.

At the same time, some basic problems of identifying and describing the individual units were resolved. Secession states were distinguished. Dispersed clan units were examined to determine whether the individual units had become effectively independent of the whole clan before the colonial era. The reunification of certain clans was examined in order to determine if the recently reunified clan had incorporated units not traditionally related. Differently named but closely related clan groups were identified.

Individual histories of some 220 clans and some seventy states were assembled in skeleton form. The reconstruction of basic histories was the principal means of organizing the collected evidence at a higher level than was achieved in the preliminary evaluation and screening of data using the person and place cards.[39] The cards on

---

[39] Lubogo has presented forty-three 'isolated histories' of the ruling families in Busoga, and some of his work was useful here.

person and place were still crucial for they contained or suggested the interconnections and cross-references which would be used with the basic histories in constructing a comprehensive chronology. They would, as well, be used in knitting together the basic histories into broader and more significant historical designs.

In traditional history, particularly where one is concerned with a culture having no traditional method of distinguishing or recording dates in terms of years and days, the construction of a chronology is a large methodological problem in its own right. In such a case, the chronology must necessarily be relative. In cultures having a linear rather than a cyclical concept of time, the minimal 'chronology' may be no more than the placing of events in a sequence of occurrence. At its best, the chronology may be built on estimated dates or eras, with allowance for margins of error.

There are certain elements which together make possible the construction of a useful and reliable chronology. First, there must be a central system operating through the past to the present, composed of elements in sequence to which events can be related. The typical system is the ruling dynasty, with the various rulers in sequence. Certain events can be related to each of the rulers. The ruling dynasties are central to the establishment of the Interlacustrine chronologies.

Second, the structure of the genealogy must be ascertainable. One must be able to know the modes of succession, the number of generations in the complete dynasty, the generation position of each figure in the dynasty, and the relationship of each figure to every other figure in the dynasty.

Third, interconnections with other dynasties must be known. It is unsatisfactory to attempt to build a chronology for an isolated dynasty. One must seek interconnections, or tie-ins, between one dynasty and another and between the figures of one dynasty and the figures of another. Such tie-ins point to contemporaneous figures or events.

Fourth, a credibly estimated date for some event in the past must be known. Such a date may be drawn from a set of radiocarbon dates, or from a dated eclipse recorded in tradition. With such a date related to a particular figure in the dynasty, the average lengths of generations and reigns can be determined. An estimated date may be established for a particular point within a dynasty by associating that point, through some evidence of tie-in, with a credibly estimated date for another dynasty.

With these requirements in mind, the problems of establishing a comprehensive and reliable chronology for Busoga were considered. There is no central dynasty in Busoga for which a central chronology can be constructed, and to which all other dynastic units, and events, can be tied. Sixty-eight dynasties or states were distinguished in Busoga. Each was at one time or another autonomous. A large number of ruling dynasties in Busoga, and, as well, a good number of commoner lineages, fulfil the four requirements discussed above. Although there are no known eclipse or archaeological dates for Busoga, there are interconnections with dynasties outside Busoga for which credibly estimated dates from archaeological sites and eclipses are available. The most important dynastic unit with dates interconnecting with the Soga states is the Buganda kingdom. There are a large number of tie-ins between the Ganda dynasty and a number of Soga dynasties. The Ganda dynasty was used as a core dynasty in the construction of a general chronology for Busoga.

The generation is the key unit for calculating time depth with respect to the Ganda chronology. Oliver has estimated twenty-seven years for each generation and suggests a basic margin of error factor of twenty years plus two years added for each generation counting back from the present.[40] The generation is calculated as the time between the birth of a man and the birth of the child who will first succeed him, typically the eldest or an elder son. The pattern of royal succession in Buganda is in general co-ordination with this concept of generation. In Buganda, it was typically one of the eldest sons of the ruler who succeeded. In the cases where a ruler was succeeded by his brother, the succession usually reverted eventually to one of the eldest sons of the first ruler among the brothers.

In a number of Soga states, the pattern of succession right through the dynasty was similar to the pattern in Buganda, with one of the eldest sons succeeding the father; or, when a brother succeeded, one of the eldest sons of the elder brother of the previous generation eventually succeeded. However, in many Soga states, the effective patterns of succession were somewhat different. There are numerous cases in Busoga of fraternal and collateral succession in which either the succession did not revert to the elder son of the next generation,

[40] R. Oliver, 'Ancient Capital Sites of Ankole', *Uganda Journal*, 23, 1, (1959), 51–63; and 'The Royal Tombs of Buganda', *Uganda Journal*, 23, 2, (1959), 124–33.

or the fraternal and collateral succession was so extended that the elder sons in the next generation did not survive to succeed. In this case, it is difficult to trace the lineal sequence of elder sons which is essential for the estimation of an average generation. Although one can still recognize and distinguish generations in this collateral situation, the significance of the generation as a fairly precise tool for measuring dynastic generations is lessened. One cannot employ the Ganda generation in assessing the chronologies of non-lineal dynastic genealogies; the collateral Soga generation is not equivalent to a lineal Ganda generation.

Collateral and fraternal succession in Busoga takes several complex forms. An example of an extended fraternal succession is the case of the abaiseMenha dynasty of Bugweri. In this dynasty, the eldest son of the *last* ruler of each generation of brothers succeeded in three generations.[41]

A second example is that of the abaiseNgobi dynasty of Buzimba.[42] The pattern here is that the eldest *surviving* son of the new generation succeeds but the succession passes through the sons of all the fraternal and collateral rulers of the previous generation. The result is a proliferating number of eligible princes and successors in each generation. This pattern is often complicated by aberrations in the actual successions caused by civil war.

In any generation, it is likely that the eldest brothers will die before the youngest, and, in the situation of collateral and fraternal succession, the succession will continually drift towards the junior end of each generation of brothers. The eldest lineages will be effectively eliminated from the throne, and, as a result, the average generation assessed for the lineage of eldest sons will not be the same as the generation length assessed for the junior ends of the collateral succession groups. What this drift towards the junior ends means for the chronology is that in such cases of fraternal and collateral succession, longer generations, relative to the estimated Ganda generation, can be assumed. Moreover, the length of these 'generations' increases as the range of collateralism increases in each successive generation.[43]

To some extent, the longer collateral generations were affected by

[41] See Figure 1, Appendix B, p. 201.

[42] See Figure 2, Appendix B, p. 201.

[43] The drift is evident in both royal and commoner genealogies. Within the abaiseMusuubo, for example, the elder lineages are some four and five generations longer than the most junior lineages though they are all credibly traced back to common antecedents.

the civil wars for which collateralism seems to have been frequently responsible. Reigns appear to have been shorter as fewer rulers lived out a normal life, and, therefore, more eligibles in each generation were able to take the throne. The shorter the reigns, the more senior was the possible first successor in the subsequent generation. The more senior the first successor in the generation, the less broad was the drift towards the junior end of the generation. As well, aberrations occurred in the line of succession. One common instance was when junior or senior brothers and their descendants were dropped from consideration.

The estimated average generation, which is a useful concept for constructing a chronology for the Ganda dynasty, is not altogether satisfactory as a means of constructing chronologies for certain Soga dynasties. The collateral generation cannot be estimated with any precision. And the collateral generation, unlike the lineal, is not constant and cannot, therefore, be averaged over a series of generations. For Busoga, the tie-in is the crucial tool. With the tie-in, a reign of a Soga ruler can be correlated with a Ganda reign for which a generation estimate is possible.

It is not the place here to postulate the origins of collateralism in the Soga royal houses; what is germane is the problem of handling such complex genealogical structures in building a chronology. The first step taken in constructing a core chronology for Busoga was to select the genealogies to be considered, and the second was to determine the credibility of each. Some 120 were selected; each of these appeared, from a first view, to be of some significance and of some credibility. Among these were most of the sixty-eight royal genealogies of Busoga, as well as the royal genealogies of Buganda and Bunyoro. Several royal genealogies in Busoga are segments of larger genealogical structures; where there was obvious evidence of such segmentation, a genealogy was constructed which encompassed all the significant component segments. Eliminated from consideration were those genealogies in which the relationships of every figure to every other figure in the dynasty were uncertain, and in which the sequence and modes of succession in the dynasty were uncertain.

Moving on to the next step, the credible tie-ins between the figures in different genealogies were established. All the data screened from the 'Collected Texts' was examined, and every alleged tie-in between genealogical units was noted on a card. Each tie-in was given a number, and this number was noted on the card. The source of the

F

tie-in data was noted. The genealogical units connected by the alleged tie-in were noted, and the generation-numbers—counting back from 1899—for the correlated figures were noted. A brief statement of the nature of the tie-in, including the names of the figures involved, was added.

Three types of tie-in evidence could be distinguished: first, evidence explicitly correlating a figure from one genealogy with a figure from another; second, evidence correlating a specific figure from one genealogy with an unspecified figure of another; and third, evidence correlating an unspecified figure from one genealogy with an unspecified figure from another genealogy. All three types of tie-in evidence were useful. The second and third types were sometimes found to contain identities—though less specific in denotation—with tie-ins of the first type. Tie-ins of the second type were sometimes correlative with other tie-ins of the second type, yielding the names of both figures involved in the tie-in. The tie-in evidence of the second and third types was integrated where possible. Together with the tie-ins of the first type, these formed a large body of refined and usable tie-ins.

A second typology of tie-in evidence then emerged: there were, first, tie-ins between one state ruler and another state ruler; second, tie-ins between a state ruler and a commoner; and third, tie-ins between two commoners.

The next step was to reduce the number of tie-ins and genealogical units to workable proportions. Close to 1,000 tie-ins and 120 genealogical units were under consideration. What were needed were the genealogical units which were the most comprehensive in terms of tie-ins: those having the most extensive network of tie-ins with other units. On the basis of a rough appraisal, thirty units considered the most extensive in terms of correlation with other units were distinguished. This narrowed the number of tie-ins to about 600. The number of genealogical units was further reduced by counting the tie-ins for each unit and isolating the fourteen units with the most tie-ins. These fourteen units were all ruling dynasties.

In the actual construction of the chronology, Buganda was accepted as the core dynastic genealogy. The Ganda genealogy was set on a chart that was devised for the chronology.[44] The known dates, most

[44] This chart appears below, Appendix C, p. 202. This particular construction was carried back to 1710 ± 32 years (according to the Buganda generation estimate). This period, from 1710 ± 32 years to 1899, is the era of extensive correlation

of them between 1860 and 1900, and the associated rulers were noted on the chart. The Ganda centred tie-ins were then added, working back from 1899. Each tie-in was marked with an arrow; the tie-in number was written next to the arrow, and the names of the rulers concerned were written at the points of the arrow. In all, twenty-four different rulers were tied-in with rulers of Buganda in the first seven generations back from 1899, counting Ganda generations. These twenty-four names were noted on the chart. Additionally, other known dates for particular rulers were added. Then, tie-ins which existed between these newly added names and other figures were noted with the horizontal arrow and tie-in number. For the first seven generations back from 1899, counting Ganda generations, some sixty tie-ins were charted. These correlated more than fifty of the 175 rulers of the fourteen dynasties over the seven generations.

With the more than fifty tied-in names charted, I moved on to the problem of estimating their reign lengths and the reign lengths of those not tied-in. These estimates were based on evidence within the texts, such as a statement that a certain chief 'ruled for less than a year and was killed,' and on the following criteria: first, a reign length or series of reign lengths had to be, at minimum, in co-ordination with the accepted tie-in data; second, where there was fraternal and collateral succession, the average length of reign of each figure in the reign of collateral succession was shorter than the average reign of lineal succession; third, the sum of reign lengths in a sequence of collateral succession was longer than the average reign of lineal succession; and fourth, where it was evident that a ruler did not succeed at a great age and where there was no evidence that he was killed in war or in a dispute, the length of reign was longer than an average Ganda generation. Using these criteria, it was possible to make a rough estimate of the dates of reign-beginning and reign-end for each ruler. These points were noted on the chart. These estimated dates probably lie within the margins of error suggested by Oliver.[45]

To this constructed core chronology for Busoga were correlated the subsidiary genealogies which had been eliminated in the early stages of the chronological work. The chronology was extended and adjusted for other genealogical units in Busoga. With this structure,

---

among the dynasties. Of the fourteen dynasties here considered, some seven go back no further than 1710 ± 32 years. For these reasons, the construction was limited to this span of time.

[45] See above, p. 63, and footnote 40.

rough dates for all major events and persons could be estimated through correlation with the core chronology.

When the massive body of diverse data was brought under control—in terms of both evaluation and organization—it was possible to turn to the problem of reconstructing the history of Busoga. Hypotheses concerning the significant events, persons, and places were generated. Some hypotheses were drawn from the assertions of informants, and some were drawn in the course of the organization, evaluation, and analysis of the evidence. These hypotheses were then tested against the diverse data. It was possible to build, around the more significant constructions which emerge from this testing, a history of Busoga.

In reconstructing the history of Busoga, two great cataclysms were seen to mark the divide between a recent epoch of sharp forms and integrated outlines—the epoch of evident history—and the older shapes and discontinuous outlines—the times obscured by myth and legend. For the northern part of Busoga, the great cataclysm was the arrival of Lwo groups associated in tradition with Mukama. These Lwo groups ultimately gave forth the founding figures of a number of Soga states. For the southern part of Busoga, the great cataclysm was the arrival of the Kintu associated groups from the east. Each cataclysm opened a new epoch in history and a new course in the formulation of historical tradition.

As events of Adamic significance, the cataclysms themselves are recalled in traditions bound up with myth and belief. Yet continuous shapes do emerge which reveal these cataclysms to be more than the mythical germs of a new epoch and of a new society. Disjointed experience gives way to integrated experience. Participant groups and individuals begin to appear in concrete rather than shapeless roles. Sequence, genealogies, and thus chronology become credible. Areas of relatively uniform culture and common experience begin to emerge. These cataclysms give a beginning to Soga history as captured in the historical tradition of the people; while partially disconnected, the historical tradition bound up with the historical experience was on the march. A new historical epoch in the progress of man and a new thread of historical tradition were born in parallel.

The two cataclysms were not contemporaneous; in fact, the Kintu cataclysm in the South preceded the northern cataclysm by several hundred years. Nor were they of similar character; the Kintu cata-clysm apparently involved a somewhat sudden introduction of new ruling groups and political forms. The Lwo cataclysm, though simi-larly an introduction of new groups and political forms, was marked by a slow shift in the North from a wandering to a sedentary pattern of existence with the subsequent emergence of a number of political centres. Traditions of the northern cataclysm have been shaped around the Mukama figure and have been given a quality of sudden-ness paralleling the Kintu impact. The parallels between the Kintu and Mukama cataclysms in the historical tradition have contributed to the emergence, more recently, of a single Adamic tradition, par-tially displacing the former two, in which the names of Kintu and Mukama are interchangeable. The merging of the two Adamic themes appears to have paralleled the nineteenth-century razing of the relatively solid divide between northern and southern culture areas.

CHAPTER III

Kintu and the Wider Region

THE earliest Busoga settlements recorded in tradition were located within the region of South Busoga—roughly the southern part of what is today Bunya County. South Busoga is also the area in which the earliest states appeared. Until the colonial era, the communities of South Busoga were oriented primarily towards Lake Victoria; the principal cultural, ethnic, and economic bonds of the peoples of South Busoga were with the Buvuma Islands, with the coastlands of Buganda, and with the coasts of Samia and Kavirondo to the east. These bonds were maintained through water communications along the lakeshores. There was a frontier to the north, and beyond that frontier there emerged groups of a quite different cultural and economic character. Only in the nineteenth century did the frontier begin to erode. Some contact between the peoples and cultures of South Busoga and those of the North did occur in earlier times, however, but only to the east of South Busoga, in the lands constituting present-day Bukooli County, and apparently without substantial effect on the Lake orientation of the area.

This Lake orientation of the communities of South Busoga had momentous impact on the early history of the area. Many of the significant events of the earliest period of South Busoga history are linked with developments in the wider region. These concern the movements of peoples, the evolution and diffusion of cultural effects, the development of economies, the foundation of political centres, and the emergence of religious forms and deities. Perhaps no event better represents this theme of South Busoga's involvement in the wider region or commands a more important place in the tradition of the wider region than the migration of the Kintu figure, and the early history of South Busoga—the area through which the Kintu figure evidently travelled—cannot be discussed without reference to this wider region.[1]

---

[1] This broader reference is to be attempted even if the available evidence is only fragmentary and the postulations only tentative. It is only with the Lwo penetration of the Interlacustrine region that tradition becomes an explicit source for

The Kintu migration has a prominent place in the traditions of Buganda, traditions which themselves have had a predominant place in the reconstruction of the region's past. Kintu is the legendary figure who is linked to eastern or western and northern origins, who is said to have come with banana, or millet, or cattle; who is connected by traditions of filiation or clientage to groups and figures right across the Interlacustrine stage. He is, as well, variously identified as God, the son of God, the father of all people, the founder of clans, the distributor of totems, and the first statesman—the founder of kingdoms.

Ganda clan traditions are the most important source of evidence on Kintu, yet they seem also to be the major source of confusion on the whole epoch in which the Kintu figure was involved. The significant, identifiable historical units of pre-Lwo times continuous with the present are totemic clans, and the traditions of these totemic clans, particularly those in Buganda, are the principal sources on the Kintu period. These Ganda clan traditions demand careful analysis and cautious handling. The clans of Buganda, competing for power in an expanding and centralizing Ganda state after the impact of the several families associated with Kimera, remained strong structures relative to clans in most other parts of the region. Although there was extensive segmentation in the Ganda clan, the centripetal pressure of the political system held together each clan in a wide and ever widening unity. The crucial centripetal factor in the Ganda political system was the practice of the Ganda kings taking, for all intents and purposes, their mothers' clans; in this, the power and prestige of the king's office was closely associated with the mother's clan, and the tradition of maternity preserved. At each time of succession, clans attempted to place their princely children on the throne and so participated in, rather than opted out of, the rigorously and dangerously competitive political system. Traditions were preserved—traditions which both held the clan together as a political force and

---

historical reconstruction. A number of dynasties were established either by the Lwo themselves or in reaction to the Lwo impact from the north beginning in the fifteenth century. Around these dynasties there developed state traditions or state-oriented traditions continuous with the present. These traditions today constitute the major body of pre-colonial tradition on the region's past. For the period before the Lwo penetration, traditional evidence where available is fragmentary, and one must look more to archaeological and linguistic evidence. Much of pre-Lwo history is obscured in apparent myth and legend. However, myth and legend often constitute the dress of historical figures and historical events.

'documented' claims based on arrangements to office and privilege in the Ganda hierarchy.

Ganda clan traditions extend back deep in time, and scholars[2] have attempted to classify the clans of Buganda according to their time of arrival in Buganda: pre-Kintu, accompanying Kintu, Kimera associated, and post-Kimera. This classificatory system is primarily concerned with the timing of first contact between corporate descent groups and the apparatus of state; it can be quite spurious when one is concerned with the peopling of the Buganda area. Buganda was a slowly expanding kingdom from its beginnings in the era of Kintu and Kimera some five to seven centuries ago. In its earliest period, Buganda comprised little more than present Busiro County and its environs, and the peoples whom Kintu 'found in Buganda' were with few exceptions found within this small Busiro area. The clans which 'came with Kintu' or were 'fathered by Kintu' all settled in Busiro County and surrounding 'home counties' of present-day Buganda. The principal difficulty with the Ganda clan traditions is that—being politically inspired traditions for the most part—they only specify the clan settlements which were within the Ganda domain at the associated stage in the expansion of the Kingdom. As a consequence, the classified 'pre-Kintu clans' in Ganda history are only the clans or clan segments which came within the earliest domain of Kintu: Busiro County and its environs. Clans or clan segments which were within the present Ganda domain but not within the central nucleus of the state at the time of the Kintu arrival would not, with a rare exception or two,[3] be considered as pre-Kintu clans unless there was outright fictionalization of the tradition. Their 'time of arrival' would be determined by the time of their absorption into the Ganda state, a process which itself could be accomplished as much by an attachment of clientage or an expansion of the kingdom as by a clan migration. And it is this expansion which becomes the crucial factor in the muddling of the Kintu traditions preserved by the Ganda clans. As Buganda expanded, areas, peoples, and their traditions were absorbed into the Ganda domain and heritage. Traditions external to the events surrounding Kintu and traditions historically associated with the

[2] Merrick Posnansky, 'Towards an Historical Geography of Uganda', *East African Geographical Review*, 1 April 1963, p. 12. Mathias Kiwanuka, 'The Traditional History of the Buganda Kingdom', Ph.D. thesis, London University, 1965.

[3] There are the cases of the Bird and Reedbuck clans which were met by Kintu in his travels to the centre of Buganda but which remained effectively outside the Buganda sphere in the Kintu period.

developments at the heart of the Ganda state were joined as one. Conversely, groups thrown off from the turbulent Ganda kingdom in later times carried Ganda tradition to the far reaches of the region.[4] It is also likely that traditions were fabricated or borrowed to facilitate the entry of new groups into the mainstream of Ganda life.

If these difficulties are controlled, the Ganda clan traditions are thoroughly exploitable, and it is possible to identify two important themes bound up within the Kintu legend as it has emerged in and through the Ganda clan traditions. The first theme associates Kintu with groups and figures—or traditions of great figures—emerging out of the encounters among diverse peoples and cultures in the grasslands of western Uganda. The second theme involves the movement of groups associated with the Kintu figure from the *east* into South Busoga and into the nucleus of the Ganda kingdom—groups apparently involved in encounters among diverse peoples in the lands between Mount Elgon and Lake Victoria on the eastern side of the region.

Involved in the encounters among the diverse peoples and cultures of western Uganda—and the consequent tumultuous backwash which swept peoples and traditions southwards and eastwards into Lake Victoria and the coastlands of Buganda and Busoga—were the iron-using Bantu speaking groups. These Bantu derived from the major dispersals of Bantu from a centre to the south of the Congo forest; the dispersals of the Bantu began perhaps 2,000 years ago and continued even into the present century. In the course of the dispersals, the Bantu were flung out across central, eastern, and southern Africa.

A light woodlands area south of the Congo forest has been proposed as the location of this nucleus of Bantu expansion on the basis of the correlation of Guthrie's Bantu language classification with the dated sites of Dimple-based and Channelled pottery wares. The evidence suggests the rapid expansion of iron-using peoples from this woodland area south of the Congo forest,[5] and the correlation of linguistic and archaeological evidence—reflecting a common pattern

---

[4] Roland Oliver has described this process of assimilation of Ganda tradition by the Bakonjo of western Uganda, 'The Baganda and the Bakonjo', *Uganda Journal*, xviii, 1, (1954), 31–3.

[5] Malcolm Guthrie, 'Some Developments in the Prehistory of the Bantu Languages', *Journal of African History*, iii, 2, (1962), 273–82. Drawing on Guthrie and the available Dimple-based carbon dates, Oliver ['The Problem of the Bantu Expansion', *Journal of African History*, vii, 3, (1966)] has convincingly placed the nucleus in the light woodlands area south of the Congo forest.

of expansion—suggests that the speakers of Bantu languages and the early iron-using peoples associated with the pottery sites were one people.[6]

On the evidence of the dated Dimple-based sites, Hiernaux, additionally drawing on the evidence of anthropobiology, has proposed that the Bantu left such a postulated centre south of the forest and expanded rapidly through and along the fringes of the moist forest.[7]

Oliver has suggested that this rapid expansion from the light woodlands into the moist areas of central and eastern Africa was precipitated by the arrival in the Zambezi Valley of the banana along with other south-east Asian food-plants. These new food-plants encouraged expansion into the moister regions; there they constituted a bountiful and nearly effortless source of food.[8]

Expanding through the moister areas, the iron-using Bantu speakers evidently reached the Interlacustrine region in the first half of the first millennium A.D. The timing of such arrivals is indicated by the early Dimple-based dates for Ndora and Cyamakuza in Rwanda and Urewe and Yala Alego in western Kenya.[9]

Sites yielding Dimple-based pottery are widely distributed around the Interlacustrine region, including a number of sites in Rwanda; the site at Nsongezi on the Kagera River on the Uganda–Tanzania border; several sites along the northern coast of Lake Victoria; a

[6] Building a deeper synthesis on the available linguistic evidence and linguistic hypotheses, and the more recently available collection of analysed anthropobiological evidence, Jean Hiernaux ['Bantu Expansion: The Evidence from Physical Anthropology Confronted with Linguistic and Archaeological Evidence', *Journal of African History*, ix, 4, (1968), 506–10] has postulated that the Bantu speakers had still earlier origins on the northern fringe of the Congo forest. He suggests that from there they passed to the southern fringe—the dispersal nucleus proposed by Oliver.

[7] Hiernaux, p. 507, notes the near contemporaneity of widely distributed sites associated with the Dimple-based and Channelled wares: Machili in the Zambezi Valley, A.D. 96±220; Kalambo Falls in northern Zambia, A.D. 345±40; Ndora in Rwanda, A.D. 250±100; Cyamakuza in Rwanda, A.D. 300±80; Kwale in south-eastern Kenya, A.D. 270±115, A.D. 260±115, and A.D. 220±115. There are also the dates for Urewe in western Kenya: A.D. 270, A.D. 320, and A.D. 390; and for Yala Alego, also in western Kenya: A.D. 400 [Brian M. Fagan, 'Radiocarbon dates for sub-Saharan Africa: VI', *Journal of African History*, x, 1 (1969), 157]. Hiernaux, moreover, has noted (p. 514) that the early Dimple-based sites in Kivu province of the Congo and in Rwanda were located 'in small clearings of the moist forests'.

[8] 'The Problem of the Bantu Expansion', pp. 368–9.

[9] For radio-carbon dates, as supplied by Hiernaux and Fagan, see note 7 above.

complex of closely situated sites (including Urewe and Yala Alego) in Central Nyanza Province of western Kenya; and sites on Lolui Island in the north-east corner of Lake Victoria.

At certain sites in Rwanda, and at Nsongezi, Dimple-based wares are found closely stratified with Late-Stone-Age Wilton industry remains; moreover, there is no evidence of an earlier Iron-Age people. These indications suggest that the peoples associated with the Dimple-based wares were the earliest Iron-Age peoples in the Lake Victoria area and that they arrived on the heels of, and perhaps had contact with, Late-Stone-Age peoples in the Lake region.

Accepting the hypothesis that the Bantu speakers expanding from the south were one and the same as the peoples associated with the Dimple-based pottery, it seems clear that by the end of the first millennium A.D., and perhaps several centuries earlier, a number of small Bantu speaking groups were established in the region, perhaps near rivers, the lake coasts, and the fringes of the moist forest, using iron implements and weapons, and probably living by a mixed economy of agriculture, gathering, hunting, and fishing. These early Bantu would have enjoyed some advantage over the pre-Bantu peoples of the region, both in their knowledge of iron-working and in their apparent knowledge of banana cultivation. These advantages over the probably foraging pre-Bantu would have continued until the pre-Bantu either learned these arts or were destroyed or pushed into environments quite unappealing to the Bantu. There is no evidence of the Stone-Age peoples restricting the movements of the Bantu arrivals.[10]

The Bantu, having left their centre of dispersal south of the Congo forest, pushed through, or expanded across, mile after mile of moist lands both open and attractive for settlement. As their population increased, they undoubtedly were forced to use their iron tools to attack marginal forest and bush so as to clear more land for occupation. The expansion continued inexorably. Eventually, though, as

[10] Merrick Posnansky, 'Bantu Genesis—Archaeological Reflexions', *Journal of African History*, ix, 1, (1968), 3–4. On the evidence from pollen analyses, Robert L. Kendall ['An Ecological History of the Lake Victoria Basin', *Ecological Monographs*, 39, 2 (Spring 1969), p. 162] has estimated that the displacement of forest along the northern coastlands of Lake Victoria began some 3000 years ago and suggests both that this was likely due to forest clearance for agriculture and that it could be attributed to pre-Iron Age cultivators. Even if this construction is correct, iron tools and new food crops would still have given the advantage to agriculturalists arriving in the mid-first millennium A.D.

they were expanding northwards through the Interlacustrine region, they found their paths of expansion blocked by peoples of comparable technology, themselves expanding southwards through the very lands which the Bantu were attempting to occupy. These peoples whom the Bantu encountered were non-Bantu, iron-using agriculturalists and pastoralists.

As evidently pre-Kintu events, these northwards and southwards expansions—and consequent encounters—are barely illuminated by the traditions of the region. Tradition does, however, throw light on certain pre-Kintu developments of momentous importance which appear to have been the direct consequences of the contact, interpenetration, and backwash evidently involved in the encounters between the non-Bantu and Bantu cultures and peoples. Out of this backwash, moreover, there emerged the groups and traditions associated with the western theme of Kintu.

The iron-using non-Bantu cultivators expanding into the region from the north and eventually confronting the Bantu speakers were perhaps the *Madi*. Crazzolara,[11] on the basis of traditional and etymological evidence, has postulated a Madi expansion from the area of Rejaf, located along the Nile in the southern Sudan. According to his construction, the Madi, a Sudanic-speaking group, moved southwards under pressure from the Eastern Lango, a Nilo–Hamitic group. Expanding southwards through present-day Acholi district of northern Uganda, they probably encountered small groups of Western Lango Nilo–Hamitic groups which had preceded them in this part of the region and which had ventured perhaps as far south as the Lake Kyoga basin. Crazzolara believes that Madi groups crossed the Victoria Nile into present Bunyoro, into Buganda, and right through the Kyoga basin;[12] and it was perhaps within this area to the south of the Nile that the expanding Bantu confronted the expanding Madi.

Ehret has also postulated a strong influence on the Lake Victoria region by Central Sudanic peoples on the basis of the adoption by Bantu speakers in the region of the Moru–Madi root word for 'cow',[13] yet he also argues that the Central Sudanic peoples preceded the Bantu in the region. The crux of his argument is that the *te* or *ti* root

[11] J. P. Crazzolara, *The Lwoo* (Verona, 1950, 1951, 1954), part 3, pp. 348–50.
[12] ibid., pp. 449–50.
[13] C. Ehret, 'Cattle-keeping and Milking in Eastern and Southern African History: The Linguistic Evidence', *Journal of African History*, viii, 1, (1967), 1–17.

for 'cow' in the Moru–Madi languages of Greenberg's Central Sudanic family was not displaced by the Bantu *engombe* root for 'cow'. He suggests that pre-Bantu inhabitants of southern Uganda may have spoken languages of this Central Sudanic group; however, there is no evidence[14]—and the argument based on the words for cattle is not evidence—of a sequence in which the Bantu post-dated Central Sudanic Moru–Madi in the region.

If the postulations of Madi and Bantu expansion into the region are essentially correct, these Madi and Bantu would not have been alone in finding themselves confronting one another in the Interlacustrine region. Also pushing southwards into the Interlacustrine region were pastoral peoples similar in economy and probably continuous ethnically with the *Hima* (*Hema* or *Huma*) pastoralists of today. These Hima are today, and were apparently in the past, the herders of the humped long-horned Ankole cow (the Sanga cow) which may have originated in the Ethiopian highlands or in a wider region including the southern part of the Sudan where the Sanga cow is also found today. The Sanga cow is found as far south as Rhodesia, and its arrival in Rhodesia is dated to the latter part of the first millennium A.D. by Iron-Age cattle figurines.[15] These Hima, and early pastoralists associated with them in Uganda, Rwanda, and Kenya, are identified as the users of Roulette ware pottery, the origins of which Posnansky has suggested are located in the Ethiopian highlands or in the southern Sudan. The classes of pottery of the Roulette motif postdate the Iron-Age Dimple-based pottery, and, according to Posnansky, presumably date from the earliest part of the second millennium A.D.[16]

The Ethiopian origins of these Hima pastoralists, while possibly suggested by the Roulette motif decorating their pottery and through their unique association with the Sanga cow, are not indicated by any traditional or linguistic evidence. The Hima were absorbed linguistically into the Bantu-speaking world. Moreover, the Hima physical type, often suggested as proof of Ethiopian or southern Sudan origins, may be due as much to diet or social selection, as to any ethnic origin. Nevertheless, the possibility of an Ethiopian or southern

[14] ibid., p. 3. Posnansky has noted the presence at Bigo, *above* the remains of Chwezi occupation and of a period much later than that during which the first Bantu iron users reached the region, of arrow heads possibly associated with the Madi. 'Kingship, Archaeology and Historical Myth', *Uganda Journal*, xxx, 1, (1960), 7.

[15] Posnansky, 'Kingship, Archaeology', p. 7.   [16] ibid.

Sudan origin for the prototype Hima people and culture cannot be dismissed.

Beginning then, perhaps, at the outset of this millennium, and certainly by 1300, these Hima pastoralists, expanding southwards, were establishing themselves right through the belt of short grass country on the western side of the Interlacustrine region between the Kafu and Kagera rivers, and were perhaps expanding into lands cleared by the Bantu and Madi cultivators. Other, possibly associated, pastoral groups were moving far south into south-central Africa. Still others were moving into areas east of Lake Victoria.

It was in the extensive contact and interpenetration between peoples and cultures wherever the expanding Bantu and Hima and Madi happened to confront one another that significant processes of change had their roots—processes which would give new shape to the older social configurations of the region. The first significant development was very likely the emergence of pastoral aristocracies and structures of economic symbiosis from the web of contacts between Hima pastoralists and the cultivators whom they encountered, structures evidenced even today in the societies of western Uganda.

The second significant process involved the apparent sharing of culture between the Hima pastoralists occupying the short grass country and the cultivating or mixed-economy peoples living in, or pushed out of, the areas favoured by the pastoralists. In the western part of the region today, most of the Hima pastoral groups have avoidances or totems associated with pastoralism: typically, finely differentiated types of cattle. If we assume that the Hima entered the region as pastoralists, it is quite possible that they entered the region with such pastoral associated totems or avoidances. But there are groups with economy, culture, and physical type very similar to the Hima model, and with traditions which claim 'Hima origins', but with totems not strictly pastoral. Two significant examples are the peoples of the Grasshopper totem and the Hinda of the Monkey totem. Both emerged as royal groups in the western part of the region in evidently pre-Lwo times. The Grasshopper groups emerged as royal pastoralists in the Busongora area of western Toro. Later, the Busongora group broke up, with important groups travelling eastwards, settling at Kisozi [Kishozi] on the River Katonga.[17] Other groups of the Grasshopper totem migrated into the centre of Buganda

[17] M. Nsimbi, *Amannya Amaganda n'Ennono Zaago* (Kampala, 1956), pp. 278–9.

before and at the outset of Kimera's reign. Tradition records them as Hima[18] but the totem suggests that they were probably not ethnically derivative from the original Hima groups entering the region with cattle totems at the beginning of the present millennium, but rather that they emerged out of the contact between Hima and Bantu groups.

There is also the case of the Hinda of the Monkey totem, who became, with the demise of Chwezi power, the founders of kingdoms through most of the southern half of the region: from Ankole to Ukerewe Island in Lake Victoria. Tradition sometimes records the Hinda as Hima.[19] However, all through the western part of the region there were groups of the Monkey totem—some of them evidently not Hima pastoralists—groups such as the Banyambo Zirankende and the Kitumba group who accompanied Kimera in his travels from Bunyoro to Buganda. It can be postulated that ethnically the Hinda derived from early Monkey totem groups such as these, but were, in the central part of the region—perhaps Karagwe—assimilated to the pastoralist culture of the Hima. Later, the Hinda groups moved south to dominate the cultivating peoples of Kianja, Maruku, Rusubi, Ihangiro, Buzinza, and Ukerewe, and moved north to dominate Nkore, the central state within the later Ankole kingdom. This postulated process of 'Himatization', which very likely had an impact on other groups both earlier and later, is a rather tenuous proposition based largely on the evidence of totem—on the premise that the totem is a more continuous element than, say, the economy of a people. But, accepting the facts of economic symbiosis, structured aristocracy, linguistic assimilation into the Bantu speaking world, one cannot reject outright the probable consequences of such contacts: inter-marriage, cultural borrowing, economic change and adaptation, fictionalization of traditions of class origins—all of these suggest the clear possibility of Himatization of non-Hima groups, as well as the possibility of a reverse process of Bantuization.

The third significant development was the emergence of powerful groups and figures of royal bearing from the contacts among Hima, Bantu, and Madi. One of the more important examples is found in the emergence of the Chwezi. The Bigo pottery associated with

---

[18] Sir. A. Kaggwa, *Ekitabo kye Bika bya Baganda* (*Clans*) (Kampala, 1908 and 1949), manuscript translation by Dr. M. Kiwanuka, p. 15.
[19] B. K. Taylor, 'The Western Lacustrine Bantu', *Ethnographic Survey of Africa: East Central Africa*, Part 13, ed. Daryll Forde, (London, 1962), p. 133.

Chwezi occupation sites is distinguished by its Roulette motif, a Hima culture trait, and this Bigo ware is continuous with the present Hima pottery types,[20] suggesting not that the Chwezi were some mysterious invaders of the region who suddenly appeared and then soon disappeared—as legend has it—but rather that they emerged from the general expansion of Hima pastoral groups southwards into areas occupied by Bantu speakers. The Renge of Rwanda, of royal bearing, were also associated with the Roulette ware and the general Hima culture. The Tuutsi, too, perhaps, emerged as a dominant group in the same way.

Still earlier than the Chwezi were the *Batembuzi*, and their emergence out of the contagion of cultures—Bantu, Madi, and Hima—is the earliest indication of central authority in the region. Crazzolara has suggested that the penetration of the Interlacustrine region by the Madi culminated in a short period of dominance over the wider region by expanding Madi groups. He identifies the Madi as the Batembuzi rulers of early Bunyoro, the loose dynasty of Nyoro tradition recalled as predecessors of the Chwezi. The Batembuzi or 'Goat-Killers' were, he argues, one and the same as the Madi–Ndri or 'Goat–Madi'.[21] Crazzolara has argued that the Madi period in the Interlacustrine region left such words as *Nyoro*, *Chope*, and *Ganda* for posterity.[22]

Posnansky has suggested the importance of the shunting action in the movements of peoples from the southern Sudan through northern Uganda. He has identified the southern Sudan region (from which the Madi, and much later, the Lwo, expanded) as a reservoir, passing streams of cultural influence to the south, east, and west. Pressures on and from the 'Nile Pool' area, as he calls it, may have caused a 'form of shunting action in which the Madi . . . may have been initially important in northern Uganda. These first movements may also have provided the loosely-knit pastoralists who had themselves derived their cattle and pottery from the north, with the stimulus to centralization.'[23]

Carrying forward this hypothesis, it is possible that the Batembuzi figures were not Madi but rather emerged as leaders of loosely knit pastoralists or of groupings of pastoral and non-pastoral peoples in

[20] Posnansky, 'Kingship, Archaeology . . .', p. 5.

[21] Crazzolara, *The Lwoo*, pp. 449–50. This is Crazzolara's construction. In Runyoro, *Batembuzi* means 'those who settle in a new place'.

[22] ibid., p. 350.

[23] Posnansky, 'Kingship, Archaeology . . .', p. 9.

response to a Madi impact across the Victoria Nile. The Batembuzi leaders, very possibly representing dominant groups rather than a true unitary dynasty as the Nyoro tradition has it, perhaps evolved out of contacts between Hima pastoralists and Bantu cultivators. The dominance of the Batembuzi groups, along with the impact of the Kintu associated groups on the region, may have culminated in the real political hegemony of the Chwezi in the fourteenth and fifteenth centuries.

The thin Nyoro traditions[24] set these Batembuzi figures in a Nyoro Genesis. Both pastoral and agricultural elements are found in the traditions of the beginnings of the Earth and of Mankind. Names of various Batembuzi 'rulers' have been given by Fisher, Gorju, Roscoe, and K.W.,[25] but there is little tradition of an explicit nature associated with any of the rulers except Isaza, the last of the first group of Batembuzi rulers, and Bukuku. The Isaza group yielded its dominance to the Bukuku or Baranzi 'dynastic group', which in turn was succeeded by the Chwezi. Two of the crucial consequences of this Batembuzi epoch were apparently, first, the cohesion of previously separate pastoral and cultivating groups, Hima and Bantu, discussed above; and second, the retreat of groups southwards, some of them venturing into Lake Victoria, finally settling in the Ssese Islands and along the Lake coasts.

These southwards movements—the postulated backwash of Bantu expansion northwards meeting the southwards expansion of the Hima and Madi—involved the migrations of prestigious groups into the immediate environs of Lake Victoria and, within the context of these migrations, the transmission of ideas of authority into the wider region, ideas which seemingly had their origins in the confrontations among diverse peoples in the western lands. This contribution of peoples and ideas to the islands and coastlands of Lake Victoria, from a source area to the west and north, has in Ganda tradition been confused with three quite distinct historical processes: first, but not earliest, the rise of the Chwezi and the dispersal of the Chwezi associated groups; second, and more recent, the arrival in the centre of

---

[24] As yet, the only comprehensive attempt to collect Nyoro tradition is a recent project undertaken by Mrs. Carol Buchanan of the University of Indiana. As of this date (March 1971), she is still processing the collected material.

[25] Mrs. A. B. Fisher, *Twilight Tales of the Black Baganda* (London, 1911); J. Gorju, *Entre le Victoria, l'Albert et l'Edouard* (Rennes, 1920); J. Roscoe, *The Bakitara* (Cambridge, 1923); K. W. 'The Kings of Bunyoro-Kitara, I.' *Uganda Journal*, iii, 2 (1935), 149–60.

G

Buganda of groups associated with the Kimera figure; and third, and earliest, the movement of the Kintu associated groups from the east through South Busoga and into the centre of the Buganda kingdom.

The Chwezi emerged as a powerful group in the short grass country of western Uganda,[26] apparently on the heels of the Batembuzi and somewhat later than the arrival of the Kintu groups from the east. These Chwezi were to make an impact on a region much broader than the pastoral lands in which they had their roots, and their influence was to survive long after the era of their living dominance had ended. The era of Chwezi hegemony has been dated to the late fourteenth century from the remains at their earthwork enclosures at Bigo on the Katonga River.[27] While the evidence relating to the sequence of major regional events clearly indicates that the Chwezi post-dated Kintu and post-dated the retreat to the Lake,[28] the Chwezi traditions tend to be syncretic—absorbing earlier and tangential traditions—and seem to associate the groups retreating to the Lake with the rise of the Chwezi hegemony. Thus, such figures as Mukasa, Bukulu, Wannema, and Kibuuka, and clans such as the Otter, Grasshopper, Reedbuck, and Civet Cat, who evidently preceded Kintu in the Buganda area, and thus preceded the Chwezi, have been absorbed into the stream of Chwezi belief and tradition. The impetus for their migrations clearly belongs to the earlier age. The memories of their greatness in the western grasslands were absorbed into and preserved in the Chwezi traditions after they had departed. Their migrations clearly represent the movement of peoples from the western grasslands to the Lake area. And here, these groups achieved a new and lasting influence.

The earliest recollected settlement in Busoga—that of Kibwika at Bukonge in South Busoga—is clearly linked to these movements from the western lands to the Lake coast and the Ssese Islands through the Reedbuck dispersals, through the name Kibuuka or Kibwika, through the particular ideas of spiritual authority which were carried by Kibwika's family to Bukonge, then to Nsumba, and

[26] Roland Oliver, 'A Question about the Bachwezi', *Uganda Journal*, xvii, 2 (1953), 135–7.

[27] Posnansky, 'Kingship, Archaeology . . .', pp. 4–5.

[28] The available evidence indicates that the groups involved in the migrations associated with Kintu (of the eastern theme) moved westwards into the centre of Buganda, meeting along the way groups earlier involved in the backwash movements southwards from western Uganda to the Lake Victoria coasts.

then to Bugulu.[29] These groups carried ideas of heroic leadership and spiritual authority into the very areas through which the Kintu groups coming from the east were to travel. In the course of encounters between these groups of western derivation and groups associated with an eastern Kintu, clan traditions were generated which transposed the migrations and heroic activities of Kintu to the short grasslands of western Uganda.

Likewise, when Kimera—the figure travelling into the centre of Buganda some years after the arrival there of Kintu—reached the heart of Kintu's world with his companions of the Monkey, Buffalo, Bushbuck, Kayozi, Squirrel, and Grasshopper totems, the linkage of traditions old and new resulted in a theme of Kintu legend which holds that Kintu, in this case identified with Kimera, came from the west and north, from the first camps of the Bito groups pushing into western Uganda as part of the Nilotic Lwo penetration of the region.

While the Ganda traditions reflect the importance of the movements emanating in the west—Chwezi, pre-Chwezi, and Kimera—to the rise of the Ganda state and to the emergence of a Ganda culture, there is a theme of Kintu tradition concerned with the movements of groups from the *east*. The western developments were certainly of crucial consequence to the region as a whole; yet the germ of the Kintu tradition of Buganda and Busoga appears to lie in the east. Here again, it was in the apparent backwash of Bantu encounters with other worlds that the groups associated with Kintu rolled back through South Busoga and into the heart of the nascent Ganda state.

[29] Kibwika is discussed below, pp. 112–13. The larger problem of the association between the Lake Victoria deity figures, including Kibwika, and the Chwezi traditions is discussed in a review article by the present writer, 'The Cwezi Cult', *Journal of African History*, ix, 4, (1968), 651–7.

CHAPTER IV

From the East

THE central theme of the Kintu legends and traditions involves the movement of groups associated with Kintu from the east through Busoga to the heart of Buganda. Kaggwa's version of the Kintu tradition constitutes the principal published text of the popular account of Kintu's origins and travels. The tradition begins with an exodus theme.

Once upon a time, God said to Kintu, his grandchild: 'Go down to Earth with your wife Nambi and produce children on the Earth.' But God warned him, 'When you go down there, do not go with your brother Walumbe [Mr. Death]. Wake up early so that he does not see you when you depart—if you go with him, he will kill all the children you produce.' And when God finished warning him, Kintu agreed to wake early to go. At the first break of light, he set off, but when he was going down, his wife Nambi remembered the millet for her hen which she had left behind. She told her husband, 'I left the millet for my hen on the porch of the house. Let me go back for it now.' Her husband Kintu refused, saying, 'Don't go back because you will meet Walumbe if you return,' but Nambi Nantutululu did not pay heed to her husband's words, and she left her husband and went back for the millet for her hen. When Nambi reached the house, she took the millet from the porch, but as she was returning, Walumbe arrived and said to her, 'Why have you left me, my friend?' And he went with that woman Nambi Nantutululu. But when Kintu went back to tell God that Walumbe was accompanying him, God said, 'Did I not tell you to wake up early and go? Now go away. Don't plead with me. Just go.' When Kintu heard this, he started to rebuke his wife. 'It is you who has brought me this Walumbe. It is you who has killed me.' When he finished rebuking her, they travelled down to the Earth. Kintu bore his children. Walumbe killed them.[1]

As Kaggwa relates it, the exodus theme contains little evidence of an explicitly historical nature. It is a religious tradition with a strong Adamic quality. Moreover, it is a national tradition giving neither advantage nor disadvantage to any particular section of Ganda society. The neutral quality of the story as a national tradition and the Adamic message may very well have been features which ap-

[1] Sir A. Kaggwa, *Ekitabo kya Basekabaka be Buganda* (*Kings*) (Kampala, 1953) . pp. 1–2.

peared long after the original event, eclipsing the historical message of the migration tradition. The transformation of the story may have been gradual, occurring perhaps in response to centripetal pressures at the court of the Kabaka of Buganda. The difficulties of discerning the historical content within the Kintu tradition are then not merely the result of a seeming fusion of northern and western and eastern themes, but are, moreover, a consequence of the seemingly ahistorical nature of the popular Ganda version of the Kintu migration.

Fortunately there are fragments of tradition which were not lost or embedded in neutralized or embellished national tradition, and these fragments offer evidence upon which some segments of the Kintu migration can be reconstructed. While a later section of the Ganda tradition of Kintu as recorded by Kaggwa does relate that Kintu travelled into the centre of Buganda from the east (from Mangira in present Kyaggwe) and therefore distinguishes this theme from northern and western themes of Kintu, the traditions of Busoga emphasize this east-to-west passage and extend the point of Kintu's origin and the origin of migration eastwards to western Kenya, thus clearly isolating this migration from the travels associated with the northern and western Kintu themes. Relying mainly on fragments of Soga tradition, historians such as Gray, Robertson, and Kiwanuka have associated Kintu with the eastern origin.[2] Now, with a larger body of Soga tradition, as well as other evidence not apparently considered before, it is possible not only to investigate in some depth the 'exodus', but also to examine, and to a considerable extent resolve, such problems as the identity of Kintu, the association with Walumbe, the dating of Kintu, and the impact of Kintu on Buganda and Busoga.

The Kintu Migration

The Kintu migration was, evidently, the migration of several clans, and it is in clan tradition, rather than in national traditions such as the one quoted from Kaggwa, that the detail is found on which to base a reconstruction. Through traditions associating themselves with Kintu by filiation or clientage, more than fifteen Ganda clans claim to have taken part in the Kintu migration. These include clans of the Lion, Otter, Elephant, Lungfish, Mushroom, Nvuma Bead,

---

[2] J. M. Gray, 'The Basoga', *Uganda Journal*, iii, 4, (1936), 309–10; D. W. Robertson, *Historical Considerations*, p. 1; and M. Kiwanuka, 'The Traditional History of the Buganda Kingdom'.

Leopard, Genet, Yam, Hippopotamus, Dog, Blue Duiker, Bean, Crow, and Heart totems, and there are a few others whose claims are tentative.[3] It seems clear, however, that only the Lion, Leopard, Lungfish, and Bean groups were involved in the process of the east-to-west-migration associated with the Kintu figure. A fifth group, the Genet clan, seems to have emerged from the Leopard clan at a later date. A few other groups may have been involved in this Kintu migration; however, the evidence on these is too fragmentary. The rest of the Ganda clans were not involved in this east-to-west migration of Kintu; rather, the others associating themselves with the Kintu tradition seem to have been involved in events related to the northern and western themes of the Kintu legend.

The evidence also suggests that the Lion, Leopard, and Genet groups together constituted one ethnic unit; it was only while they were moving westwards that they segmented into three groups. The Kintu figure appears to have been intimately associated with this complex, and within the complex, a link with the Leopard segment in particular is indicated. It is less clear that Kintu was a living leader of the migrants; it is possible that the Kintu figure may have been a deity or symbol of this complex of groups passing from east to west, perhaps the spirit of a once living leader.

While the evidence of Kintu's living presence is superficial, there is striking evidence of the common ethnicity of the Lion, Leopard, and Genet groups. First, there is the sharing of secondary totems. The secondary totem of the Lion groups is the Leopard, the secondary totem of the Leopard group is the Genet Cat, and the secondary totem of the Genet Cat group is the Leopard. There is also narrative evidence. Kiwanuka relates the tradition that the Genet clan in Buganda was founded by Leopard clan members escaping persecution in the reign of Kabaka Kateregga [1629–56±].[4] Nsimbi relates a similar tradition but has the Genet clan emerging from the Leopard clan in the reign of Kabaka Nakibinge [1548–75±46] or Kabaka Mulondo [1575–1602±44].[5]

Additionally, Ganda tradition, particularly clan tradition, provides considerable evidence relating Kintu to this Lion–Leopard–Genet complex. Clan tradition relates that Namuguzi, a purported founder

---

[3] The list of clans has been constructed from the material presented by Kaggwa, *Clans* (Kampala, 1949), and by M. Nsimbi, *Amannya Amaganda*. There are today some forty clans in Buganda, each defined by a major and secondary totem.
[4] Kiwanuka, pp. 182–3.   [5] Nsimbi, pp. 212–14.

of the Lion clan in Buganda, was a son of Kintu.[6] There is also the Leopard clan tradition that Kkeya of the Leopard totem was a son of Kintu.[7] Kaggwa relates the tradition that Mwanje, son of the same Kkeya, was founder of the Leopard clan.[8] Perhaps the most important indication from Ganda tradition is that 'Members of the Lion and Leopard clans are the ones who settled wherever Kintu made his capitals.'[9] This seems particularly true of the Leopard clan settlements. Leopard clan estates in Buganda—including Nnono, Buvvi, Bukesa, Mangira, and Butwala—are recalled as important stopping places of Kintu in the episode in the popular tradition which begins with Kintu's departure from Bweramondo on the eastern side of present Buganda. In this sequence of stops and marches, Kintu reaches the heart of Buganda.

And when Kintu finished giving his grandchildren land, he left Bweramondo and went to Butwala, and built there and spent about two months there. And he left Butwala and reached Ntunda and stayed there for about three years. When he left Ntunda, he reached Mangira and he built there and spent about eleven years there . . . he left Mangira and walked and reached Buvu [Buvvi] and built there and stayed there for many years. He used to go to Buddu and Kiziba from that place and afterwards he came back to Buvu. He would go to the Ssese Islands and explore all over that area. And then he came back to Buvu and spent many years, about fifteen, there. Afterwards he left Buvu and reached Bukesa and built there and stayed there about six years . . . And when Kintu left Bukesa, after killing Bemba Omusota [Bbemba the Snake], he went and built at Nnono Hill, and he stayed there for some seven years. And when he left there, he went and built at Magonga and established a capital there which has lasted up to the present.[10]

There is also the tradition which records that Kintu, before travelling to Bukesa, stopped at Kanyanya and built at Lwadda Hill in present Kyaddondo County.[11] Kanyanya and Lwadda Hill are among the most important clan estates of the Lion clan in Buganda.[12] Additionally, there is the tradition that Kintu, while at Bukesa, called Ssebuganda, putative founder of the Lion clan, to come to Bukesa.[13]

In the Ganda traditions, Magonga is the most important capital of Kintu, and it was at Magonga that Kintu distributed a number of

[6] Kaggwa, *Clans* [MS. translation], p. 1. [7] Nsimbi, p. 208.
[8] Kaggwa, *Clans* [MS. translation], p. 59. [9] ibid., p. 1.
[10] Kaggwa, *Kings*, pp. 3–4.
[11] Nsimbi, p. 215.
[12] ibid., pp. 215–16. [13] ibid., p. 216.

estates to his numerous client groups. It was at Magonga that Mwanje of the Leopard clan, with his clansmen, performed the traditional rites for Kintu down through the ages. A later Mwanje of the Leopard clan invited Kabaka Mawanda [1737–64±32] to come to meet and speak with Kintu at Magonga.[14] And at Magonga the Lion clan kept the small drum called *Nnalubaale* which is reported to have been given to Kintu.[15]

There are other indications that Kintu was intimately associated with the Leopard–Lion complex. In Buganda, no person from the Lion clan was eligible for the throne, and boys born of a royal marriage with the Lion clan are said to have been strangled at birth.[16] This suggests that the Ganda royal lineage—which, from our perspective, appears to be of matrilineal bent—was still incipiently a Lion clan lineage with the consequence that no offspring of an incestuous marriage between a Kabaka and a woman of the Lion clan could be tolerated. The abaiseKiyuuka of Busoga have a tradition bearing this out:

The abaiseKiyuuka [of Lion totem] ran away from the Kabaka of Buganda. He had taken a girl of the abaiseKiyuuka. Then he saw Nambogwe [her father] to say that he wanted to marry her right away. His prospective father-in-law said that this was impossible, 'How can you marry your daughter?' The Kabaka decided to kill them, and he tried.[17]

Bearing on the same point is the tradition which relates that Kabaka Kateregga [1629–56±40] persecuted the Leopard clan because the Leopard clansmen claimed to belong to the royal family.[18]

Roscoe relates the story that Kintu declared that the Eagle should be considered a sacred bird and would become a royal totem. The dressed eagle, the lion skin, and the leopard skin 'have formed the rug [*ekiyu*] upon which the King sits or stands for State ceremonies; and the animals and birds in question have been looked upon as sacred to royalty. Indeed, formerly, no one was allowed to possess any of these skins; they were a royal monopoly, and were sent to the King.'[19] In Busoga, the abaiseKyema clan which ruled a small part of South Busoga had both the Eagle and Lion totems. There is no Eagle clan in Buganda and no other group recognizing the Eagle in

[14] Kiwanuka, p. 256.
[15] John Roscoe, *The Baganda* (2nd edn., London, 1965), p. 141.
[16] ibid., p. 142.   [17] STBTH, i. 112.
[18] Kiwanuka, pp. 182–3.   [19] Roscoe, *The Baganda*, p. 141.

Busoga. However, the Eagle is recalled in the traditions of the Liisa royal group in the western part of the region.[20]

There are other Soga traditions which associate the Kintu figure with the Lion–Leopard complex. Among the early settled groups in South Busoga were the abaiseIumbwe, who emerged as the ruling families in the Bunyuli and Bukasango states, and the aforementioned abaiseKyema, who emerged as the ruling family of the Bukyema state. These groups were all of the Lion totem. Several Soga traditions recall that Kintu was the forefather of the abaiseIumbwe of the Lion totem,[21] and the abaiseKyema of the Lion are also traced back to Kintu.[22] The four Leopard totem groups now present in Busoga all emerged from a centre at Wamango in South Busoga, or from Leopard groups dispersing from Wamango, and all of the Leopard groups of South Busoga trace their origins to Kintu.[23]

Taken together, the evidence quite clearly indicates a close association between Kintu and the Lion–Leopard groups and the existence of one traditional complex, perhaps a consanguineous group, comprising the Lion, Leopard, and Genet groups.

There is a second group to be considered. The Ganda traditions concerning Kintu speak of Nambi, the wife of Kintu, and Walumbe, the fearsome anti-Kintu force. In Ganda tradition, there is a strong claim that Nambi was a daughter of the Colobus Monkey clan, and there are suggestions that Walumbe was in some way associated with the same clan.[24] But Ganda tradition leaves a convincing record that the Colobus Monkey clan preceded Kintu in Buganda. It would be

[20] The Liisa tradition relates how three brothers and a sister of the Liisa clan chased the eagle from Kyabukuju in Mpororo in south-west Uganda. Three of them continued the chase right to the capital of Ndahura, the Chwezi king, who was then ruling. The eagle here may represent a group or figure. P. K. Kanyamunyu, 'The Tradition of the Coming of the Abalisa Clan to Buhwezu, Ankole', *Uganda Journal*, xv, 2 (1951), 191–2.

[21] STBTH, i. 68; Lubogo, p. 102.

[22] This tradition is found in the original Luganda manuscript (p. 171) of Lubogo's *History*, a copy of which has been deposited by Omw. Lubogo in the Africana Collection, Makerere University Library. The Luganda MS., which differs from the published English translation in a number of respects, will henceforth be cited as 'Lubogo [Luganda MS.]'.

[23] Lubogo, p. 107.

[24] Nakabaale of the Colobus Monkey clan is the priest of the Walumbe shrine at Ttanda in Ssingo County, Buganda. Walumbe is supposed to have disappeared down a hole at Ttanda. Nsimbi, pp. 137–8, 192. In Soga tradition as well, Walumbe is associated with holes. Could this in some way be associated with the Lungfish clan's purported origins at Bumogera, recalled as an area of man-made holes and trenches? See below, pp. 97–100.

unlikely, therefore, that the Kintu figure coming from the east would have come with a Colobus Monkey clanswoman as his 'wife', although once in Buganda Kintu may very well have married a woman of that clan.

In these possibly symbolic traditions, 'wife' may represent a favoured marriage tie between two groups. In some Soga traditions, the 'wife' of Kintu is called Nambubi.[25] Soga traditions also relate that it was Nambubi, the wife of Kintu, who was mother of Namunhole Iumbwe, the founding figure of the abaiseIumbwe ruling group in Busoga.[26] This *Nambubi* name is of significance, for it is the most common name given to daughters of the Lungfish clan throughout the islands off the coasts of Buganda and Busoga.

While in both Ganda and Soga tradition Walumbe is referred to as the brother-in-law of Kintu,[27] the Soga traditions additionally associate Walumbe with the Lungfish totem. The traditions of the abaiseMaganda record that Walumbe is their most important clan deity, and they are of the Lungfish totem.[28] Still another tradition relates that Walumbe was a mwiseMaganda,[29] and in South Busoga, segments of the Lungfish totem have guarded the shrine of the Walumbe deity, evidently for centuries.[30]

A Soga tradition records that Walumbe, travelling with Kintu, reached the area of Buswikira in South Busoga.[31] The most important Kintu shrine in Busoga is at Buswikira in South Busoga, and it is there that Kintu is reported to be buried, though no more than an emotional identification with that place has been demonstrated. At the same place, there is the very important Walumbe shrine kept by the abaiseMaganda, and some believe that Walumbe is buried there. Walumbe is also associated with Buyanirwa, a few miles to the west. One tradition records that Kintu, when he fled or disappeared from Buganda, returned to Buswikira and found at Buyanirwa a large group of abaiseMaganda of the Lungfish totem whom Kintu had to

[25] STBTH, i. 1 and 69; Lubogo, p. 102.

[26] STBTH, i. 69; Lubogo, p. 102.

[27] Sir A. Kaggwa, *The Customs of the Baganda*, ed. M. M. Edel, trans. E. B. Kalibala (New York, 1934), p. 112.

[28] STBTH, i. 72; CTBTH, Text 297.   [29] CTBTH, Text 802.

[30] CTBTH, Test 297. A reconstruction of Lungfish clan history in South Busoga indicates that at first the family of Mudoli of the Lungfish totem cared for the shrine, but that later they were overwhelmed by a stronger Lungfish group migrating from Buganda, the abaiseMaganda, with whom they evidently committed incest.

[31] STBTH, i. 72, 133–5.

defeat when they tried to resist his rule.[32] Kyema, the founder of the Bukyema state, is said to have been born at Buswikira, and he is re-called as a son of Kintu.[33] In many texts, Buswikira is identified as the centre of Kintu's activities in Busoga. While this close identification of Kintu and Walumbe in the immediate vicinity of Buswikira is suggestive of a relationship developing between Lion–Leopard and Lungfish groups prior to their reaching Buganda, there is scant evidence of a link existing east of Busoga, though the 'origins' of both groups seem to lie in the region between Mount Elgon and the Lake Victoria coast.

The most useful source on the Lion–Leopard movements from the east is Higenyi's 'History of the Banyole', an unpublished history of the peoples of Bunyole County in eastern Uganda. Higenyi records in some detail the migrational routes of the groups who were to emerge in South Busoga as the abaiseIumbwe rulers of the Lion totem. At a relatively recent date, perhaps 250 years ago, a number of families, including parties of abaiseIumbwe, left the Iumbwe domains in South Busoga—Bunyuli and Bukasango—and travelled to what is now Bunyole County east of Busoga, the area of Higenyi's immediate interest.[34] Higenyi records that the peoples of the Lion totem (abaise-Iumbwe) travelled to South Busoga from the Kenya side of Mount Elgon in two groups, Munyole's and Nanyumba's. Higenyi's text, while supplying little genealogical evidence suggestive of chronology, does give a fairly extensive description of the routes taken. Higenyi relates that,

The Banyole came from the Masai tribe on the Kenya side of Mount Elgon. The population of the Masai grew to an enormous size and some of them had to migrate to other areas where there was room for them to settle. Some of them went to a country called Buwanga but the centre of the Masai was Kitale. The Banyole came from an area called Bunyifa. Dyeri was our forefather from whom we descended and he lived in that village Bunyifa in Buwanga. His wife was Mayi [mother]. Dyeri had a son, his eldest [Mu]Nyoa[le] Nnyea, and a second son Nanyumba. And a third, Masinde.

Higenyi describes the break-up of the family of Dyeri in terms of a

---

[32] Lubogo, p. 102.

[33] Lubogo [Luganda MS.], p. 171.

[34] The peoples of South Busoga, including the abaiseIumbwe, were almost completely wiped out by the Sleeping Sickness epidemics of this century. Higenyi could draw upon representatives of groups which left South Busoga long before the outbreak of Sleeping Sickness.

stereotypic Lwo story.[35] The story, in this form, may have emerged
at a relatively recent time as a consequence of the penetration of eastern Uganda by Nilotic Lwo arriving from the north. Higenyi describes how Munyole's group left Nanyumba's group at Bumbo in
Bugishu, which they apparently had reached from the east. They
passed through Bugwere to Budumba near the Mpologoma River.
From there, they travelled through present-day Busiki until they
reached Wambete in South Busoga, where they finally settled.
Nanyumba's group, on the other hand, took a southern route, leaving
Munyole's group at Bumbo in Bugishu and travelling from there to
Maseno in Central Nyanza, to Bukhubalo in present-day Samia–
Bugwe County, to Bukooli, and finally to Wambete in South Busoga,
where they established a settlement.

Lubogo, drawing on Soga rather than Nyole sources, relates the
tradition that Kasango Iumbwe, the putative founder of the abaise-
Iumbwe, left Mount Elgon because of overcrowded conditions and,
from there, wandered south-westwards, reaching Nambale in
Bugishu where he stayed for a time. Later, he moved to South Busoga
where he made his home at Nambale.[36] Munyole of Higenyi's text
appears to be one and the same as Kasango Iumbwe of the Lubogo
text. The Kasango Iumbwe group emerged as the ruling house of the
Bukasango state on the eastern side of South Busoga. The Nanhumba (Nanyumba) name was the title which was later applied to the
rulers of the abaiseIumbwe state of Bunyuli on the western side of
South Busoga and seems here to represent the second 'Banyole'
group. In Soga tradition,[37] Mubiko is recorded as the founder of the
ruling family on the western side, having been given his domain by
Kintu. These two abaiseIumbwe groups—of Bukasango and Bunyuli—were evidently of the same patrilineage.

Mount Elgon also figures prominently in the migrational traditions of the Leopard group. One Soga tradition relates that Nalwebe,
the purported forefather of the Leopard groups in South Busoga,
travelled with Ngiya of the Small Millet totem from the Mount Elgon
area to Bugiya in South Busoga.[38] Lubogo relates that Kintu travelled
from Mount Elgon to South Busoga at Mpundwe from where he
distributed four contiguous areas to four sons of the Leopard totem.[39]

[35] This is the story of the two brothers and their spears, and beads, the elephant,
and the disemboweled baby. Crazzolara, *The Lwoo*, pp. 62–4.

[36] Lubogo, p. 80.

[37] Lubogo [Luganda MS.], p. 138; Lubogo, pp. 81–2, 102.

[38] CTBTH, Text 714.   [39] Lubogo [Luganda MS.], p. 104.

A source from Buddu, western Uganda, relates that Kintu emerged from a complex living on or behind Mount Elgon and that one of the forefathers was Lubowa of the Leopard totem.[40]

The traditions of migration of the Lungfish clan, which is apparently associated with Walumbe, are perhaps the most solid of the Ganda clan migrational traditions. While there are some conflicts among the variant Lungfish traditions, there is considerable common ground. Nsimbi relates the tradition that the Ndiira family of the Lungfish totem came from the area of Mount Elgon and travelled to Kirinya Hill near Jinja, in south-western Busoga, where Ndiira died. Mubiru succeeded his father there, and from Kirinya they migrated eastwards under the new leadership to Bumogera near Kisumu where Mubiru and his sons did the work of fishing and forging axes.[41] At Bumogera, the son of Mubiru is supposed to have lost his axe in the lake; as a result of this loss, his people decided to leave in their canoes, and they paddled across the Lake to Buvuma Island, where Kisanje established himself as the ruler at Maggyo. From there, they went to Busagazi on the Kyaggwe coast.[42]

The tradition related by Kaggwa begins with the Lungfish people at Bumogera under the leadership of Gabunga. According to the tradition, Gabunga's people left Bumogera and travelled to Nalwebe's in South Busoga.[43] From there, they went to Busagazi on the Kyaggwe coast.[44]

Ggomotoka records a tradition which has Mubiru Kisanje coming with his brothers, including Mubiru Gabunga, from Bumogera. They reached Kigulu Island and then went to Magogo, then to Ddolwe [Lolui] and then to Buvuma, arriving at Namusoba harbour.[45]

Picking up the story at Busagazi in Kyaggwe, Nsimbi relates that Mubiru left Busagazi and travelled inland to Mangira, in Kyaggwe, where he found Kintu and asked him to give him a place in his country.[46] Kaggwa[47] relates a similar story. The tradition continues: Kintu sent Mubiru with Kalyango of the Leopard clan, and Kalyango was to guide Mubiru to a place of settlement. They returned

---

[40] J. M. K. Bapere, 'Kintu n'abantu be yali nabo e Bukedi ku lusozi Masaba', *Munno*, April 1929, pp. 66–7, quoting Suka Masiira of Kabuwooko, Buddu.

[41] Nsimbi, p. 252.   [42] ibid., pp. 252–3.

[43] Nalwebe was of the Leopard totem. Kaggwa calls him Nanhumba's brother. Kaggwa, *Clans* [translation], p. 35.

[44] ibid.

[45] J. T. K. Ggomotoka, 'Buvuma Island', [manuscript included in CTBTH].

[46] Nsimbi, pp. 253–4.

[47] Kaggwa, *Clans* [MS. translation], p. 35.

to Busagazi, boarded their canoes, and travelled along the coast, stopping at several places. They also inspected the islands along the coast. Kalyango left Mubiru at Kiwumu near the Lake, and, in the next generation, Mubiru's son Ssematimba moved to Jjungo, which remained the chief estate and headquarters of Gabunga of the Lungfish clan, the admiral of the Ganda fleet.[48]

The evidence indicates that the Lungfish people made an important contact with the Kintu figure and the Leopard clan at Mangira in Kyaggwe. There are additional indications that contact was made earlier in South Busoga or possibly even earlier in the lands east of Busoga. The reported route of the Lungfish group from Mount Elgon to Kirinya Hill would have passed through South Busoga and could have been a movement accompanying the Lion–Leopard migration.[49] There is the tradition of the Lungfish migrants meeting Nalwebe of the Leopard totem in South Busoga. It is more certain that a Walumbe–Kintu contact was made east of Mangira at Buswikira or Buyanirwa as the dual shrine sites and the traditions would suggest.

While it is difficult to determine whether the westward movements of these peoples—so evidently associated with Kintu and Walumbe—constituted a unitary migration, a diffuse movement, or a slow westward expansion, the other reconstructed migrations in the region do appear to have been slow and diffuse, and the movements of the Lion–Leopard and Lungfish groups may very well have followed a similar pattern.

The Origins of Kintu and Walumbe

The 'origins' of the Lion–Leopard complex and the Lungfish group have been suggested in some of the traditions already considered. The Mount Elgon and Bunyifa–Kitale areas have been indicated as origins of the Lion–Leopard groups. Mount Elgon and 'Bumogera' have been suggested as possible origins of the Lungfish group. While the precise origins of Kintu and Walumbe and their associated groups must be uncertain, it is possible that both groups emerged from the early Bantu speakers settling on the eastern side of Lake

[48] Kaggwa, *Clans* [MS. translation], pp. 35–6; Nsimbi, pp. 254–5.

[49] The Lungfish group, however, appears to have been lacustrine in culture over a considerable period of time, and the asserted movement from Mount Elgon would run against the tide of evidence, unless, of course, this movement antedated their settlement at Bumogera and their adaptation to a lacustrine way of life, which is, in essence, the account related by Nsimbi.

Victoria. This early Bantu presence has been indicated by the evidence of the Dimple-based pottery ware found at Urewe, Yala Alego, and other sites in Central Nyanza.[50] The Dimple-based ware at Urewe has been radiocarbon dated to the fourth century A.D.[51] The evidence suggests that the Lungfish group was involved in a lacustrine culture, though perhaps influenced to some extent by the pastoralist culture dominating the higher ground of western Kenya. The Lion–Leopard complex, on the other hand, appears to have avoided the Lake and the Lake shore, confining themselves to the higher lands; there, they were open to considerable contact with the pastoral groups occupying the Western Highlands of Kenya from an early time.

Bumogera appears to be one key to the 'origins' of an early Lungfish group; the problem is that it is unclear where Bumogera was located. Nsimbi has written that Bumogera is found near Kisumu.[52] Kaggwa reports that when the Gabunga, the admiral of the Buganda fleet and a Lungfish figure, died, his jawbone was removed and one tooth was removed from it to indicate that they were 'Bamogera'.[53] This evulsion of teeth was a custom common to peoples all through Busoga (with the exception of the peoples of Busiki County) and through most of the islands on the eastern side of Lake Victoria, among peoples to the east of Busoga right up through the Kalenjin Cushitic speakers of western Kenya and southern Ethiopia. Among the Lungfish people of Buganda, the custom apparently survived, if only in the symbolic rite of removing one tooth from the jaw of the leading clan figure after death. Most of the peoples who evulse in the region remove two or four teeth; however, the people formerly occupying Lolui Island in Lake Victoria and the Lungfish people in Buganda are apparently unique in removing just one lower incisor,[54] and it is perhaps to Lolui that one should turn in seeking Lungfish 'origins'. Several significant details on the culture and history of the peoples of Lolui Island were obtained in a recent interviewing survey of a few of the survivors of the Sleeping Sickness epidemic which

[50] M. D. Leakey, W. E. Owen, and L. S. B. Leakey, 'Dimple-based Pottery from Central Kavirondo', *Coryndon Memorial Museum, Occasional Paper* 2 (Nairobi, 1948).

[51] Brian M. Fagan, 'Radiocarbon Dates for Sub-Saharan Africa: VI', *Journal of African History*, x, 1 (1969), 157. The material at Yala Alego has been radiocarbon dated at A.D. 400.

[52] Nsimbi, p. 252.   [53] Kaggwa, *Clans* [MS. translation], p. 36.

[54] La Fontaine reports that some Bagisu removed one or two lower incisors. J. S. La Fontaine, 'The Gisu of Uganda', *Ethnographic Survey of Africa, East Central Africa*, Part 10, ed. Daryll Forde, (London, 1959) p. 60.

cleared Lolui in the early years of this century, and these details would tend to reinforce the hypothesis of association between the Lungfish group and Lolui Island. The informants reported that the people of Lolui came originally from the east, from the Mount Elgon area; that elements of the Lungfish, Lion, Monkey, Bird, and Civet Cat totems lived on the island before evacuation; and that the gods of Lolui Island were Mubiru, Muwanga, and Namunamira, whose medium was Wamango.[55] The correlations between Lolui and the Lungfish clan are impressive: the one lower incisor removed, the Mubiru figure, the presence of Lungfish people on the island, the origin near Mount Elgon, and the Ganda tradition, related by Ggomotoka, that the Lungfish group migrating from Bumogera stopped at Lolui [Ddolwe].[56] There are also several unexpected correlations of exceptional significance between the Lion–Leopard complex and Lolui: the presence of Lion people on the island and the figure of Wamango, the medium of the Namunamira deity, who in Soga tradition is identified with the earliest settlement of Leopard groups in South Busoga. These are the only lacustrine connections between Lungfish and Lion–Leopard groups on the eastern side of the Lake.

There is an important Dimple-based pottery site on Lolui Island,[57] one perhaps associated with the Dimple-based sites found in nearby Central Nyanza. These sites suggest an early and important series of Bantu settlements around the north-east coast of Lake Victoria. Interestingly, Posnansky has reported that Lolui Island has very poor soil for the production of pottery; he has suggested that the pots were imported.[58] Excellent pottery clays are found at the Central Nyanza sites; remains at the Nyanza sites indicate that they were primarily sites of pottery making—no associated settlement sites in that area have been unearthed. It is not entirely impossible that the Lolui peoples visited sites such as those of Central Nyanza, made their pots, and returned to their settlements on Lolui, or that there was some sort of economic symbiosis or trade between the Lolui Islanders and a pot-making group on the mainland (whose settlement remains would still have to be found)—one possibly associated with the Central

---

[55] Lolui Island Project: interview by Miss L. Anderson, Mr. Nabugusi, and Mr. Temple; copy of typescript in CTBTH.

[56] J. T. K. Ggomotoka, 'Buvuma Island' [Manuscript included in CTBTH].

[57] M. Posnansky, 'Bantu Genesis—Archaeological Reflexions', *Journal of African History*, ix, 1 (1968), 1.

[58] Posnansky, 'Bantu Genesis', 3.

Nyanza sites. Posnansky has suggested, on the basis of the persistence in form and decoration of the Dimple-based pottery on Lolui, that 'after the Dimple-based ware users settled on the island, probably in the last half of the first millennium A.D., there seems to have been no new influence affecting the island until the middle of the second millennium A.D.'[59] The sequence of events in early Buganda would have the Lungfish people migrating westward from Bumogera–Lolui before the middle of the second millennium A.D. Presumably then, on the basis of the Posnansky hypothesis and the chronological sequence, the Lungfish people reaching Lolui, or residing there, were part of the general Lolui Bantu culture and did not represent some cultural influence alien to the early producers and users of Dimple-based pottery on the eastern side of Lake Victoria. Developing the hypothesis still further, one can postulate that Lolui was within the province of the Lungfish people some time after the middle of the first millennium A.D., the time when the Bantu speakers, with their Dimple-based ware, were apparently establishing themselves in the region.

There remains the elusive problem of the Bumogera reference. There are a few additional though scanty references to Bumogera in Ganda and Soga tradition. The Sheep clan in Buganda has, like the Lungfish group, the tradition of Bumogera origins, and this is interesting, for the Sheep clan has the Lion as its secondary totem. Tradition has the Sheep clan passing through the Lake from Bumogera to the Ssese Islands.[60] The founder of the Sheep clan was Sekkoba, and, while there is no available evidence which could relate Sekkoba's journey with the Kintu–Walumbe movements, it is interesting that Ikoba of the Bean totem, the founder of the abaiseIkoba clan and state, and possibly associated etymologically with Sekkoba of Sheep tradition, is associated with similar eastern origins (though not specifically Bumogera) and with the Kintu–Walumbe movements.[61] There is evidence that the Bean groups came from Sigulu Island in the north-east corner of Lake Victoria. As the Bean groups moved westward by canoe, families established themselves at various points on the lake coasts and on the islands—at Bukoba, at Lingira Island, at Bugaya Island and on other islands of the Buvuma group, and on the Kyaggwe coast.[62]

[59] ibid.   [60] Nsimbi, pp. 293–4.
[61] Kaggwa, *Clans* [MS. translation], p. 102; CTBTH, Texts 108, 616.
[62] CTBTH, Text 111; Lubogo, p. 130. Ggomotoka, 'Buvuma Island', CTBTH.
H

On Bugaya Island and Sigulu Island are found iron-working sites, stone-enclosure ruins, and palisaded village remains.[63] It is not improbable that a Bean group carried these techniques related to defence from Sigulu to Bugaya. These defensive works are similar to those found in western Kenya and eastern Uganda.

The abaiseNhikodo of the Giraffe totem, who claim to have come from the area between Mount Elgon and Lake Victoria, and who, in this region, fought with and were defeated by a strong Bean group, the abaiseKyewe, have a tradition which relates them to Bumogera and to this region of earthworks and trench defences. The testimony records that the Baganda who came to the eastern edge of Busoga and beyond on raiding forays used to call them 'Bamogera'. The source records,

This name came as follows: whenever the Baganda came to attack us, our infantry, who had climbed the trees, warned us, and we had to go down into our trenches. The trench was known as *lukoba*. The Baganda nicknamed us *Bamogerattaka*. *Bamogerattaka*—'They peep through the soil.' We used to peep through the soil but in fact we used to be on the treetops, not peeping through the soil at all. This name comes from the method of our fighting.[64]

While this explication of the word is not altogether clear, the proposition that the Baganda gave these trench and tree-top fighters this nickname because of their special method of fighting is plausible. Persse, in his article on the Bagwe of eastern Uganda, has described such defensive works as consisting of 'moated villages surrounded by circular mud walls about eight feet high. There were some thirty or more huts in each village, and there was a bridge of tree trunks with guard rails providing access to the gates in the wall.'[65]

Several serious problems emerge in respect to this Bumogera reference. First, it is ostensibly a Ganda reference applied to an area far from the heart of Buganda, and the explication of the term may be based on what the Baganda saw of the defensive strategies of these peoples in the nineteenth century. The word may not refer specifically to clans emerging from that area centuries before. The word may have replaced an earlier word describing the region; perhaps the

[63] Personal communication from Dr. M. Posnansky; Ggomotoka, 'Bugaya Island', CTBTH.
[64] CTBTH, Text, 754.
[65] Captain E. M. Persse, 'The Bagwe', *Uganda Journal*, iii, 3 (1936), 283–4.

basic root was altered at some recent time to give the word that twist of meaning which the mwiseNhikodo source has conveyed.[66]

There is, secondly, the problem of the spread of the defensive works systems throughout the wider region. The pattern of works found all along the routes of the Bean clan migrations may represent the diffusion of a type of village construction. But many of these defensive works may have been more or less natural developments in the prevailing circumstances of danger in the region of western Kenya and eastern Uganda. Certainly the area in which the defensive earthworks abound has expanded and altered over the centuries, making it difficult to define a specific location of concentrated earthworks dated at one particular point in the past. The question of whether there is some historical continuity between the different types of defensive structures and their builders and occupiers cannot be resolved unless material evidence from within such structures is associated. The only clear point is that they were all apparently of the Iron Age. The Bumogera term can probably be added to the long list of general, geographic reference words in use in the region with no precise or consistent application. However, one should not dismiss the Lungfish clan tradition associating Bumogera with the Lake shore.[67] Nor can one dismiss the indication that the early Lungfish people were axe forgers. One of the most important centres of iron-working in the Interlacustrine region was located in the Samia Hills not far from the north-east coast of Lake Victoria. The Samia Hills area was apparently the source of ore, iron, and hoes for all the surrounding region including South Busoga and the islands in the north-east corner of the Lake. The early Lungfish peoples—recalled in tradition as blacksmiths and fishers, certainly superior boatmen, and clearly associated with Lolui Island—would appear to fit very neatly into the iron-working, lacustrine world around the north-east corner of the Lake. The only references which would carry them away from the Lake are, first, that of the trenches, possibly, but not necessarily suggesting a location well to the north, perhaps midway between the Lake coast and Mount Elgon; and second, a tradition associating the

---

[66] In Luganda, *kumoga* means 'to peep'. *Bamogera* means 'they peep through', and *Bamogerattaka* means 'they peep through the soil'. It is interesting that among the Sidama Kaffa of southern Ethiopia, the *moga* is the open area around a defensive trench encircling a village. G. W. B. Huntingford, 'The Galla of Ethiopia: The Kingdoms of Kafa and Janjero', *Ethnographic Survey of Africa, North-East Africa*, Part 2, ed. Daryll Forde, (London, 1965), p. 57.

[67] Nsimbi, pp. 253–4.

Lungfish clan with cattle. A Lungfish tradition relates that Mubiru Kisanje reached Buvuma Island with his cows.[68] And the Lolui Island survey data includes the remark that, on Lolui, 'The god Mubiru took the form of a black bull.'[69] Carrying the hypothesis forward, it is possible that the Lungfish peoples living along the lakeshore north of the Kavirondo Gulf had contacts with the pastoralist peoples living inland in the Western Highlands, an area not far from the Lake Victoria coast and quite close to the Dimple-based pottery sites in Central Nyanza.[70]

It seems quite possible then that before their departure for the west, the Lungfish people were established along the coastlands to the east of Lake Victoria between Berkeley Bay in the north-east and the Kavirondo Gulf. What also seems probable is that Lolui Island, and perhaps Sigulu Island as well, were components of a cultural complex including the coastlands and that the Lungfish people had their 'origins' within this sphere. The Lungfish people very likely derived from early Bantu speakers entering the region. They were clearly lacustrine in culture, and though they may have made contact with pastoral groups living east of the coastland belt, the pottery tradition on Lolui suggests that they did not carry an alien influence to the islands.

The associated Bean groups were also part of this lacustrine cultural complex around the north-east corner of the Lake. Their westwards expansion was probably contemporaneous, and closely involved, with the westwards movements of the Lungfish group. Like the Lungfish group, the Bean peoples evidently made some contact with the pastoral groups in the higher lands to the north-east and perhaps themselves emerged from groups occupying the higher ground in the vicinity of Mount Elgon.

This region around Mount Elgon is again and again indicated as the 'origin' of the Lion–Leopard complex—this area includes the aforementioned Bumbo to the west, Nambale to the south-west, Bunyifa to the south, and Kitale to the east of Mount Elgon. On the basis of traditions of western Kenya peoples, Ogot has postulated the existence of a region of early Bantu occupation running from Mount

[68] Ggomotoka, 'Buvuma Islands', CTBTH.

[69] Lolui Island Survey, CTBTH.

[70] Posnansky has pointed out that there is no evidence of cattle accompanying the earliest iron-users into the region. 'The Origins of Agriculture and Iron-working in Southern Africa', *Prelude to East African History*, ed. M. Posnansky, London, 1966), p. 93.

Elgon to Lake Victoria. He suggests that the Luyia–Gisu groups were in the Elgon area before A.D. 1000 and may have been the earliest settled Bantu speakers in the region.[71] Gideon Were has suggested that elements which eventually emerged as the Bantu-speaking Gisu and Vukusu were in the region of the Uasin Gishu Plateau east of Mount Elgon before moving westwards towards Mount Elgon under pressure of Nilo–Hamitic groups.[72] The traditions of the Bagisu and Bavukusu are not clear, nor are the histories of the historically associated peoples of Buluyia.[73]

One point that seems clear is that such early Bantu speakers as there were in the north-east corner of the Interlacustrine region—that is, between the Lake, Mount Elgon, and the Uasin Gishu plain—did come into contact with Kalenjin-speaking groups (and probably Cushitic speaking groups as well) in the Elgon region. These contacts very likely commenced as the earliest Bantu speakers arrived or expanded into the area; and the contacts have continued up to the present. J. E. G. Sutton has suggested that Caucasoid groups emerged from the Ethiopian highlands and reached Kenya perhaps in the second millennium B.C. He describes these peoples as Cushites on the evidence of their burial cairns and on the proposition that they were responsible for the diffusion of the north-east African culture complex of circumcision, initiation, and age-sets. Sutton suggests that the Kenya highlands group were, in language, Eastern Cushitic.[74] They probably introduced, besides the cultural elements mentioned above, cairns, grain cultivation, long-horned cattle, sheep and goats, basic irrigation techniques, and pastoral construction works such as wells, dams, and rain ponds.[75]

[71] B. A. Ogot, *History of the Southern Luo*, pp. 137–8.

[72] *A History of the Abaluyia* (Nairobi, 1967), pp. 42–3.

[73] Two major attempts have been made to record and digest the tortuous traditions of the Baluyia of western Kenya: Were, op. cit.; and J. Osogo, *A History of the Baluyia* (Nairobi, 1966). These two attempts have failed to assemble anything like a satisfactory history of these heterogeneous peoples living in western Kenya between Mount Elgon and the Luo of Nyanza. The major problem seems to be that the writers have attempted to reconstruct history at levels which are, for the purposes of reconstructing migrations and settlements and describing historical units, largely artificial, and they have depended on evidence too narrow to produce a credible result. It is impossible, at present, to use the complex Luyia data in reconstructing earlier groupings or in resolving the problem of the Kintu 'origin'.

[74] J. E. G. Sutton, 'The Archaeology and Early Peoples of the Highlands of Kenya and Northern Tanzania', *Azania* (1966), 47–8.

[75] ibid.

Sutton suggests the possibility of a Cushitic Iron Age in the region on the basis of the Engaruka ruins which probably date to the first millennium A.D., but he also suggests that iron working may have been introduced from the north by the Kalenjin and from the south by the Bantu pioneers in the region.[76] These Kalenjin were probably the first Nilo–Hamitic speakers in the region. Sutton has suggested that each successive wave of new immigrants, such as the Kalenjin, may have integrated itself in time with the 'indigenous substratum', such as the Cushitic and earlier groups.[77] The Bantu were very likely part of such a process of acculturation and integration, perhaps effecting an identity of experience with the early Bantu speakers of western Uganda. Some were certainly integrated into the Nilo–Hamitic speaking world. Some Bantu-speaking groups may have absorbed peoples or cultural elements of the Kalenjin–Cushitic 'substratum'. Certainly, such contacts, and the acculturation and integration which perhaps was their principal consequence, were not of a regular pattern, nor were they of a particular moment in history; there is evidence of such contact on both sides of the Rift Valley and these contacts apparently continued into the present century. The Bantu-speaking Gisu of the Mount Elgon area have a number of cultural features suggestive of extensive contact with the Kalenjin–Cushitic world: the ritual killing of cattle,[78] circumcision,[79] scarification, evulsion of teeth, lip-plugs, and dress.[80]

It is quite possible, on the basis of the evidence available, that the Kintu figure and the Kintu associated groups emerged from just such contacts in this region around the southern and eastern reaches of the Mount Elgon area, and from there moved westwards to make a major impact on Busoga and Buganda. The *Kintu* name, a basic Bantu word meaning 'thing', may be associated with the *Muntu* name associated in tradition with the founding figure of the Gisu and Vukusu groups.[81] Both are terms probably symbolic of inherent *Bantu-ness* in an apparent situation of Bantu contact and involvement with non-Bantu speaking groups.

[76] ibid., 48.   [77] ibid., 53–4.
[78] La Fontaine 'The Gisu of Uganda', p. 16.
[79] ibid., pp. 41–6.
[80] ibid., p. 60. Evulsion of teeth and scarification of women were common practices throughout most of Busoga and most of the islands on the eastern side of the Lake. Lip-plugs were common on the islands of Lake Victoria (Ggomotoka, 'Bugaya Island', CTBTH), and among the peoples of the Kyaggwe coast (Kaggwa, *Clans* [MS. translation], p. 106).
[81] Were, p. 43.

Ganda and Soga traditions record that Kintu was associated, variously, with the banana, millet, cattle, and hunting. Oliver[82] has postulated the arrival of the banana in the Interlacustrine region from the south. The tradition that Kintu brought the banana from Mount Elgon would tend to associate him with the important banana cultivation area on and around Mount Elgon. The Mount Elgon–Kintu-banana tradition immediately suggests the possibility that the banana reached the Lakes region from Ethiopia, a possibility suggested by Wainwright.[83] While this seems unlikely, it is possible that the Kintu movement from the Mount Elgon area may have, in some way, been the initial impulse towards the banana becoming an important food-plant in Buganda and Busoga. But Kintu, in both the Ganda and Soga traditions, seems to have been associated more closely with the cultivation of millet. It is, of course, possible that the Kintu complex may have emerged in an area of contact between banana cultivators near Mount Elgon and the millet-growing, cattle keepers to the east on the Uasin Gishu Plateau.

There are a few interesting correspondences between the cultures of south-west Ethiopia and this region around Mount Elgon, the postulated 'origin' of the Kintu complex. Among the Luyia and Gisu peoples, the Supreme God is Were or Wele. Among the Kaffa of South-west Ethiopia, the Sky-God is Yero or Yaro; among the northern Mao, the Supreme Being is Yere or Yeretsi. And there are the aforementioned Gisu cultural effects drawn very likely from the postulated Kalenjin–Cushitic substratum to which the peoples of south-west Ethiopia are related. Oliver once suggested the importance of the linkages between the small kingdoms of south-west Ethiopia including Damot, Enarya, Kaffa, and Janjero, and the emergent political cultures of Ankole, Rwanda, and the other Interlacustrine states, and the kingdom of Monomotapa lying in southern Africa between the Limpopo and the Zambezi Rivers.[84] Oliver pointed to the important elements of the 'divine, high-priestly, self-sacrificing king; . . . the cult of spirit possession; . . . the transmigration of the king's soul into a lion; . . . the royal fire and new-moon ceremonies; . . . the queen mother and the official queens with their

[82] Roland Oliver, 'The Problem of the Bantu Expansion', *Journal of African History*, vii, 3 (1966), 368–9.

[83] G. A. Wainwright, 'The Coming of the Banana to Uganda', *Uganda Journal*, xvi, 2 (1952), 145–7.

[84] Roland Oliver, 'The Riddle of Zimbabwe', *The Dawn of African History*, ed. R. Oliver, (London, 1961), pp. 56–9.

courts; ... the office-bearers, the pages and the nobility of royal favourites'.[85]

The close relationship between Kintu and the beginnings of the state in Buganda and Busoga, and perhaps throughout the wider region, is significant. There is the link between Kintu and the Lion–Leopard totemic groups, and these avoidances could be associated with the belief that the king's soul migrates into a lion. There are the traditions of origins of the Lion–Leopard groups in the region of the Kalenjin–Cushitic substratum, and there is the evidence of linkage between certain Bantu-speaking groups and the Kalenjin–Cushitic substratum; the Sidama kingdoms probably emerged from the Cushitic substratum. The hypothesis is unproven, yet it seems possible, on the basis of the very fragmentary evidence available, that Kintu constituted a link between the Bantu world pressing northwards and eastwards through the Mount Elgon region and the cultures associated with the Cushitic substratum lapping the margins of Mount Elgon and Lake Victoria. The process of acculturation of the Kintu complex—in the postulated circumstances of contact between Bantu and Cushitic or Kalenjin groups—would have ended with the movement of the Lion–Leopard group westwards.

Dating Kintu

The impact of Kintu on South Busoga and Buganda evidently preceded the rise of the Chwezi power in the grasslands of western Uganda. This Chwezi period has been dated, by remains at the enclosure of Wamara at Bigo to A.D. 1350–1500.[86] On the basis of this dating, the entrance of Kintu onto the Interlacustrine scene probably could not have been later than 1450. Traditional evidence provides still another indication. The Ganda evidence records that Kimera ruled some nineteen generations back from the death of Mutesa in 1884—through generation-dating 1386–1413±58. The Kintu impact may have preceded the reign of Kimera by one or more centuries; it certainly did not postdate it.

Lubogo has recorded [87] the royal genealogies of several groups in South Busoga associated with Kintu. The depth of the royal genealogy of the abaiseIkoba (Bean) ruling family of Bukoba is given as twenty-seven generations. The depth of the royal genealogy of the

[85] ibid., pp. 57–8.
[86] Merrick Posnansky, 'Kingship, Archaeology and Historical Myth', 7.
[87] *A History of Busoga.*

abaiseKisui (Leopard) ruling family of Busamo is given as thirty-one generations. The royal genealogy of the abaiseIumbwe (Lion) ruling family of Bukasango includes sixteen generations. The royal genealogy of the abaiseIumbwe (Lion) ruling family of Bunyuli includes twenty generations. The ruling family of the Bukyema state, the abaiseKyema (Lion–Eagle), includes some twenty-two generations. While the depth of these lineages would generally correspond with the Ganda genealogy, there are few significant tie-ins indicated among these Soga lineages which could provide credible substance for chronological analysis.

The ruling genealogy of the Lungfish family of Buvuma includes twenty-five names from the founder to the beginning of the colonial era; however, Ggomotoka does not make clear the generations of the rulers named.[88]

In the absence of specifically datable material evidence associated with the Kintu figure or the events surrounding the migration, it is impossible to do better than the roughest of estimates of the timing of the arrival of Kintu in the centre of Buganda. With the crude estimates of generations of the Lion, Leopard, Bean, and royal lineages all falling within the range of twenty to thirty generations, coupled with what we can reconstruct of the sequence of major events in the wider region—which indicates a Kintu arrival in the centre of Buganda before the Chwezi period for which we do have radiocarbon dates—an estimated date of A.D. 1250 ± 150 may be offered for the arrival of Kintu. But one problem of dating the Kintu impact on Busoga and Buganda is that it may very well have been gradual. The evidence does not exclude the possibility that the Kintu epic occurred over several generations during which Lion–Leopard groups moved slowly, extending their settlements westwards. The traditions of Kintu in Buganda do suggest a considerably long period between the establishment of the Mangira settlement in Kyaggwe and the founding of the Magonga settlement in the heart of Buganda. A second important dating problem arises in attempting to determine the length of time elapsing between the Kintu impact on the heart of Buganda and the arrival there of Kimera and his followers, an event which can be dated on a firmer basis of evidence.

The Impact of Kintu on Buganda

It is unlikely that the arrival of any considerable group of migrants

[88] 'Buvuma Island', in CTBTH.

would have gone unnoticed in either South Busoga or Buganda. The extant tradition of Kintu itself is evidence that notice was taken. Differences in culture were perhaps marked, and the language and dress of the Kintu–Walumbe migrants would have excited immediate attention. The iron-working skills of the Walumbe group and the planting skill of the Kintu group—both reflected in the Kintu tradition—would have given them advantage, though probably not immediately. The solidarity of a people on the march—insular, mobile, unencumbered—would likewise have conferred advantage, in this case immediate. We can do little more than infer the qualities and baggage of the migrants (until material evidence is recovered), but we can get a measure of their strength and their weakness through assessing the experience of contact with already settled people— experiences which the record of tradition has preserved.

Taken alone, the experience of contact at the heart of what is today Buganda suggests that Kintu was imbued with special qualities, that he possessed a gift or essence, that quickly brought the people whom he met to his feet, that his knowledge and interest in planting and possibly iron-working constituted unsurpassable material advantages, that he was most importantly destined to rule. The area at the centre of Buganda was not an empty land when the followers of Kintu arrived. Already settled in the area were groups of the Civet Cat, Colobus Monkey, and Manis totems. These groups were probably more numerous than the Ganda traditions would have us believe. It is likely that they had experienced a pattern of slow growth and expansion over a long period of time, perhaps from the moment of arrival of Bantu speakers in the region, an arrival of which they were probably part, given the linguistic history of the area. These settlers, the traditions indicate, fell under the domination or influence of a centre of serpent worship at Nagalabi Hill, the recollected residence of the *Bbemba Omusota* [Bbemba the Snake] figure of Ganda tradition. Bbemba was the force which Kintu succeeded in defeating and replacing once he had arrived in the area, and it was in the aftermath of this victory that Kintu appears to have erected his own brand of divine leadership among the groups which he had found there.

The people Kintu met in the centre of Buganda were probably iron-users practising a mixed economy.[89] The higher level of iron

[89] The pre-Kintu Baganda were called *Abalasangeye*, 'those who kill colobus monkeys'.

technology which the Lungfish groups may be assumed to have introduced would have assisted in the expansion of the efforts of forest
clearance, allowing for the extension of the areas of millet and banana
cultivation.[90] Kaggwa suggests that Kintu introduced the practice of
celebrating the 'new moon'.[91] a rite associated with an agricultural
people.

Before Kintu, the Civet Cat and Colobus Monkey groups, and
possibly the Manis group as well, were each unified under the
authority of a clan head. With no surviving record of association
with a particular clan, the Bbemba figure may very well have been a
unique figure in the community, a ritual specialist, a ritual overlord,
without kin, yet linking distinct families which would otherwise have
no unifying institution. The Kintu tradition does suggest that, at the
time of the Kintu arrival, this Bbemba was beginning to lose his
authority.[92] Upon the arrival of the Lion–Leopard groups amidst
these clan settlements, marriage ties were established between the
Kintu group and the pre–Kintu peoples. Tradition records the marriage of Kintu and Nambi of the Colobus Monkey clan. This marriage
tie was perhaps crucial in building a following for Kintu, and there
may have emerged from just such a simple tie as this—between the
Kintu figure and the people he found—the important role of Queen
Mother in the Ganda state.

Kaggwa has described how the various clans attended Kintu at
Magonga.[93] This may have been in response to the establishment of a
new religious order, centred on the divine Kintu, which replaced the
earlier serpent worship; and this is the earliest recorded instance of
the pattern of political service and clientage characteristic of Buganda
society. It was very likely at Magonga that the family traditions of
the Leopard group were elaborated and embellished, taking the
shape of a national tradition centring on the Kintu figure. While the
way in which the eastern, western and northern themes of migration
were joined to one popular Kintu tradition must defy anything but
the most abstract explication, what seems likely is that the Magonga
priests were responsible for bridging two crucial ideas of Kintu: one,
that of the family head, or *muzimu* or spirit of an earlier leader, of the
migrating Lion-Leopard group; and the other, that of the more uni-
versal figure praised in the creation myths of many Bantu-speaking

[90] One of Kintu's putative sons, Mulanga, is reported to have learned how to
work iron. Kaggwa, *Kings*, pp. 4–5.
[91] Kaggwa, *Customs*, p. 1.   [92] Kaggwa (*Kings*, pp. 3–4) describes this conflict.
[93] Kaggwa, *Customs*, pp. 9–11.

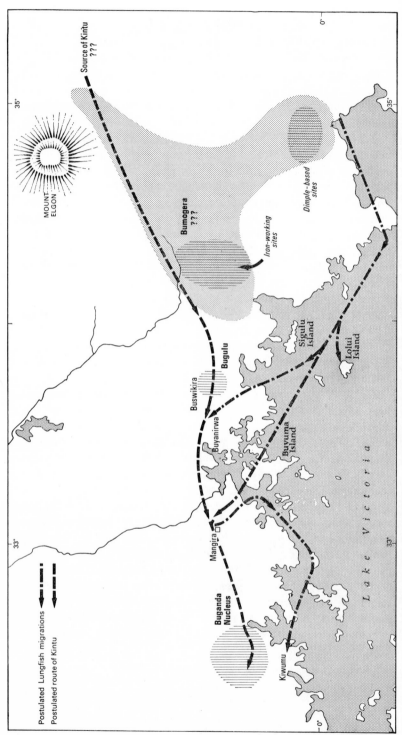

MAP VI. The Central Kintu Theme: Migrations of Kintu and Wdumbo. Associated

peoples and recalled variously as Kintu, Muntu, Kantu, and Mundu.

In Ganda tradition, Kintu and his putative successor Cwa Nabaka both disappeared; this may very well mark the beginning of a pattern of royal suicide, though one which was apparently extinguished or hidden after the penetration of families associated with the person of Kimera. Kimera and the groups associated with him arrived at the centre of Buganda, possibly as late as two centuries after Kintu's arrival there. Kimera founded a new dynasty and a new order influenced by the political culture of the western grasslands· This Kimera impact altered the face of what had been a new Ganda political community. Kimera shifted the emphasis away from the Magonga shrine kept by the lineage of Mwanje of the Leopard totem, substantially replacing Kintu's aides with his own followers from the north and west, and partially effacing the crucial role of the Lion–Leopard complex in the emergence of the Buganda kingdom. This picture of an immigrant lineage taking control of the seat of political power and leaving the displaced ruling line with what was to become the most important religious seat is not an uncommon one in the wider region.

But success in Buganda is not the whole story of Kintu. The Kintu figure did pass through South Busoga[94] and there we get a different image of the character, a sense—out of comparison with the Buganda experience—that it was opportunity at the moment of arrival in Buganda more than cultural baggage, military advantage, or divine destiny that determined the success of Kintu, or of the groups of which he may have been a symbol. Significantly, in areas other than the centre of Buganda the impact of the groups associated with Kintu and Walumbe was neither great nor of direct or immediate consequence. In Bunyuli in South Busoga, the impact was indirect, the effects secondary. Descendants of the Kintu migrants established colonies well to the south of the migrational route and from these centres expanded their domains at the expense of groups previously settled there. In Bugulu, to the north-east of Bunyuli, the appearance of the Kintu and Walumbe migrants appears to have made no substantial impact on the emerging community which they found there; rather the reverse seems the case, with the impact being made on the followers of Kintu. And it is within Bugulu that one is to find the source of the exodus phase of the Kintu tradition.

[94] The outlines of the movements associated with the central theme of Kintu are traced in Map VI.

CHAPTER V

Kintu in Busoga

As the Kintu figure and the small group of Lion–Leopard people under his living or spiritual leadership made their way westwards, they apparently reached the Bukhubalo Hills[1] east of present-day Busoga. Following the sun, they would have crossed the Lumboka River[2] into what is now Bukooli County. Skirting Nagugi[3] and Nang'oma Hills,[4] they very likely sighted Irimbi Hill[5] rising 750 feet above the Namaseri Valley[6] floor. Looking west from the Lumboka River, they would have noticed Irimbi as a dominant feature only some ten miles away across rolling land. Continuing on, they would have found the Luvunya Valley[7] which, in the dry season, offers easy passage. In a normal wet season, a ford could have been made at several points. Continuing on towards Irimbi, they would have met either the Kigusa or Namaseri streams.[8] The Kigusa allows easy crossings all year round while the Namaseri is a broader valley with fording more difficult. Crossing the Kigusa at its most convenient ford, the Kintu group would have found themselves travelling parallel to a branch of the Namaseri River, the Irimbi. Following its course along the south side, they would have been driven further from Irimbi Hill and along the rising slopes of Materere Hill.[9] Moving west through this Irimbi Valley between Ivumangabo Hill[10] and Kitumba Hill,[11] they would have noticed a line of ridges running south and a number of hills to the west. Pushing on towards these hills just a few miles to the west, the Kintu group would have passed along the Nakaseni Valley into the heart of the domain of Igulu.[12]

---

[1] The Bukhubalo Hills include Sitambogo (33° 55·7′E, 0° 29·8′N), Sikyendera-muwe (33° 56·2′E, 0° 30·1′N), Nahoma (33° 57′E, 0° 30·7′N), Nebinga (33° 55′E, 0° 31′N), Mukanga (33° 57·8′E, 0° 31·3′N), Nawanga (33° 56·2′E, 0° 31·8′N), and Buyindi (33° 56′E, 0° 32·6′N).

[2] 33° 54·5′E, 0° 28′N.   [3] 33° 53·5′E, 0° 25·5′N.   [4] 33° 52′E, 0° 25·5′N.
[5] 33° 45·2′E, 0° 27′N.   [6] 33° 47·5′E, 0° 27·5′N.   [7] 33° 51′E, 0° 25·8′N.
[8] 33° 47·5′E, 0° 27·5′N.   [9] 33° 46′E, 0° 25·6′N.
[10] 33° 45·5′E, 0° 27·4′N.   [11] 33° 45·5′E, 0° 26′N.

[12] This reconstruction of the Kintu migration from the east to Bugulu is based on a number of sources including CTBTH, Texts, 14, 71, 74, 79, 84, 132, 134, 147, 148, 259, 304, 333, 354, 480, 515, 595, 600, 601, 603, 610, 614, 615, 616, 617, 624, 672, 697, 716, 717, the Higenyi text, and Lubogo, pp. 102–8, 131–4. See Map VII.

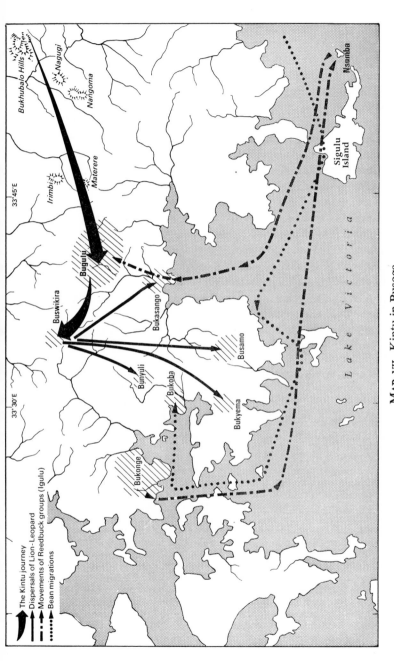

MAP VII. Kintu in Busoga

Bukhubalo Hills

Nagugi

Nangoma

Materere

Irimbi

33°45'E

Bugulu

Buswikira

Bukasango

Busamo

Bunyuli

Bukoba

Bukyema

Bukonge

33°30'E

Nsamba

Sigulu Island

Lake Victoria

The Kintu journey
Dispersals of Lion–Leopard
Movements of Reedbuck groups (Igulu)
Bean migrations

Igulu was the clan name of the abaiseIgulu, a Reedbuck group. On the periphery of Bugulu, and perhaps within the province of Igulu's authority, were settled several groups including the abaiseButanda and the abaiseNdolera of the Reedbuck totem, the abaiseMatende of the Rabbit, the abaiseMukenge of the Iduudu Bird, and the abaise-Mukubembe of either the Iduudu Bird or the Otter totem.[13] Kintu found an Igulu whose prominence and dominance among these several groups were based on two elements: deification or ennoblement, and a prestigious potting tradition.

First, the abaiseIgulu had a tradition of spiritual prominence. They had migrated to South Busoga from Nsumba Island[14] in the northeast corner of Lake Victoria some generations before the arrival of Kintu. Nsumba was the site of a great religious shrine which was guarded and maintained by the abaiseIgulu from the time of their arrival there until the beginning of the present century.[15] The religious bearing of the abaiseIgulu was carried with them by descent and migration, from their famed forebear Kibwika whose descendants had at one time apparently achieved a spiritual and military hegemony over the coastlands of South Busoga and the islands in the northern part of Lake Victoria from their base at Bukonge[16] in South Busoga.[17] Kibwika himself had migrated from the Ssese Islands,[18]

---

[13] CTBTH, Texts 22, 710, 320, 495, 479.   [14] 33° 55′E, 0° 07′N.

[15] Sleeping sickness cleared the lakeshore of inhabitants in the early years of this century and cut off the regular pilgrimages to lake shrines such as Nsumba, thus considerably interrupting the traditions which flowed around these shrines and around the pilgrimages themselves. CTBTH, Texts 88, 94, 95, 97, 98, 111, 280, 622, 623, 625, 710, 712, 624, 96 reflect the spiritual importance of the Nsumba shrine.

[16] 33° 24′E, 0° 21′N.

[17] A number of sources reflect the pre-eminence of Kibwika among the Reedbuck families in Busoga. (CTBTH, Texts 84, 93, 147, 148, 304; and Lubogo, pp. 85–7, ascribe to Kifunvu, the 'father' of Kibwika, many of the activities that are generally associated with Kibwika.) Moreover, several sources suggest the pre-eminence of Kibwika in the South Busoga and Lake areas. Lubogo, p. 86, relates that Kibwika's father Kifunvu conquered Buvuma and Bugaya Islands and gave them to Kibwika to rule. Lubogo, p. 88, relates the tradition that Kibwika ruled the Buvuma Islands and Ssese from his mainland base at Bukonge. CTBTH, Text, 84, relates that Kibwika was the ruler of Butamba, or the southern part of Busoga. Kibwika may be associated with the Kibuuka god of Interlacustrine tradition, who, in Ganda legend, left the Ssese Islands as a war god to help the Kabaka's forces who were fighting Bunyoro (J. Roscoe, *The Baganda*, pp. 217, 301–8).

[18] The settlement of Kibwika at Bukonge appears to be a part of the migrations and settlements of the Reedbuck peoples, which seem themselves to be a part of a broader movement of peoples from western Uganda to the lakeshore and the islands of the Lake. See Chapter III above.

one of the areas of settlement of groups in the backwash of Bantu advance through western Uganda. The Ssese Islands became one centre of the pantheons of deities who were to dominate the cosmologies and religions of much of the Interlacustrine region right up to the present.[19] The abaiseIgulu, through their ancestor Kibwika, carried this religious culture with them to Nsumba and established a new deity centre there. They drew within the orbit of the Nsumba deity diverse groups living on and near the coastlands of the northeast corner of Lake Victoria. Nsumba Island, less than a square mile in size, was very likely too small for the growing clan and its immediate followers. A body of the abaiseIgulu, perhaps instructed by an oracle, set off in their Waiswa canoe for a new settlement.[20] Only the privileged central core of the abaiseIgulu remained on the island to continue their guardianship of the deity.[21]

The Waiswa canoe which set out from Nsumba evidently contained a few abaiseIgulu pioneers, a few wives, some brothers of the wives, and some children. A dug-out canoe suitable for lake travel would have been able to carry fifteen or twenty people. Several clans were represented including the abaiseIhemula of the Bird totem, the abaiseKinhama of the Mushroom, the abaiseKalenzi of the Millipede, the abaiseMukubembe of the Iduudu Bird or the Otter, and the abaiseNdolera of the Reedbuck totem.[22]

[19] For a somewhat more extensive reflection on the place of the Ssese pantheon in the history of the Interlacustrine region, see the present author's review article, 'The Cwezi Cult', *Journal of African History*,' ix, 4 (1968), 651–7.

[20] CTBTH, Text 88. Text 624 relates that an oracle guided the voyage: 'At Nabubi, the *musambwa* Nabubi told us, "I have a husband and he is called Nsumba." He was at Nsumba and so we went there. Nsumba told us, "Go back. You will see the harbour where I shall direct you to land and you will land there." He guided us and our canoes landed at Bugoto.'

[21] CTBTH, Text 188 reports that Nsumba was more recently within the domain of the Banda state ruled by the abaiseKibiga. The authority on Nsumba under abaiseKibiga tutelage was Masibo, a mwiseKabodha of the Reedbuck totem. Kabodha is a common clan name among the abaiseIgulu.

[22] CTBTH, Texts 94, 199, 154, 480, 710. Text 94 relates that eight clans were represented in the canoe. Text 199 relates that twelve were represented. The problems of identifying the clans participating in the voyage are considerable. Some of the clans which recall a separate seat in the canoe split off from a migrating clan *after* reaching Busoga. An example is the abaiseMutamba. Second, the Waiswa canoe continued to be significant in lake travel after the initial voyage, and clans may be recalling participation in later, distinct voyages. The Waiswa canoe name was later used by Lukalango, ruler of Bukasango south of Bugulu, who gained control of the Bugoto landing. In the nineteenth century, the name was used by the Kabaka of Buganda as a designation for one of his important canoes. And, of course, the Waiswa name is an extremely common name throughout the region.

I

Paddling west and north, they entered MacDonald Bay.[23] Travelling further, they reached Bugoto point,[24] a small finger of land reaching out a mile into the Bay. Landing there, they marched northwards,
very likely moving between the Bukumbi[25] and Nakyandiba[26]
Rivers, perhaps aiming for Kyoga Hill[27] which reaches up 500 feet
above the valleys and offers a fine view of the surrounding country-
side.[28]

The second element giving prominence to the Igulu group among
the peripheral settlements around Bugulu was their potting tradition.
Right up to the present day, the abaiseIgulu have been known for
their excellence in pottery.[29] They established their settlement near
Kyoga Hill on fine potting clays and continued a pursuit which may
have been practiced by their ancestors at Nsumba, Bukonge, the
Ssese Islands, and in the lands of western Uganda.

Undoubtedly, the early development of Bugulu as a centre of
specialized production established it as a place of relative wealth and
enormous prestige among the far flung settlements of Bantu-speakers
around the Lake. Their position as specialists perhaps opened the
way to the building of close, symbiotic ties with groups living on the
margins of the principal abaiseIgulu settlement. The founders of
some of these groups came with the original pioneers in the canoe
and may have already had strong ties, through marriage or through
spiritual devotion, with the abaiseIgulu. The centripetal force of a
specialized craft may have drawn these peripheral groups who
accompanied them still closer. Other settlers came later with the
return voyages of the abaiseIgulu pilgrims who visited their Nsumba

---

The traditions surrounding the principal voyage relate that the Waiswa canoe was
discarded at Bugoto and eventually returned to its original state as a muvule tree.
This is a stereotypic story, commonly applied in stories of canoe-borne migrations, and reflects the permanence, the continuity, of the spirit contained in the
muvule tree, in the canoe after it is shaped or constructed from the tree, and in a
state existing long after the canoe is discarded. The spirit is credited with guiding
the canoe and carrying its passengers safely across the Lake. The problem of using
the canoe name as evidence is discussed in Chapter II, pp. 45–6.

[23] 33° 40′E, 0° 17′N.   [24] 33° 38′E, 0° 19·5′N.
[25] 33° 39′E, 0° 20·8′N.   [26] 33° 35′E, 0°21′N.
[27] 33° 36′E, 0° 24′N.
[28] Text 88 is among the sources which mentions the voyage from Nsumba to
Bugoto landing. This source relates that the migrating group went from Bugoto
directly to Namasaka Hill, immediately adjacent to Kyoga Hill. Such a direct
journey would follow the route between the Bukumbi and Nakyandiba Rivers
which is proposed above.
[29] CTBTH, Texts, 304 and 624.

shrine, and this pattern of migration apparently continued into the present century.[30]

The settlements in Bugulu appear to have followed a general pattern. Each was established on a separate *mutala*, or rise of land between streams. Each group was apparently responsible for the day-to-day affairs of its own kin on its own *mutala*.[31] However, they looked to the abaiseIgulu as their spiritual leaders and were perhaps drawn within the orbit of the Igulu family by the relative wealth of the abaiseIgulu potters.[32] After all, Busoga was an open frontier. There were a few settlements to the south and west in the record of tradition but none apparently so early to the north. One can postulate that there was a variety of pressures and forces which attracted these groups and held them within the expanding province of Igulu. The abaiseIgulu had established marriage ties with many of these groups far back at Nsumba and these ties remained important, AbaiseIgulu pilgrims returned from Nsumba with new wives and new families and new in-laws.[33] Thus, new clans were introduced to the Bugulu area, but usually within the protected sphere of the abaise-Igulu pilgrim. Beyond the factors of spiritual dominance and wealth.

[30] See notes 15 and 22 above.

[31] This is an inference from functional analysis of the clan and state in Busoga and in the Interlacustrine region in general. There is both a functional and structural hostility between the clan and the state, and the histories of Busoga, Buganda and the western kingdoms all reflect the gradual displacement of clan function and unity in correspondence with the growth of the state. There is the additional evidence which emerges from an analysis of clan shrines; rarely in this area does one find the shrines of two or more clans on one geographical *mutala*.

[32] The patterns of clan settlements surrounding Bemba at Buddo Hill in immediately pre-Kintu Buganda are perhaps comparable to the patterns of settlement at Bugulu. An illuminating parallel can be drawn with the abaiseMuhaya *nkuni* figure, Kazinga, which is located near the boundary between Bugweri and Bukooli Counties in Busoga (33° 37·9′E, 0° 32·7′N). Although traditionally the *nkuni* of the abaiseMuhaya and the place of one of their early settlements in Busoga, it has since become something more than a clan shrine. It is now an important spirit shrine respected by peoples from various clans living within a few miles of Kazinga. The abaiseMuhaya are not the sole worshippers of Kazinga. In fact, today, they no longer even supply the caretaker for the shrine. This simple but momentous shift from an ancestor or clan shrine or deity to a community deity appears to have been a constant factor in the social, cultural, and political development of the peoples of the wider region.

[33] The 'Book of the abaiseIgulu' [in CTBTH] lists the mothers of several of the early Igulu rulers: abaiseMubaiti, abaiseKyema, abaiseIgaga, abaiseKaima, abaiseMugogo, abaiseKasango, and abaiseKaziba, all of them settling in Bugulu or on the Bugulu margins. Other sources include the abaiseNdolera (Text 710), the abaiseMuhindi (Text 428), the abaiseMugogo (Text 382), the abaiseKaima (Text 151), the abaiseKanale and the abaiseIgaga (Texts 20, 64).

the arrangements and relationships among these groups may have
been knit together by this complex of interlocking, preferred marriages and by the obligations of the individuals and groups involved
in these marriage alliances.

The Bugulu through which Kintu evidently passed was, in his time,
emerging as a distinct society with a distinct culture. A structure
broader than the clan was in the process of emergence. New groups
were being integrated as they arrived. The Igulu potteries, with their
traditions, styles, and terminology, distinguished the area from other
parts of the region. The elements of wealth associated with the
pottery and the status associated with spiritual authority were perhaps welded together in the minds of Igulu's followers. For them,
God was *Kibumba*, the *Potter*, the Soga name for the Supreme Deity.[34]

When Kintu reached the Nakaseni Valley along which he very
likely passed into Bugulu, the authority of Igulu was apparently no-
where near the height of power in political or geographical terms that
it would reach in later days. With most clans still settled on separate
mitala, Igulu's authority was weak. With open frontiers inviting
further exploration and settlement, Igulu's hold over these disparate
settlements was fragile. Well before the arrival of the Kintu group,
the abaiseIgulu had faced a crisis which immediately weakened their
clan but which would, apparently, strengthen their political hand in
the long run. The crisis involved succession, the importance of which
was increased by the value given to the fine potting clays at the heart
of Bugulu by these pot-making families. A section of the abaiseIgulu
were excluded from the best lands as the extended families of the
abaiseIgulu segmented. A quarrel developed and the emergent
Mutamba group either departed or was driven away.[35] They travelled
some fifteen miles to the north-west and settled at Igombe.[36] Such
divisions, which evidently became more common with the ever-
increasing pressure of population on each *mutala*, eroded the role of
kinship in the organization of people on the *mutala*. The diminution
of the kinship function in South Busoga led inexorably to the enlarge-
ment of the political function. Eventually, the central authority was
in a position to determine the character of settlement on the *mutala*.
Mutala homogeneity gave way to *mutala* heterogeneity as new

[34] Or occasionally, *Kiwumba* or *Kibumbi*. CTBTH, Text 822.
[35] CTBTH, Text 624. The traditions of the abaiseMutamba are complex; they
have been affected by a somewhat disruptive overlaying of tradition by groups
fleeing Buganda some 200 years ago.
[36] 33° 30·5′E, 0° 30′N.

families were settled on the *mutala*. This heterogeneity eroded the earlier patterns of clan autonomy and *mutala* homogeneity still further.[37]

There were other abaiseIgulu segments besides the Mutamba group which broke away and emerged as distinct clans. For all, the major cause of fission appears to have been the struggle for control of land and power at the centre of the Igulu domain.[38]

When the Kintu group reached Bugulu, they found an area which was already in the process of cultural and political consolidation, and, as a result, the immediate impact of Kintu and his people on Bugulu was apparently less severe and immediate than was their impact on other areas. The Kintu group evidently settled briefly on the margins of the abaiseIgulu core settlement at Bugulu, and it appears to have been these migrants who fell within the orbit of the spiritual authority of the Igulu figure. It is possible to see the whole exodus theme of the Kintu tradition in terms of the interactions and transactions taking place on the periphery of Bugulu. First, the Igulu of Bugulu and the *Ggulu* (Heaven) of Ganda tradition may be one and the same. Second, it is possible, even likely, that it was in this area that the marriage tie between the Lion–Leopard group associated with the Kintu figure and the Lungfish group associated with the Walumbe figure was established through the real or symbolic marriage of Kintu and Nambubi.[39] The traditions suggest that it was the Igulu figure, perhaps through an oracle, who advised Kintu to leave. Kintu left with Nambubi. The traditions record that Kintu left *Ggulu*; however, it seems likely that what Kintu left behind was the domain

[37] This postulated shift from the homogeneous to the heterogeneous *mutala* would have provided the *mutala* head with new functions relating to being a judge and intermediary in the local affairs of his followers. Kinship functions only applied to kin. Non-kin on the *mutala* necessitated new forms of authority in respect to local justice and land distribution. One can postulate that such a process of shift from homogeneous to heterogeneous was gradual; one or two non-kin might be absorbed into the dominant clan. The momentous shift comes when the new group is large enough to withstand absorption. Fallers (*Bantu Bureaucracy* pp. 162–3) discusses the tension between the dominant *mutala* lineage and the *mutala* chief arising from the duality of rule: through the clan and through clientage.

[38] There are some twenty-nine clans in Busoga which are of the Reedbuck totem. Many of these are probably derivative from the abaiseIgulu, and among these are the abaiseButanda, the abaiseKantu, the abaiseKaziba, the abaiseMukasa, the abaiseMukonzi, the abaiseMusoga, the abaiseNdhoka, the abaiseMutamba, the abaiseNdolera, and the abaiseNkumba.

[39] This marriage is discussed above, p. 90.

of Igulu, the dominant figure and spiritual authority in the Bugulu area.[40]

Kintu departed, travelling west. Nambubi hesitated, and, while asking to return for her millet to feed to her hens, she was probably more concerned about this break with her brothers of the Lungfish clan. She returned to Bugulu, and, when she again departed, the Walumbe figure, or the Lungfish group, followed. Kintu and Nambubi, with the nemesis Walumbe, reached Buswikira,[41] ten miles to the north-west, perhaps passing Busimo Hill[42] on the way. Buswikira is a rise of land cut off completely from surrounding country by wide, swamp-filled valleys. Here the group stopped, and this place was to become, in the traditions recalling Kintu, the 'landing place' of Kintu and Nambubi in their travels from 'Heaven'.[43]

Apparently, Kintu and Nambubi camped on one side of Buswikira and Walumbe and his group on the other.[44] Struggles between the Kintu group and the Walumbe group evidently drove the Walumbe associated Lungfish people a few miles west to Buyanirwa[45] where they established a permanent settlement.[46]

The influence of the Kintu figure and the Lion–Leopard groups in South Busoga was to expand from this camp at Buswikira. In South Busoga, small groups of the Lion and Leopard totems spun off the Buswikira settlement and established new settlements to the south. A group associated with the Kasango Iumbwe figure travelled south and established a new centre at Kirongo.[47] Later, two segments of

[40] This interpretation of the Kintu migration connects the standard version of the Kintu legend—quoted above, which appears largely symbolic, with the evidenced activities of the Kintu associated groups in Busoga and with the important figure of Igulu. The actual events involved were not heroic; rather, they were relatively commonplace. The momentous impact of Kintu on the heart of Buganda ennobled the commonplace, and the heroic Kintu tradition may have been passed eastwards to Busoga or may have developed independently among the peoples living in South Busoga.

[41] 33° 31·3′E, 0° 28·5′N.   [42] 33° 35′E, 0° 27·7′N.

[43] One version of the standard tradition is quoted above, p. 84.

[44] Today, the most important shrine of Kintu is found on one side of Buswikira Hill and an important shrine of Walumbe is found on the other side.

[45] 33° 31′E, 0° 28·3′N.

[46] STBTH, i, pp. 72, 133–4. The clan which emerged from the Lungfish settlement at Buyanirwa was the abaiseMudoli-Maganda. Their traditions are complicated by the overlaying of traditions from a runaway group from Buganda. However, the abaiseMaganda sources, quoted in CTBTH, Texts, 293, 296, 298–300, do record that Buyanirwa is the place of their most important *nkuni*. Walumbe is discussed at some length in Chapter IV, above.

[47] Kirongo is located at 33° 36·5′E, 0° 20·5′N. Lubogo, p. 102, discusses this Iumbwe migration as does CTBTH, Text 134.

this original Iumbwe family divided, one to become the abaiseIumbwe rulers of Bunyuli[48] and the other the abaiseIumbwe rulers of Bukasango,[49] located south of Bugulu.[50] Another small group, who were to emerge as the abaiseKyema rulers of Bukyema in the South near Bukalenzi,[51] left the main body at Buswikira. A Leopard totem group left Buswikira and travelled south, establishing a settlement at Busamo Hill.[52]

The colonization of the southern reaches of South Busoga by these Lion and Leopard groups was perhaps contemporaneous with the establishment of a Kintu hegemony at the centre of Buganda.[53] The 'cultural baggage' of these colonizing groups was likely similar to that of the Lion–Leopard migrants reaching the heart of Buganda, but the character of their new settlements and the patterns of emerging dominance in South Busoga did not resemble the developments at the nucleus of the expanding Ganda kingdom. Though we have only scant tradition throwing light on these developments in South Busoga,[54] we do know that these Lion–Leopard colonies carved out domains by colonization and conquest.

[48] Bunyuli was ruled by Nanhumba (a title apparently more recent than the office), and the domain expanded from a centre near Kityerera (33° 32′E, 0° 22′N).

[49] Bukasango, ruled by Lukalango, expanded from a centre six miles south of Bugulu on the eastern side of present-day Bunya County.

[50] Text 132, CTBTH, discusses this division as does Lubogo pp. 102 and 105. Higenyi, in his 'History of the Banyole' (CTBTH), suggests that divisions in this family occurred during the migrations from the Mount Elgon region, well before reaching South Busoga. Higenyi relates that the Nanyumba and Munyole groups split during their travels and arrived in South Busoga separately. Text 132 relates that the ancestor of the Lukalango branch was Namunhole. The traditions of conflict and turmoil in South Busoga, in which the abaiseIumbwe lie at the centre, and the stereotype themes related in the Higenyi texts, suggest that the split did occur in South Busoga, and that the tradition which Higenyi relates is merely an explanation, perhaps in stereotypic dress, of a split between brothers during a migration, borrowed from Lwo traditions by a group of abaiseIumbwe returning to the east in more recent times.

[51] 33° 32′E, 0° 17·8′N. The Bukyema state is discussed in Lubogo, p. 126; and CTBTH, Texts 273–5.

[52] Busamo Hill is located at 33° 34·5′E, 0° 14·6′N. These Leopard totem people were the abaiseKisui. The abaiseMugalo and the abaiseMuleemo also emerged from the group settling at Busamo Hill. Lubogo, p. 107, comments on the origins of the abaiseKisui and their establishment at Busamo. CTBTH, Text 250, records that the *nkuni* of the abaiseKisui is Wamango, located near Busamo.

[53] See above, pp. 104–5, for a discussion of the chronological data.

[54] The destruction of the population of South Busoga by Sleeping Sickness carried away both the structures of state and the traditions of both commoners and rulers. The evidence does seem conclusive, however, that these early Soga colonies were of the same stream as the Kintu settlement in Buganda.

Perhaps contemporaneous with the Lion and Leopard colonization of South Busoga were the westward movements of peoples of the Bean totem from the north-east corner of the Lake.[55] These canoe-borne groups followed the coast, stopping at Gwabazimu[56] in South Busoga; continuing on from there by canoe, they eventually reached Hannington Bay.[57] They landed at Mayovu,[58] and there the abaise-Ikoba of the Bean established a lakeside settlement which was to become the centre of an emergent kingdom. Other Bean groups pushed westwards, settling in the islands off the Kyaggwe coast and on the coast itself.[59]

With these significant settlements, the outlines of South Busoga were laid. A number of settlements dotted the region. The open areas and frontiers were considerably reduced from the days when Bugulu and Bukonge were small and isolated settlement areas. In most situations, major river valleys came to mark the frontiers between the emergent domains. Smaller river valleys and swamps marked off the *mitala* on which new groups settled.

The traditional evidence suggests that competition and conflict among these disparate settlements became increasingly rife, and that the emergence of centralized states was dependent on the ostensibly voluntary attachment of settlements of distinct families to a central lineage, and, perhaps more importantly, on conquest. The earliest recollected conflicts involved the abaiseIumbwe who were at Kityer-era and the abaiseKalenzi, a pre-Kintu group who were a few miles to the south-east at Bukalenzi.[60] Beginning some nineteen generations back from 1892, in the reigns of Mubiko at Kityerera and Mbadhi at Bukalenzi, this conflict continued for some ten generations. Small victories were won by one side or the other in the Nabule Valley;[61] neither side was immediately successful in terms of conquest. How-ever, the centre of the Bukalenzi domain and the direction of its expansion shifted south away from the abaiseIumbwe centre and towards Nakalyango Hill.[62] The abaiseKalenzi were of the Millipede

---

[55] See above, pp. 97–8, for a discussion of the Bean–Kintu connection.

[56] 33° 35′E, 0° 13·5′N.   [57] 33° 25′E, 0° 18′N.   [58] 33° 29′E, 0° 19·5′N.

[59] Important Bean clan settlements of an apparently early date include Nam-beta, Nakisunga, Kiringo, and Lumuli in Kyaggwe County (Kaggwa, *Clans* [MS. translation], p. 102), and Bugaya Island (Ggomotoka, 'Bugaya Island', in CTBTH), where island taboos and customs, as well as traditions, suggest that a Bean group preceded a Lungfish group on that island.

[60] 33° 32′E, 0° 17·8′N.   [61] 33° 31′E, 0° 18·5′N.

[62] 33° 34′E, 0° 15·5′N. CTBTH, Text 154, discusses the war between Bunyuli and Bukalenzi; also, Lubogo, p. 109.

totem and had migrated from the east some generations before Kintu; they were perhaps part of the initial migration of abaiseIgulu and followers from Nsumba.[63]

In the eighteenth generation back, Nanombe, the abaiseIumbwe leader of Bunyuli, attacked the abaiseWamwena who were living on Hannington Bay just south of Kityerera. These abaiseWamwena were of the Convolvulus totem and had settled in South Busoga some generations before Kintu. They were lacustrine people and had a tradition of intimate association with the waters of the Nile River. They had come to Bumwena[64] in Busoga from the northern tip of Buvuma Island. The principal groups of the abaiseWamwena had settlements near the falls at the head of the Nile and are, in tradition, recalled as the 'parents of the Nile River'.[65] Perhaps more experienced at warfare on the Lake than on the land, they were easily overrun by the abaiseIumbwe, and their settlement was brought within the orbit of abaiseIumbwe dominance.

Some years later, Kaigwa, brother of Nanombe, set off on a new campaign of conquest, this time against the abaiseKyema of Buk-yema.[66] Skirting the abaiseKalenzi settlements, they attacked and defeated the abaiseKyema.[67]

Turning to the north in the reign of Mboli, some fifteen generations back, the abaiseIumbwe attacked and defeated a Reedbuck group which was attempting to establish a settlement at Busaka[68] across the Naiwailogo River,[69] just two miles north of Kityerera. The Reedbuck families which were associated with Kibwika had been for perhaps ten generations expanding their domain in a north-easterly direction. With the rise of the Lungfish group in the central part of the northern lakeshore area, and with the arrival of the lacustrine Bean groups, the power of Kibwika's descendants was apparently on the wane. With their control over the Lake communities dissipated, attention was turned towards the open frontiers to the north. The growth of abaise-Iumbwe power just a few miles to the east, as evidenced by the increasing tempo of military conflict, was surely seen as a threat to the Kibwika domain. The most definitive natural boundary between the

---

[63] CTBTH, Text 154, asserts that the abaiseKalenzi, travelling in the Waiswa canoe, were part of the abaiseIgulu-led migrations through the Lake.

[64] 33° 32′E, 0° 16′N.   [65] CTBTH, Text 798.

[66] Bukyema was one of the Lion-Leopard domains associated with the Kintu presence at Buswikira.

[67] Lubogo, p. 103.   [68] 33° 32′E, 0° 22·8′N.

[69] 33° 32′ E, 0° 22·5′N.

two states was the Naiwailogo Valley, with its Namugombe branch.[70] Perhaps the leaders of the Kibwika state wanted to exclude the abaiseIumbwe from the security of a natural boundary and, at the same time, keep open a route of contact between the domain of Kibwika and their kinsmen at Bugulu to the east.[71] However, the Reedbuck party sent to colonize Busaka was overrun and forced back across the two valleys.[72]

Soon after, in the reign of Mboli's nephew Kamadi, the abaiseIumbwe turned westwards and attacked the abaiseIkoba who were expanding from their Bukoba nucleus into Ituba village[73] along the eastern side of Naiwailogo. The abaiseIkoba, under the leadership of Batwagulaine,[74] drove off Kamadi's army. Kamadi died in the conflict and was succeeded by his brother Nsabadi who fought to avenge his brother's death. His army defeated the abaiseIkoba and drove them out of Ituba village; however, Nsabadi was killed amidst the campaign. His brother Kalali succeeded and, avenging Nsabadi's death, attacked the abaiseIkoba again, driving them farther west onto the head of land which was to become the heart of the emergent Bukoba state.[75]

Thirteen generations back, Mukuha succeeded his father Kalali as ruler of Bunyuli and turned to fight the abaiseKizibu at Buzibu[76] south of Kityerera. In a series of battles, Mukuha and his brothers succeeding him were killed. Kagulire, the last of the brothers, picked up the pieces and finally defeated the abaiseKizibu, bringing their village within the abaiseIumbwe domain.[77] The resistance of the abaiseKizibu suggests the continued strength and resilience in this period of domains peopled by a single clan and organized on a kinship basis; yet the ultimate power clearly was in the hands of the aggressive groups associated with the Kintu presence in South Busoga.

This process of expansion continued inexorably through this

[70] 33° 30'E, 0° 21·4'N.
[71] There is no evidence establishing that the Bugulu group was in contact with its parent Kibwika group, nor even that they realized that only fifteen to eighteen miles separated the two domains. Political frontiers often limited contact between 'relatives' living even closer than that in pre–colonial Busoga. Trade, though, may have been one feature of life which did bring the two groups into contact. The importance of the Nsumba shrine as a source for a number of Bugulu groups and the rise of a strong Bugulu state may have reduced the significance of the Kibwika parentage and the Bukonge 'origins' in the minds of the abaiseIgulu rulers of Bugulu.
[72] Lubogo [Luganda MS.], p. 139.   [73] 33° 30·7'E, 0° 21·2'N.
[74] Literally, 'They have scratched us.'   [75] Lubogo [Luganda MS.], p. 139.
[76] 33° 32·2'E, 0° 18'N.   [77] CTBTH, Text 271; Lubogo, pp. 103–4.

period; the traditions suggest that the abaiseIumbwe—while occasionally suffering the consequences of their aggressive campaigns of conquest—had secured an expanding central base of power on which they could draw in these successive campaigns. It is likely that as this central base around Kityerera was becoming stronger, settlements based on kinship exclusivity were being dissolved and the initial clans were dispersing around the centre. Apparently, the enlarging state was gradually assuming the function of defence for a number of formerly exclusive clans.

In Bukoba to the west of Bunyuli, in Bukasango to the east, in Bugulu to the north-east, in Bukyema and Busamo to the south, similar patterns of expansion were under way.

This expansion was the aftermath of the Kintu penetration of South Busoga. The aggressive families which left Buswikira, associated with Kintu's journey from the east, attempted to carve out and expand domains in the South, unleashing a whole new process of change and creating upheavals in the political and social fabric of the region. Kibwika of the Reedbuck totem, whose family had established itself at Bukonge in South Busoga a century or two before the appearance of the Kintu groups and achieved a hegemony over the central part of the Lake, was now evidently cut off from further expansion on the South Busoga mainland by the new arrivals. The Lungfish groups established on Buvuma Island, and later Bugaya Island, developed as lacustrine powers and displaced the Kibwika hegemony over the Lake peoples.

The security of the clan evidently gave way before the increasingly violent conflicts. Only the state could guarantee the security of the settlements, and only with such security could the new communities grow. Many families fled these lands as a consequence of the abaise-Iumbwe wars, migrating eastwards into north-eastern Busoga and Bunyole in eastern Uganda. However, with the impact of Kintu, the significant political forms were shaped and would not be radically transformed until the nineteenth century when Ganda invasions, over-population, and an improvement in the opportunities in the North would throw open South Busoga to extensive demographic and political change and would send peoples of the South to the North in large numbers for the first time.

CHAPTER VI

The Appearance of Mukama

IN the traditions of the peoples of northern Busoga, Mukama, like Kintu in the South and in Buganda, has emerged as an Adamic figure. Mukama's presence in Soga culture and his role in Soga history are multiple. Mukama is recalled as the father of the princes who founded the great states across the northern face of Busoga. Mukama is the giver of all things; Mukama is the awaited one, the messiah looked to as negotiator between this world and another. Mukama is the foreigner, the light-skinned figure, the bearer of new cultural and political ideas. Mukama is the herdsman, the milker, the hunter, the wanderer. Mukama is the cripple, the miscreant, the possessed one, both feared and respected.[1] Mukama is the personification of cultural, ethnic, and political links between Busoga and Bunyoro. Mukama is the apotheosis of Ganda participation in and hegemony over Soga affairs.

A persistent theme of the Soga historical tradition concerns the travels of Mukama through Busoga. A common rendering of the tradition relates that Mukama travelled into Busoga from the east, eventually reaching Nhenda Hill[2] in the centre of the country. 'Leaving there [Nhenda] . . . Mukama moved on downwards; he had a child in the valley which can still be found in Busoga. A woman had a child in a bamboo grove in the valley of Lumbuye and she was given a bamboo shoot and they called the child Ibanda.'[3] The infant Ibanda was left in Busoga as a foreordained ruler. Mukama continued his westward journey to Bunyoro.

This narrative of Mukama's travels reflects only one dimension of a much larger historical development: the appearance of a new social force in northern and eastern Busoga between 1550 ± 50 and 1700 ±

---

[1] The Mukama deity is regarded as intimately concerned with the health and fitness of a newly born infant. Mukama is, as well, a central figure in the traditional spirit-possession beliefs and practices of the people of Busoga.

[2] 33° 30′E, 0° 33′N.

[3] CTBTH, Text 595. Variants of this popular tradition are related in Texts 134, 483, 603, 610, 718.

40 in the form of pastoral peoples of Nilotic Lwo origins flowing in from the north, west, and east.

Several significant historical themes underlie this grand traditional theme identifying Mukama with the arrival and impact of the Lwo pastoralists. One is that of demographic change: the expansion of peoples of Nilotic Lwo origins into the region south of Lake Kyoga. A second theme concerns the passage of aristocratic Lwo figures and families into and through Busoga. A third theme involves the emergence of states, dominated by Lwo royal families, out of the new configuration of Lwo immigrants and pre-Lwo in Busoga. A fourth theme is the emergence of a culture, imported and syncretic, centred on these early Lwo immigrants.

The grand Mukama theme is not only laden with important historical themes related to the development of the northern Busoga communities; it also comprises many historical threads. Bound together in the monolithic tradition of Mukama are the diverse streams of Lwo advance into northern Busoga.

As with the 'Kintu cataclysm' in the South and Buganda, the 'Mukama cataclysm' opened a new epoch in history and set a new course in the formation of a historical tradition. For the era preceding the Lwo arrivals, the evidential tradition relating to northern Busoga is sketchy and lacks depth. There is evidence recalling pre-Lwo settlements, and there are firm links between those early settlers and peoples settled in Busoga today. However, chronological evidence is virtually nil. Groups settling before and after the principal Lwo arrivals can be distinguished with some certainty, yet the nature of the timing and circumstances of the pre-Lwo settlements in the North is difficult to establish.

But with the arrival of the Lwo, a central focus—the Mukama figure with the associated royal houses—begins to emerge. Within the context of the state, and against the Mukama backdrop or baseline, the traditions of the North take on a new momentum, and, with the added dimensions of time and circumstance better understood, the traditions assume a sharper focus. In the terms of the emerging historical tradition, the journey of Mukama constitutes a cataclysm. It is with the Lwo advance, symbolized by Mukama, that a new epoch of history in the North is opened.

The arrival of Nilotic Lwo pastoral groups on the eastern margins of Busoga was part of a much wider process of expansion and migration of Lwo peoples from their 'cradleland' along the Nile River in the southern Sudan. These pastoralists, perhaps set in motion by feuding in their homeland or pressures from peoples living to the north and east, moved southwards through and into areas resembling their homeland along the rivers and swamps of the southern Bahr el Ghazal.

The Lwo migrations very likely began in the fifteenth century.[4] The character of the migrations seems to have been dominated by certain persistent features. First, the Lwo tended to move in small groups. The migration was not a flood, but rather a composition of small groups following disparate routes at various times over the several centuries of extensive migration.[5] Second, the migrating Lwo groups were forever cleaving into smaller units. Segments of larger groups broke off, leaving their camp for new lands over the horizon. Internal tensions among the travelling Lwo seem to have been the major cause of this pattern of fission.[6]

While fission was a persistent problem among the migrating Lwo groups, the Lwo, carrying with them the prestige of a pastoral culture, readily absorbed various non-Lwo groups encountered in their travels.[7] Another constant feature was the Lwo 'wanderlust': the Lwo seem to have been driven onwards by a feeling that a better homeland was just ahead.[8] Another common pattern among the migrating Lwo was their establishment of temporary camps from which parties were sent to survey the surrounding lands, and from which raiders were sent to seize both cattle and human booty in the neighbourhood of the camp.[9]

In the fifteenth century, groups of Lwo began arriving at Pubungu on the Nile in northern Uganda. Here, an important camp was established, a camp which is recalled in the traditions of many Lwo

[4] B. A. Ogot, *A History of the Southern Luo*, pp. 44–7.   [5] ibid., pp. 53–7.
[6] Crazzolara, *The Lwoo*, records the traditions of several of these divisions: pp. 35–9, 42–4, 62–6, 88–90.
[7] Crazzolara, pp. 45–9, 72–5, discusses the role of prestige in the absorbing of non-Lwo met on the march.
[8] For example, Crazzolara describes the debate at Pubungu between the younger adventurers who wanted to push on to new lands and the older folk who wanted to halt the 'seemingly endless journey' (pp. 59–61).
[9] Lucy Mair, in her volume [*Primitive Government* (Baltimore, 1962), p. 131], in discussing the Nilotic Nuer, gives a glimpse of the linked processes of expansion and raiding. 'In the early part of the nineteenth century, sections of the Nuer were seeking new grazing grounds for their cattle. The Nuer warriors invaded the Dinka country, captured a cattle kraal, and used it as a base for attacks on any herds within reach. They usually stayed there several weeks but sometimes for the whole of a dry season. But sometimes they did not go home at all.' (p. 131.) Cf. E. E. Evans-Pritchard, *The Nuer* (London, 1940).

peoples now dispersed across the region stretching from the Congo–Uganda borderland in the north-west to western Kenya in the south-east. Groups broke away from the Pubungu camp, some travelling west and settling among the Sudanic-speaking Lendu–Okebu–Madi peoples, others travelling north and east, settling in the present Lango and Acholi Districts of Uganda.

Some of the Lwo who were camped at Pubungu left there and pushed directly south and east, crossing the Nile into Pawiir. Pawiir, lying to the south and west of the Victoria Nile as it flows north, then west, from Lake Kyoga to Lake Albert, became a new area of settlement and a new centre of dispersal for the migrating Lwo. One group, the *Jo-Bito*, penetrated the Kitara domain of the Chwezi in the late fifteenth century and assumed control of the apparatus of state, abandoned by the Chwezi rulers as they fled their royal enclosures.[10] Many of these Lwo families which had traversed the Nile into Pawiir, and particularly those such as the Jo-Bito which drove still further south, were linguistically absorbed into the Bantu-speaking world.

Other Lwo flowed eastwards through the open savannah grasslands north of Lake Kwania and Lake Kyoga. By the close of the fifteenth century, Lwo peoples had consolidated a hold on the region north of Lake Kyoga and west of the Omunyal River, on Pawiir south of the Nile, and right through the grasslands of western Uganda as far south as the Katonga River.[11]

Some four or five centuries ago, Lwo families began to leave this area to the north and west of Lake Kyoga, travelling east along the northern shores of Lake Kwania and Lake Kyoga. Joined in the area of the Kaberamaido peninsula by other Lwo migrating south from Acholiland, they moved east, south-east, and then south around the fingers of Lake Kyoga into the corridor between Mount Elgon and the Mpologoma River. Many Lwo passed along the western face of Mount Elgon, perhaps avoiding the lowlands of the corridor which were open to the assaults of cattle raiders from the East.

Leaving the Mount Elgon foothills, the early Lwo traversed the corridor and reached the Malaba River. Very likely seeking a safer haven than the corridor for settlement, some Lwo crossed the Malaba River into the more readily defensible grasslands along the eastern fringe of present-day Busoga. Here, according to Ogot, Lwo groups

[10] This transfer of authority is discussed at some length by Oliver, 'A Question about the Bachwezi', *Uganda Journal*, 17, 2 (Sept., 1953), pp. 135–7.
[11] Ogot, p. 61.

settled twelve to fifteen generations back, probably in the late six-teenth century.[12] Budoola and Banda on the eastern side of Bukooli became camping grounds for the early Lwo arrivals.

Northern Busoga was not an empty land when these Lwo pastoralists broke through its eastern margin. Diverse groups were occupying parts of northern and eastern Busoga. Hunters roamed the interior while fishing people meandered on the rivers of the Mpologoma system. More permanent settlements were established by cultivators along the Mpologoma, Malaba, and Kibimba Rivers, along the Victoria Nile, and among the hills peripheral to the Bugulu community in the South. Cultivators had migrated into northern Busoga from the Mount Elgon area, from South Busoga, and from Kyaggwe across the Nile. Other cultivating groups emerged from the hunting and fishing communities in the Busoga area. While this pattern of pre-Lwo migration and settlement appears to have been part of a more general pattern of scattered occupation in the wider region between the River Kafu in the west and Mount Elgon in the east, several significant complexes of pre-Lwo occupation in northern and eastern Busoga can be discerned.

Since before the arrival of Lwo pastoralists in eastern Uganda, an amorphous group of clans has occupied the papyrus islands of the rivers and river banks of the Mpologoma system along the eastern side of Busoga. These are the *Bakenhe* fishing people. The Bakenhe clans, while of a common culture, were evidently of diverse origins. Several of the Bakenhe groups had drifted away from the principal areas of settlement of Bantu speakers in the Interlacustrine region. A number of Bakenhe families left islands in Lake Victoria and travelled across the north-east corner of the Lake and overland to the river system of eastern Uganda, perhaps in response to the rise of Lungfish hegemony over the larger part of Lake Victoria. These Bakenhe settlements were impermanent. Floating on meandering papyrus islands, dependent on the canoe and canoe-borne mobility, the Bakenhe moved through the rivers between Lake Kyoga and the higher lands of western Kenya as time, current, and conditions would permit. The rivers functioned as avenues of dispersal while serving as insulated routes of continued communication and contact.

New groups were continually joining the Bakenhe, many of them refugees from the turbulent age in the development of the Buganda kingdom. Some groups fled the onslaughts of Ganda armies ranging

[12] ibid., pp. 73–4.

over the eastern parts of Kyaggwe and Bugerere and across the Nile in Busoga. Others left the Bantu-speaking communities on Mount Elgon and the communities north of Lake Kyoga. Still others were refugees from the advance of early Lwo groups into eastern Uganda and western Kenya.

The transience of the Bakenhe makes it extremely difficult to determine both the sequence of Bakenhe settlements and the particular times of arrival in the river area of individual Bakenhe families. The evidence does suggest that many important Bakenhe groups preceded the early Lwo pastoralists in eastern Busoga. The abaiseKiruyi, a Lwo clan and one of the early arrivals among the Lwo pastoralists, wrested control of Nsango, located in the confluence of Kibimba and Malaba Rivers, from earlier occupants some ten generations back from 1892. The evidence indicates that a Bakenhe family of the abaiseMulumba–Nangwe, had preceded them there. One tradition relates that Ibanda and Lukedi, prominent Lwo figures, arrived at Nsango and found Dugo there.[13] Dugo of Nsango was a mwise-Mulumba–Nangwe.[14] Dugo's family was one of the dispersed abaise-Mulumba–Nangwe groups which had, at an early time, given up the Bakenhe way of life and had subsequently settled at different points along the eastern river system.

There is additional sequential evidence for Bakenhe groups further north. The abaiseMukubembe dispersed northwards along the Mpologoma and some of these abaiseMukubembe families settled in the Busiki area before the arrival of Nemwe, a mwiseIgaga.[15] Nemwe's appearance at Namagero marking the beginnings of state formation on the western bank of the Mpologoma, was roughly contemporaneous with Lwo arrivals to the north and south.

Still further north, Bakenhe groups such as the abaiseBalwa, the abaiseIruba, the abaiseBabiro, the abaiseMulyanda, the abaise-Mbeya, and the abaiseMumbya had preceded the Lwo arriving in that area.[16]

---

[13] CTBTH, Text, 616. Nsango is located at 33° 52·3′E, 0° 39′N.

[14] CTBTH, Text 687.   [15] CTBTH, Text 482.

[16] CTBTH, Text, 126. Text 731 relates a tradition of the abaiseNgobi rulers of Bukono which mentions the earlier presence of Bakenhe in Busoga. 'Kitimbo [founder of the Bukono dynasty] came from Bunyoro side. They left there and went to Masaaba. From Masaaba [Mount Elgon], Mukama travelled back to Bunyoro. They crossed the lake at Iyingo. They made canoes out of muvule trees. They had canoes. The canoe makers were found in this country. And there were fishermen called "Abakenhe". Those are the people who were experts with canoes. Even now they are expert.'

K

The continuing pattern of arrival of new groups among the Baken-he, while evidently under way before the arrival of Lwo near the waterways on the eastern side of Busoga and clearly running on into the present century, is difficult to detail. But, while the Bakenhe had no common origins and had arrived on the rivers at different times, they did share a common experience which drew them into a rela-tively homogeneous culture. Most Bakenhe families had sought refuge from the very competitive and dangerous political world on firmer ground. On the rivers, insulated from the turmoils of politics, strife, and war in Buganda, Busoga and the countries of Bukedi to the east, the patterns of Bakenhe life were very much determined by the economy of the river. Fishing was the primary economic pursuit, and the Namukenhe fish was the foremost object of their fishing toils. The canoe, hewn from the muvule tree, was a fundamental tool of life. Later, with the rise of states along the river margins, the command of canoes permitted the Bakenhe to serve as important functionaries in the state organization—controlling harbours and ferriage, hand-ling trade, and fishing.

The Bakenhe were water nomads, but before the emergence of the northern states of Busoga, some Bakenhe were settling more perma-nently on the firm land along the eastern river system. These settled Bakenhe constituted a bridge, in terms of culture and contact, con-necting the interior hunters and cultivators and the early Lwo pastor-alists with the Bakenhe nomads of the rivers. Settled Bakenhe probably practised a mixed economy of fishing and cultivation and were involved in the emerging pattern of interdependence among the different economies of the region.

This process of change from the nomadic life on the rivers to a more settled life on the firmer land was one which has continued up to the present. While more permanent settlements were established all along the eastern rivers and along the shores of Lake Kyoga and near the effluence of the Nile into Lake Kyoga, there were several areas of concentrated settlement. The lands adjacent to the Kibimba River constituted the most important centre of Bakenhe occupation in the Uganda area. Nsango, in the confluence of the Kibimba and Malaba Rivers, was settled by families of the abaiseMulumba–Nangwe of the Mushroom totem, and the abaiseMulamba of the Egret totem. The abaiseMulumba–Nangwe migrated to the Kibimba–Malaba confluence from Kyamuvuma in the Mount Elgon area. From Nsango, they spread north along the river and later travelled west into the centre of Busoga.[17] These abaiseNangwe were displaced from their position of dominance at Nsango by the Lwo pastoralists arriving in the eastern Bukooli area.[18]

Another group settling at Nsango was an abaiseMulamba family which had travelled from the Mount Elgon area under their leader Fuuna. The *nkuni* shrine of the abaiseMulamba clan spirit, Afusa, marks the location of their early settlement at Nsango.[19]

Another important Bakenhe settlement in the Kibimba area was that of the abaiseMudwana at Kigulu.[20] Kigulu became an important ferry site on the Kibimba, and the strategic value of the site is suggested by the abaiseMudwana role as arbitrators in disputes arising among the Bakenhe in the Kibimba area.[21] The abaiseMudukiri of the Iyobyo plant totem, travelling from Nsumba Island in the north-east corner of Lake Victoria, and the abaiseMululwe, who travelled from Sagitu Island,[22] established settlements at the Kibimba–Malaba confluence.[23]

Ihemba Hill,[24] a mile and a half west of the Kibimba River, was another important centre of settlement in the eastern Bukooli area, and several of these settlements preceded the Lwo arrivals at the hill. Adjacent to the Kimira crossing of the Kibimba River and thus lying along one of the principal avenues of penetration of Busoga, Ihemba Hill was to become one of the first points of Lwo impact in Busoga. Families of the abaiseMudwana and abaiseMudope, and families of the Rabbit totem: the abaiseKaliro and the abaiseMbeya; and groups of the Otter totem: the abaiseMagobwe, the abaiseIbira, and the abaiseKagongwe; and the abaiseMuhemba of the Spider totem, all

[17] The abaiseMulumba-Nangwe, of the Mushroom totem, segmented into a number of sub-clans, each having different mushroom totems. In this century, active clan organizers have reunited, under the banner of the Nangwe mushroom, many of the fragmented Mushroom families. The Mulumba group which travelled from Mount Elgon to the Kibimba River area, ultimately establishing a more permanent settlement at Nsango, appears to have been the parent group of most of the Nangwe lineages which have been reunited. These dispersed lineages include a Nangwe group, a Buhaso group, a Wanamboira group (which travelled north from Nsango and settled at Lugulu, 33° 47·5′E, 0°42·5′N, dispersing widely from there), and the Bulumba (Mulumba) group.

[18] CTBTH, Texts 616, 687.   [19] CTBTH, Texts, 12, 508.
[20] 33° 51′E, 0° 36′N.   [21] CTBTH, Text 12.
[22] 33° 40′E, 0° 00′N.
[23] CTBTH, Text 12. These abaiseMululwe may have earlier been associated with settlements on Lolui Island (33° 43′E, 0° 09′S). Sagitu Island is situated between Lolui and the South Busoga mainland and lies less than ten miles north of Lolui.
[24] 33° 48·3′E, 0° 36′N.

appear to have left their floating homes and river bank settlements, establishing more permanent homes at the hill.

Many of these families settling at Ihemba were also represented on the eastern side of the Malaba River in the Busolwe and Budama areas. The abaiseMudope had travelled to Ihemba from the eastern side of the Malaba.[25] Later, perhaps, four generations back from 1899, groups of abaiseMudope left the Ihemba centre and travelled north along the river, planting important settlements in Busiki near the banks of the Mpologoma River.

Both the Otter and the Rabbit groups appear to have had an important place in the life of the communities along the Mpologoma River. While the abaiseIbira, the abaiseMagobwe, and abaise-Kagongwe of the Otter totem, all from the eastern side of the river, settled at Ihemba, the abaiseNhanzi of the Otter totem settled at Bulamba Hill[26] on the southern margins of the Kibimba River system,[27] and their *nkuni* shrine was at Bulamba Hill. The abaise-Muyagga, with the same Bulamba *nkuni*, appear to have been part of this same settlement complex.[28] It is possible that these and several other of the ten Otter groups in Busoga were part of a shattering of a unified Otter group in the eastern Uganda area. That all of the five Otter groups which point to origins outside northern Busoga have traditions of migrations from Lake Victoria, suggests the common experience and possibly common identity of the Otter groups.

Similarly, the traditions of Rabbit clans, the abaiseIruba, abaise-Kaliro, abaiseMuganza, abaiseMbeya, and the abaiseMulinda, indicate a shattering along the eastern river system, though the earlier origins of such a postulated Rabbit complex are obscure. Several of the Rabbit groups point to South Busoga, while other Rabbit families point to eastern Uganda and the Mount Elgon area as earlier homelands.

The area of Namukonge Hill[29] and the adjacent harbour at Kimira on the Kibimba River were also important points of Bakenhe settlement. The abaiseMuyoga controlled the Kimira harbour and its crossing to the Nsango area. West of the Kibimba, the abaiseItego of the Shrub Vegetable totem established a settlement at Namukonge Hill a mile from the river. Their *nkuni* Nyenda was located at a small

[25] CTBTH, Text 352, records that the abaiseMudope of the Guinea Fowl came from Budama, establishing themselves around their *nkuni* at Ihemba. They were evidently in the Lake Kyoga area before they reached Budama.
[26] 33° 52′E, 0° 21·5′N.   [27] CTBTH, Texts 749–51.
[28] CTBTH, Text 12.   [29] 33° 51′E, 0° 33′N.

hill at Namukonge.[30] A short distance to the north of Namukonge, the abaiseMuiggi of the Colobus Monkey totem established a settlement around their *nkuni* shrine at Kayango Hill.[31]

Bakenhe, then, occupied an important place in the area of the Kibimba and Malaba Rivers along the eastern side of present-day Bukooli County. While it is difficult to reconstruct a complete picture of these pre-Lwo settlements at one time, or to place all the Bakenhe migrations and settlements in a chronological or even sequential framework, it is possible to speak of processes or patterns: diversity of origins, refuge, nomadic life on the rivers, transformation of culture from fishing to mixed cultivation, establishment of more permanent settlements, and control of strategic points on the rivers. The evidence suggests that these settled families, along with the water nomads, were drawn together by traditions of common flight, by common interests in the river life, by a web of marriage ties among the diverse Bakenhe families, and by a growing interdependence between the pure water nomads and the more settled cultivating groups of the shore. The strong men of this wider Bakenhe community came out of groups such as the abaiseMuyoga, the abaise-Mukoma, and the abaiseMudwana, all in control of fine ferriage points on the river—therefore able to dominate the spheres of contact with groups settled on firmer ground. Other groups such as the abaiseMulumba–Nangwe controlled considerable areas between the Kibimba and Malaba Rivers and all along the Mpologoma River. With land plentiful, they were able to attract groups of new settlers. Another powerful group was the abaiseMuiggi family, who, like the abaiseMudwana, guarded an important religious shrine along the river to which Bakenhe of many clans came to make offerings.

Several other clans, evidently pre-Lwo, were established outside this area of intensive Bakenhe occupation, but not far from the Kibimba River. Iramu Hill in the Igwe forest,[32] located a few miles south-west of the Kibimba River, was settled by abaiseMufumba of the Giraffe totem who had migrated from Isime Island[33] in the Lake.[34] They were later joined at Igwe by other groups, foremost among them an abaiseMutamba family who had fled eastwards from

[30] CTBTH, Text 130.
[31] CTBTH, Text 433. Kayango Hill is located at 33° 51′E, 0° 34′N.
[32] 33° 48·5′E, 0° 30·5′N.
[33] 33° 48·5′E, 0° 30·5′N.
[34] CTBTH, Text 354.

Busakira in South Busoga after the colonization of that area by a group of refugees from Buganda.[35]

A group of abaiseKidoido of the Frog totem, who had migrated from the west, were settled at Kisimbiro Hill near Magoola[36] by the time of the arrival of Lwo in that area. A tree at Kisimbiro was the *nkuni* of the clan. Members of the clan dispersed to near-by hills after the arrival of the first Lwo at Kisimbiro Hill.[37]

At Busoga Hill[38]—located some fifteen miles south-west of the Kibimba River and on the periphery of the Bugulu state—were a group of Reedbuck people, the abaiseMusoga. These abaiseMusoga were apparently part of the exodus of families, particularly of Reedbuck derivation, from the Bugulu centre. They had travelled north and east settling in areas beyond the control of the Bugulu rulers.[39]

These scattered settlements in the interior were to be points of pronounced Lwo impact several generations after the arrival of Lwo on the eastern margins of Bukooli.

On the northern margins of Bugulu, and beyond the control of Bugulu and the other South Busoga states, a new centre of settlement was emerging in the years before groups of Lwo pastoralists were reaching the interior of Busoga. Centred on the abaiseMusuubo settlement at Kikalangufu,[40] the configuration of adjacent settlements—together called Kizenguli in tradition—was taking shape as an emergent state under a dominant abaiseMusuubo lineage. The abaiseMusuubo, having as their totem a small bird,[41] had migrated from the area around the north-east corner of Lake Victoria[42] and were very likely part of a dispersal of Bird groups from the region between the Lake and Mount Elgon. Groups such as the abaise-Ihemula had left the same area and had been drawn within the orbit

---

[35] CTBTH, Text 624.   [36] 33° 42·2′E, 0° 33′N.

[37] CTBTH, Texts 193–4. Kisimbiro later became an important shrine of the Bukooli ruling family, the abaiseWakooli, who were part of the Lwo onslaught into eastern Busoga. Texts, 785, 786, 787, 788, 789, 790.

[38] 33° 39′E, 0° 30·8′N.

[39] Traditions of the abaiseMusoga, recorded in CTBTH, Texts 597–601, are not explicit in regard to this migration, but the evidence of similar names from abaise-Igulu and abaiseMusoga genealogies suggests that a relationship existed within nearby Bugulu.

[40] 33° 36·1′E, 0° 28·5′N.

[41] Called, variously, Namuhaya, Namusuubo, Namusisi, Kasombamoya, Munhale, Kinhole, or Kasanke. It is often referred to as the Shrike, or Kimbagaya.

[42] CTBTH, Text 617.

of the early Reedbuck group at Nsumba Island.[43] Another clan with the same Bird totem, the abaiseMuhaya, passed across the Lake, settling for a time in Bunyuli.[44]

In his manuscript, 'The History of Bwema Island Belonging to Omutaka Lugonda Nnangoma at Bwema in Buvuma', Ggomotoka relates that Lugonda Nnangoma of the Bird clan travelled around Lake Victoria from his Bwema home, and left a family on Sigulu Island (adjacent to Nsumba) through a son, Ggulu, whose mother was a 'Kavirondo'. According to Ggomotoka, Ggulu was the father of many of the Bird lineages dispersed throughout the north-east corner of the Lake and Busoga. This story appears to have been reconstructed within the emergent tradition of the Bird clan family on Bwema Island, descendants of whom were evidently the principal Ggomotoka sources for the story. According to Ggomotoka, Lugonda Nnangoma was a young man in the time of Kabaka Kyabaggu in Buganda. The recentness of Kyabaggu's reign—some five generations back from 1884—would appear to preclude the possibility of a young contemporary being the parent of some eighteen independent lineages (by Ggomotoka's count), several of which have traditions recalling more than ten generations back from about 1900. Ggomotoka has apparently assumed that all dispersed Bird groups tracing their origins back to the Lake came from the single parentage of Nnangoma of Buganda, living at that one moment of Bird clan peril in Kyabaggu's reign.[45]

There is considerable evidence that Bird groups were settled beyond the borders of Buganda long before the described incident in Kyabaggu's Buganda. The abaiseMukose of Busoga were just one of the Bird groups settled outside of Buganda long before Kyabaggu; some of these groups absorbed refugees from the Kabaka's fury, and certain traditions in Bird totem groups in Busoga reflect the presence of elements fleeing the Buganda of Kyabaggu and Semakokiro. It is likely that Ggomotoka's Lugonda Nnangoma returned from the north-east corner of the Lake to Bwema Island with the Ggulu

[43] CTBTH, Texts 94–8 point to Nsumba as an early stopping point in the migrations of the abaiseIhemula. Texts 94–6 point to an earlier Ihemula settlement at Busimbi near Mount Elgon. The location of Busimbi is not precisely identified.

[44] CTBTH, Texts 415, 421.

[45] Kaggwa (*Clans* [MS. translation], p. 100) relates that it was Semakokiro, the Kabaka four generations back from 1884, who was the king who took vengeance when a bird landed on his house at Kitende. Nsimbi, *Amanya Amaganda*, p. 202, concurs.

tradition, having borrowed it from the tradition of an Igulu prominence on Nsumba.

This area of Kizenguli became a focus for settlement in the centre of Busoga. A family of the abaiseMuhaya—with the same totem as the abaiseMusuubo—travelled north from their settlement in Bunyuli and settled at Busolera[46] just a few miles north-west of the abaiseMusuubo settlement at Kikalangufu.[47]

At Buwongo,[48] just two miles north-west of Kikalangufu, there were settled a group of abaiseMukose of the Shrike totem. Buwongo was one of the principal centres of the abaiseMukose in Busoga, and the settlement was centred on their shrine there. There is a tradition which mentions the room cut out of stone at Buwongo in which the abaiseMukose gathered on important occasions.[49]

A few miles to the north-east of Kikalangufu, a group of abaiseKisendo millet growers of the Serval Cat totem were established at Wante[50] along the Kitumbezi River. A tree enshrined their *nkuni*.[51]

A group of abaiseMususwa of the Hyena were settled on Isegero Hill[52] where their *nkuni* shrine was located.[53] Isegero is located some two miles south-east of Kikalangufu.

AbaiseMukuve of the Egret totem, a family of abaiseKaziba of the Reedbuck totem, and a group of abaiseWampande of the Monkey totem settled in the immediate vicinity of Kikalangufu.[54]

The abaiseMusuubo were evidently the dominant group in this area of Kikalangufu Hill. The abaiseMenha, who were later to emerge as the ruling family of Kizenguli as well as the lands to the

---

[46] 33° 34′E, 0° 34·6′N.   [47] CTBTH, Text 415.   [48] 33° 34·7′E, 0° 29·6′N.
[49] CTBTH, Text 468. One source (STBTH, i. 137) relates, '. . . an important place called Buwongo. There is a hill there which is significant in its rock formation. On top, it is covered with stones but there is an audience room which is as big as this house. Also, God made rooms and covered the top with stones. In case it rained, people could sit inside without harm. In this house God put down stones, which are like chairs, on both sides and in the middle there is something like a passage. It was a splendid place to visit. This is where the abaiseMukose who have now spread all over Busoga came from. That is where they came from. During the time of taking sacrifices they go there from all over Busoga. They might number a thousand or more. They offer cattle, goats, chickens, and other things. In the past, this place was called Buwongo because all sacrifices [*Kuwonga* = to sacrifice] in Busoga were carried out at Buwongo.'
[50] 33° 39·5′E, 0° 35′N.
[51] STBTH, i. pp. 100–101. The source further relates, 'We had no special drumbeat but our forefather had a lot of millet and we had to go daily to cut it, and we said, "Kisendo produces quite enough millet".' ['*Kisendo yaisa obulo kamala.*']
[52] 33° 37·7′E, 0° 28′N.   [53] CTBTH, Texts 604–10.
[54] CTBTH, Texts 333, 181, 581, 794–6.

north after their arrival in the country, have a tradition which records the abaiseMusuubo as their head *bataka*.[55] An abaiseMusuubo tradition suggests that by the time the abaiseMenha were arriving in their domain, their own authority over the various clans was collapsing.

After distributing people about, Busi [a mwiseMusuubo] settled in Bugweri and in Bugweri he had a mwiseNhulya as his *Katikkiro* [Nhulya was the name given to the abaiseMenha by the abaiseMusuubo]. He did not like to sit very much; rather, he [Busi] spent all his time playing on a swing [*Lusuubo* = swing]. His chieftainship was considered a joke. It was taken away by the abaiseNhulya. When he died, people appointed Nanhulya's son to the office because he used to give them many things to eat. This Musuubo spent his time playing on a swing. That is how we lost the chieftainship.[56]

It is not clear whether the early abaiseMusuubo leaders had achieved a dominance over other clans in the area because they preceded them in the Kizenguli area or whether the migrating abaiseMusuubo had carried with them from the east the prestige of rulership and a knowledge of statecraft. The abaiseMusuubo traditions do associate their overland migration and early activities with those of the Kintu figure.[57] It is possible that the commoner families coming from the south and settling in Kizenguli carried with them the experience of living as the subjects of a ruling house in a centralized political community.

Beyond these intensively occupied areas—eastern Bukooli and Kizenguli in central Busoga—occupation of the country appears to have been scattered. There was some replication of the pattern of Bakenhe life and occupation all along the Mpologoma River and along the shores of Lake Kyoga, though apparently much less intensive in scale. The lands of Kisiro and Bugangu, on either side of the Mpologoma River just north of the Kibimba–Malaba confluence, were occupied by several clans. At Lugulu Hill,[58] situated just two miles west of Mpologoma, were the settlements of several clans, each settlement marked by an *nkuni* shrine.[59] The eastern bank of the Mpologoma at Bugangu was apparently occupied by a number of

[55] STBTH, i. 145.

[56] CTBTH, Text 614. This transfer of power is discussed below pp. 155, 164–7.

[57] CTBTH, Texts 614–17.   [58] 33° 47·5′E, 0° 42·5′N.

[59] The abaiseMubaiti of the Serval Cat totem, the abaiseMulumba-Nangwe of the Mushroom totem, and the abaiseMudope established settlements in the Kisiro–Lugulu area.

families which had migrated from Mount Elgon and had established themselves within the Bakenhe world of the river. The abaise-Muhingwa of the Shrub Vegetable totem and the abaiseMulega of the Cobus Cob were among the groups settling at Bugangu.

The lands to the north of Kisiro and to the west of the Mpolo-goma River as far north as the Naigombwa Valley were occupied by a number of clans of diverse origins. Naminhagwe, along the river, was occupied by a group of abaiseMukubembe who were part of the general Otter clan dispersals along the eastern side of Busoga.[60] At Bugiri, just a few hundred yards north-west of Naminhagwe, at Nawambiri, just two miles south of Naminhagwe, and at Bunhagwe, a few hundred yards to the west, were settled families of the abaise-Mukose who had reached the Mpologoma River from Buwongo in Bugweri. These abaiseMukose of the Shrike totem were later joined by other families of abaiseMukose from Buwongo in Bugweri and by Shrike refugees from Buganda.[61]

AbaiseKyewe of the Bean totem, having crossed the Mpologoma from Bunyole, settled at Namagero,[62] a rocky outcrop near the river; at Bunhagwe, two miles to the north-west; and at Lwatama, also along the river, but some twelve miles by river further north.[63]

These three clans—the abaiseKyewe, the abaiseMukubembe, and the abaiseMukose—occupied an area along the Mpologoma River in which the abaiseIgaga, future rulers of Busiki, made their initial appearance. The three clans were to play a vital role in the emergence of the Busiki state. The arrival of the abaiseIgaga family on the western bank of the Mpologoma River appears to have been more or less contemporaneous with the arrivals of Lwo in adjacent areas to the north and to the south.

To the north of these Naminhagwe settlements and on the eastern side of the Mpologoma River were settled several Bakenhe groups, including the abaiseBalwa and the abaiseIruba. Near Kikalu Hill[64] on the western side were families of the abaiseNkwanga of the Elephant totem and the abaiseMugabwe of the Gorilla totem.[65]

Traditions concerning the areas to the north and west of the Naigombwa Valley, the demarcation between present-day Bulamogi and Busiki Counties, suggest a sharp division between the peoples of

---

[60] CTBTH, Texts 479–82. The *nkuni* stone of the abaiseMukubembe called Lwendera is located at Naminhagwe, 33° 46·5′E, 0° 54·3′N.

[61] CTBTH, Texts 458, 463, 77, 476.

[62] 33° 46·5′E, 0°50·1′N.   [63] CTBTH, Texts 77, 276–9.

[64] 33° 39′E, 1° 02·5′N.   [65] CTBTH, Text 731.

the river—the Bakenhe—and the peoples of the interior, the hunters or 'meat people', the *Banyama*.[66] When Lwo pastoralists and hunters began to trickle across the Mpologoma River between Naigombwa and Lake Nakuha to the north-west, they found the abaiseMukose settled at Gadumire[67] and an abaiseIgaga family at Izinga near the Mpologoma River.[68] These abaiseIgaga and abaiseMukose were apparently among the hunting groups of the interior. Among the Bakenhe on the rivers and on Lake Nakuha were abaiseIruba of the Rabbit, abaiseMabiro of the Small Lungfish, abaiseMulyanda of the Small Mushroom, abaiseMbeya of the Rabbit, abaise-Mumbya of the Oribi Antelope, and abaiseMulwa of the Vulture totem. This pattern of Bakenhe occupation, along with the Banyama pattern evidenced in the Gadumire area, apparently continued right across northern Busoga and all along the Lake Kyoga coasts. Many of the clans notable among the Bakenhe in the Kibimba area—such as the abaiseNangwe, the abaiseMulwa, the abaise-Mudope, and the abaiseIbira—were represented in the Kyoga waters, perhaps reaching there at an early date.

Thus, when the Lwo began arriving in northern and eastern Busoga, they found centres of intensive occupation in eastern Bukooli and at Kizenguli, and they found scattered settlements and transient groups all across the interior and along the Mpologoma and Kyoga waterways.

[66] CTBTH, Text 562; Lubogo, p. 19.

[67] At Gadumire, 33° 31′E, 1° 07·3′N, was the *nkuni* of the abaiseMukose group who reached there. Text 460, CTBTH.

[68] Texts 62, 68–9, 562; Lubogo, pp. 18–19, 68–70. Izinga is situated at 33° 35·5′E 1° 04·8′N.

CHAPTER VII

A Lwo Camping Ground

IN the sixteenth century, Lwo pastoralist groups began to push south around the eastern fingers of Lake Kyoga and through the Mount Elgon foothills which lie on the eastern side of the corridor running north and south between Elgon and Busoga. Leaving the foothills, they traversed the corridor with their cattle and reached the Malaba River. Crossing the Malaba at several points, these Lwo migrants began arriving in the late sixteenth century on the relatively protected side of the river in the Budoola area of present-day eastern Bukooli. Already occupied by Bakenhe fishing peoples and settled cultivators, eastern Bukooli was to become, for the Lwo, an important new camping ground and a new centre of dispersal. For many of the Lwo, the Budoola camps were merely temporary—families soon left the camps with their cattle, some pushing west to deeper involvement in the Bantu-speaking world; or to the east, to Nyanza, where descendants of the Lwo migrants would come to represent a powerful force in the future life of Kenya; and to the north, where a handful of Lwo families settling just across the Malaba would become the nucleus of a new Lwo community, the Padhola.

The Lwo camps in Budoola would be significant germinal points of new political, cultural, and demographic developments in Busoga. But the Malaba River crossings were not the only Lwo entry points into what is now Busoga. Lwo groups trickled in from the north-east and from the north-west, down the Nile into south-western Busoga, through the centre of Busoga to Bugweri and the hills of Luuka and Kigulu. What distinguished the Budoola settlements is, first, that they apparently preceded the other Lwo arrivals in Busoga, and, second, that from them emerged the group central to the monolithic Soga tradition of Mukama.

The traditions of the Padhola of eastern Uganda and the Luo of western Kenya, as recorded and analysed by B. A. Ogot, suggest that elements of two migrating Lwo groups—the *Owiny* and the *Omolo*—crossed the Malaba River and established camps in eastern Bukooli in the sixteenth and seventeenth centuries. Within a generation or two of arriving at Budoola, the Owiny group, which had apparently been the first to arrive at Budoola, split into two sections. The first, the 'Owiny segment', left Budoola within three generations of having arrived there and, travelling southwards through Samia–Bugwe, reached Alego in Nyanza as one of the spearheads of Lwo advance into the Nyanza region of western Kenya. The other fraction, the 'Adhola group', comprised two prominent clans, the Amor and the Ramogi. After the Owiny clans left for Nyanza, these clans of the Adhola fraction remained behind in Budoola for a generation or so before recrossing the Malaba River and settling in West Budama as a spearhead of permanent Lwo settlement there. Ogot, in reconstructing the history of these groups settling in western Kenya and Padhola, suggests that the split in the Owiny group may have occurred because the Owiny element was more adventurous. Ogot argues that the Adhola clans, on the other hand, did not leave Budoola until they were forced to by pressure from the Bagwere and the Banyole who were moving northwards and from the Basoga whose settlements were gradually extending southwards.[1]

According to Lwo tradition, another migrating Lwo group, the *Omolo*, stopped for a time in eastern Bukooli. The Omolo remained in the area of Banda[2] for two or three generations in the late sixteenth and early seventeenth centuries before moving eastwards and southwards into western Kenya.

The Lwo traditions record the presence of these groups in eastern Bukooli between 1500 and 1700 yet, naturally enough, tell us little about the contributions of these groups, or associated or descended groups, to developments in Busoga. For this, we must turn to the traditions of Busoga and particularly to the traditions of those clans which appear to have emerged from the complex of Lwo settlements in the camping grounds along the eastern side of Bukooli.

Traditions suggest that seven clans, all prominent in Busoga today, emerged from the complex of Lwo settlements along the eastern side of Bukooli and were absorbed into the Bantu-speaking world of Bukooli. These clans—the abaiseMudoola, the abaiseNaminha, the

[1] B. A. Ogot, *A History of the Southern Luo*, pp. 75–6.
[2] There is a village, Banda, located at 33° 53·5′E, 0° 16′N, but the term is used more generally to refer to the lands between Budoola and Lake Victoria which were at one time under the rule of a dominant lineage of abaiseKibiga.

abaiseBandha, the abaiseKiruyi, the abaiseWakooli, the abaise-
Kiranda, and the abaiseKibiga, all of the Bushbuck totem—have
traditions which carry them back to the pastoralist settlements in
eastern Bukooli, to the same settlements as those recalled in the
traditions of the Padhola and Kenya Luo. These traditions indicate
that families of Lwo origins were gradually leaving the core area of
Lwo settlements and were, in several cases, assuming a dominant
position among the Bantu-speaking groups with whom they came in
contact.

Within a generation or two of the initial Lwo arrivals in Budoola,
the abaiseMudoola were evidently emerging as a dominant group
among the Lwo and perhaps also among the Bakenhe and the other
groups who preceded them in the neighbourhood of the Kibimba
River and the Bukhubalo Hills. The abaiseMudoola were very likely
associated with the Adhola group of Lwo tradition, and they may
have emerged as the dominant group on the Budoola lands after the
departure of the Owiny fraction. The abaiseMudoola settled initially
at Nagugi Hill,[3] and Nagugi became their *nkuni* shrine;[4] Nagugi was
located just one mile from Nang'oma Hill[5] which had apparently
been at the centre of the Owiny camps and which later came within
the domain of the abaiseMudoola.[6] In Lwo, the expression *won ng'om*
means 'the landlord' and suggests that Nang'oma Hill may have been
the settlement site of a group which had control over the use and
distribution of land in the area of the Budoola camps—namely, the
Owiny group and then the abaiseMudoola.

The abaiseMudoola themselves figure largely in the history of the
Lwo settlements in Bukooli. Yet, in a more important sense, the
emergent abaiseMudoola clan became, over four or five generations
following their arrival on the western side of the Malaba, a key
bridge between the migrating Lwo on the eastern side of Busoga and
the founders of states in the centre of Busoga, who, in Soga tradition,
are recalled as the abaiseNgobi sons of Mukama. One tradition,
recorded by Lubogo, links the Lwo migrations first with the Mukama
figure and second with the Lwo settlement at Nang'oma Hill. Lubogo
describes the journey of the Mukama figure to Busoga:

He travelled through Teso, Bugwere, and along the River Mpologoma and
entered Bunyuli [Bunyole County in eastern Uganda], thence to Budama.

---

[3] 33° 53′E, 0° 27·2′N.   [4] CTBTH, Text 349.
[5] 33° 52′E, 0° 25·3′N.   [6] CTBTH, Text 189.

From the latter country, he [Mukama] travelled along a land route and arrived in Busoga.

On his arrival in Busoga, Mukama first went to Nangoma Hill in Bukooli. He stayed on this hill for a short time surveying the country and hunting wild animals ... From Nangoma he travelled to Walugoma in Bunya.[7]

Ogot has observed that Lubogo's outline of Mukama's travels parallels his own reconstruction of the Lwo migrations,[8] and he suggests that the Mukama figure may be a personification of the Lwo generally. In Soga tradition, one strand of Mukama tradition records *Kigenhi* or *Kigenyu* as an ancestor of the Mukama who was father of the princes who founded the Luuka and Buzimba states seven generations back from 1899.[9] In the traditions of the abaiseMudoola, their clan founder is recorded as Kigenhi.[10] According to the traditions of the abaiseNgobi of Kigulu who are one of the Soga groups claiming descent from Mukama, Kigenhi antedated Prince Ngobi, their ancestor, by some four or five generations,[11] and this would suggest that Kigenhi may have been living in Budoola eleven to thirteen generations back from 1899—a date in co-ordination with Ogot's estimates of Lwo arrivals in eastern Bukooli.

Several abaiseNgobi traditions relate that Kigenhi, or Kigenyu, was the son of Kimumwe.[12] Kimumwe is recalled as the founder of the abaiseNaminha, who were among the first of the Lwo clans in the Budoola area to move off to the west and to become absorbed into the Bantu world. The abaiseNaminha founders apparently left the Lwo camps at Budoola, settling at Kitumba,[13] some twelve miles west of Budoola. Kitumba Hill, the *nkuni* of the abaiseNaminha, became the centre of a community of settlements dominated by a ruling line of abaiseNaminha.[14] The abaiseNaminha, who evidently settled at Kitumba ten to twelve generations back from 1899, remained dominant in their Mayole community until deposed by the abaiseWakooli some 250 years ago.

Shortly after the abaiseNaminha arrived at Kitumba, a group of abaiseBandha reached Mayole from the Lwo camps and was given a

[7] Lubogo, p. 139.   [8] Ogot, p. 74.
[9] Daudi Waiswa, 'History of Busoga', in CTBTH; and 'Book of the abaiseNgobi of Kigulu', in CTBTH.
[10] CTBTH, Text 349.
[11] 'Book of the abaiseNgobi of Kigulu', and Daudi Waiswa's 'History of Busoga'.
[12] 'Book of the abaiseNgobi of Kigulu', and Daudi Waiswa's 'History of Busoga'. Also CTBTH, Text 717.
[13] 33° 44·5′E, 0° 26′N.   [14] CTBTH, Texts 669–73.

place to settle at Kisaho,[15] a hill just a mile and a half north of Kitumba. One tradition of the abaiseBandha records their passage from Mount Elgon,

through Kangaiwa, through Kibuli, through Malaba, and through Kayango. At Kayango, he [Bandha] had a rest. From there he came to settle at Kigereke. At Kigereke, he killed a goat and he put some meat in a bag made from intestine. He left the place with the food in his bag to go and look for fertile land on which to settle. He then reached Kisaho. It was where he ate his meat from the bag [nsaho]. This was the food he had carried. That was the reason why this hill was called 'Kisaho'.[16]

From Kisaho, groups of abaiseBandha dispersed around Bukooli: Muhofu's family went to Buhofu and Buwekula; Ivumbi's family went to Nakivumbi; and Mugona's family went to Bukwiirize.

But Kisaho was not, apparently, the principal settlement of the abaiseBandha. Also important were the dispersals along the eastern side of Bukooli. Several traditions relate that the founder of the clan was Muhuma, and that he distributed his sons along the eastern side of Bukooli.[17] And the name *Muhuma* is the one which the abaiseBandha give to their daughters' sons.[18] One tradition relates that Muhuma, the clan founder, was the son of Molo.[19] In Lwo tradition, the Omolo group of migrating Lwo settled for two generations at Banda just to the south and west of Budoola.[20] It is possible that this Bandha clan name is associated with the Banda place-name recalled in the traditions of the Omolo groups, and that the Omolo at Banda were the source of the abaiseBandha settlers at Kisaho and other points. Supporting this hypothesis is one tradition[21] which relates that abaiseBandha families held a series of villages running from Mount Elgon to Bukooli: Kangaiwa, Kibuli, Malaba, and Kayango. This claim suggests that the abaiseBandha may be closely linked to the Parang group of Omolo Lwo who remained behind in the western foothills of Mount Elgon when the Omolo group travelled across the corridor to eastern Busoga. The clan shrine of the Parang group is at Molo in East Budama. The shrine marks the place where their leader Omolo died.[22] The postulated link between the Bandha group of Soga experience and the Omolo group of Lwo experience cannot be dismissed.

[15] 33° 43'E, 0° 28'N.   [16] STBTH, i. 4.
[17] CTBTH, Texts 13, 16.
[18] *Kahuma* is the name given to their daughters' daughters.
[19] CTBTH, Text 13.   [20] Ogot, p. 73.
[21] CTBTH, Text 16.   [22] Ogot, p. 90.

Evidence from Lwo tradition has suggested to B. A. Ogot that an Omolo group, the *Kagor* or *Wahori*, remained behind when the main body of Omolo left for Kenya in the seventeenth century, and that from this clan there may have emerged the abaiseWakooli ruling house of Bukooli.[23] Some evidence from Busoga supports this association between the abaiseWakooli and the Omolo group. First, the migration routes of the abaiseWakooli and the abaiseBandha, which appears to have been an Omolo group, are essentially the same. The abaiseBandha traditions relate that they passed from Mount Elgon, to Kangaiwa, through Kibuli, through Malaba, to Kayango where they rested.[24] The abaiseWakooli tradition of migration takes them from Mount Elgon to Kangaiwa (or Tororo), to the Malaba River, to Kigulu Hill and to Kayango.[25]

Moreover, the abaiseBandha have an explicit tradition of having separated from the abaiseWakooli:

... when we reached here we separated. The others called themselves abaiseWakooli. And we called ourselves abaiseBandha. This was because of marriage. We had no other way of marrying. We separated ... we had the same Bushbuck totem. The tradition concerning childbirth is also the same. When a woman is pregnant, she does not eat salt until she gives birth. Again she does not look at the sun until the cord drops off. The placenta is buried against an *Ndhibaigalwa* [a type of banana] ... on the right in the case of a boy, and on the left in the case of a girl. ... And the woman does not look at the sun before the cord drops off. If she goes out she covers her head with a tray. If she should look at the sun, the child will have crossed eyes. The kind of banana that must be eaten is called *Ntinti* which with simsim is mixed for chewing. Or we can eat *Naminwe* in case *Ntinti* cannot be found. ... We do not eat a hen but the abaiseWakooli eat it. When a woman delivers, they eat a hen in the case of a girl and a cock in the case of a boy. That is the only difference.[26]

Although the traditions of the abaiseWakooli, or Kagor, or Wahori, assert that the clan founder, Okali, took the office of ruler upon reaching Bukooli, there appears to have been a considerable time lapse between the Omolo arrivals and the coming to power of the abaiseWakooli which may suggest the very gradual emergence of

---

[23] ibid., pp. 73–4   [24] STBTH, i. 4.
[25] CTBTH, Texts 784, 791.
[26] STBTH, i. pp. 3–4. The special place of the hen in the ritual of the abaise-Wakooli is interesting. One of the early sites of settlement of the abaise-Wakooli was Kisimbiro Hill. The abaiseKidoido of the Frog totem were settled at Kisimbiro when the abaiseWakooli reached there and the hen figures rather prominently in the funeral rituals of the abaiseKidoido. (STBTH, i. 89.)

L

the Wakooli clan into prominence among the Lwo and Bantu-speaking groups of eastern Busoga. The traditions of the abaiseWakooli record an ancestry reaching back to *Okali*, a name which is both a Lwo praise name and an inversion of Wakooli, Kagor, or Wahori. Several of the abaiseWakooli genealogies count nine generations from Okali through Ochwa, Kasaali, Otakinyi, Mukama, Nhabe, Kaggazzi, Kibwe, and Muluya to Mwondha Mukwaya, the first mwiseWakooli to hold evidenced power and the earliest to emerge as a distinct person in the recollected traditions of the clan. It is likely that these early abaiseWakooli figures were no more than leaders of small groups of relatively unsettled pastoralists herding cattle between Nang'oma Hill and the Kitumbezi River, which today divides Bukooli from Bugweri County.

The earliest abaiseWakooli settlements appear to have been at Kisimbiro near Magoola,[27] where the abaiseWakooli met the abaise-Kidoido, and at Namakoko, Bukooli Hill.[28] Both of these points of early settlement were situated along the northern frontier of Mayole. It is likely that during the early years of abaiseNaminha rule in Mayole, the abaiseWakooli pastoralists were assuming a prominence throughout this area just to the north of Mayole.

A number of clans were living or settled within the abaiseNaminha domain in the years before their displacement by abaiseWakooli. Among them were the abaiseMusoga of the Reedbuck totem who were at Busoga Hill,[29] located some twelve miles to the north-west of Kitumba Hill. The abaiseMusoga would, within several generations, carry traditions associated with the Lwo advance into Bukooli to a new area of settlement at Butembe in south-west Busoga.[30] The abaiseBandha were at Kisaho and served in the position of *Katikkiro* in the Mayole state. Among the other groups were the abaiseIhemula at Busimbi near Kitumba, the abaiseMuganza at Namuganza,[31] the abaiseKidoido at Kisimbiro, and the abaiseMususwa at Isegero.

The sites of these settlements suggest an abaiseNaminha domain as large as 100 square miles, yet it is difficult to reconstruct the patterns of authority within this domain. Relatively few client settlements are evidenced; naturally enough, there is little indication of groups which

[27] 33° 42·2'E, 0° 33'N. [28] 33° 41'E, 0° 30·3'N. [29] 33° 39'E, 0° 30·8'N.

[30] The descendants of Ntembe, founder of the Butembe state, record a tradition asserting that *Wunhi*, a Lwo figure was the founder of the abaiseMusoga clan in Busoga.

[31] 33° 44'E, 0° 29·9'N.

may have been settled in Mayole but left at a later time for other lands, perhaps as a result of the extensive fighting involved in the aftermath of the transfer of power from Naminha's to Wakooli's family. But it is clear that a considerable portion of the authority of the abaiseNaminha was centred on their pastoral culture and, in particular, on their spiritual resources. The abaiseNaminha *nkuni*, Kitumba, became an important shrine for the larger community, and long after the abaiseWakooli had displaced them as rulers, the Kitumba spirit remained important in Bukooli.[32] One tradition, quoted frequently, relates that Naminha of Mayole had considerable powers of predicting the future[33] and Lubogo relates that Naminha was both a ventriloquist and a foreteller of the future.[34] The royal symbols of the abaiseNaminha also must have carried considerable authority. One, the *Nkandaiga* royal drum, became one of the royal drums of the abaiseWakooli.[35]

By the time the abaiseWakooli pastoralists and hunters began settling along the northern frontier of Mayole at Kisimbiro and Namakoko, the abaiseNaminha had clearly emerged as a power in their own right. Yet the abaiseNaminha rituals of birth suggest that they were creatures of two worlds—one the world of the Lwo cattle keeper, the other of the Bantu-speaking banana cultivators.

Our traditions were that when a woman delivers, someone goes for milk and he holds the milk with only one hand. This is only the right hand. On the occasion of the 'coming out', we use a small fish called Nkejje and a banana of the Ntinti type and it is put there and it is called 'Naminha's bunch'. . . . That is what I witnessed. If a woman delivers, she does not eat Millet.[36]

Two popular stories, together evidencing this meeting of two worlds, witness the transfer of power in Mayole from the abaise-Naminha to the abaiseWakooli. One, the story of Naminha's thorn covered reception floor, suggests the strong stroke of Buganda's hand in the life of Mayole. The other, the story of Naminha's beads, attests to the continuing strength of Lwo culture in the life of Bantu-speaking Bukooli.

In the story of the thorns or spikes, Naminha is recalled as a cruel ruler:

[32] CTBTH, Text 793.
[33] Lubogo, [Luganda MS.], p. 6; Lubogo, p. 5.
[34] Lubogo, p. 5; CTBTH, Text 791.   [35] CTBTH, Text 670.
[36] CTBTH, Text 670. The 'coming out' refers to the important occasion marking the first time a child is brought out of the house in which it was born.

That man Naminha had a custom of worship. He arranged pointed spikes before him. People who came to worship Naminha were ordered to put their hands on these spikes and to say, 'Praise be to Naminha' ['*Wesinge Naminha*']. And the hands were on the points of the spikes. 'Wesinge Naminha.' Some who were clever placed their hands between the spikes when bending down. But those who did not know how to do that put their hands right on the spikes and the pain was horrible. That was how Naminha was worshipped.

When people saw that, they asked Okali . . . 'Dear friend, have you not heard of this cruelty?'

'I have never heard of it because no one has ever told me,' Okali answered.[37]

This story is found again and again in the traditions of the early clans in Bukooli. The abaiseMususwa rendering records the name of the Naminha as Kubengiriho, but is otherwise identical.[38] An abaise-Wakooli version is largely identical except that the cruel Naminha is merely the *Katikkiro* of Wakooli; when Wakooli learns of the cruelty, Naminha is dismissed and replaced by Tesaga, a mwiseMusoga.[39] An abaiseNaminha version is similar, but Naminha's custom of the spikes is paralleled with that of Kabaka Kagulu Tibuchwereke of Buganda. Moreover, this tradition relates that this Naminha ruled in the time of Tibuchwereke.[40] This raises the most interesting problem related to the story of the spikes—the suggested association between Buganda and Mayole.

Kaggwa[41] records that Kabaka Kagulu Tibuchwereke made mats of rings of spikes and placed them before him and when people came to visit or came to bring cases before his court, Kagulu ordered them to kneel on the spike mats and to greet him with the words 'Praise to the Kabaka' ['*Asinze Kabaka*']. If his visitors failed to greet him properly while kneeling before him on the mats, Kagulu had them speared to death. In Ganda tradition, this practice is recalled as the last straw in Kagulu's cruel reign. The chiefs and their people fled the palace and refused to visit the Kabaka, and, ultimately, they saw the Kabaka flee the capital for lack of support.[42]

While one may make the observation that both the Kagulu and Naminha stories suggest the general loss of respect for the ruler and his ultimate loss of power, it is a larger problem to make a connection between the cruel practice of Kagulu and the identically cruel practice

[37] STBTH, i. 21.　　　[38] CTBTH, Text 610.　　　[39] CTBTH, Text 792.
[40] CTBTH, Text 672.　　　[41] Sir A. Kaggwa, *Kings*, p. 46.
[42] Kaggwa, *Kings*, pp. 45–8.

of Naminha. There are some indications of possible contact between the ruling house of Mayole and the ruling house of Buganda in Kagulu's time. First, Kagulu ruled some seven generations back from 1884 [1710–37 ±34], and this would seem to make him a contemporary of Mwondha of Bukooli who, in the story of the lost beads, is the mwiseWakooli who displaces the Naminha of Mayole. Mwondha lived six generations back from 1899, but in generations three, four, and five of the Bukooli house, several brothers or collateral brothers succeeded, very likely extending the lengths of those generations. The generation depth of Mwondha's reign is in co-ordination with that of Kakaire, the first mwiseMenha ruler of Bugweri, who also ruled six generations back from the 1890s, with several of the Menha generations apparently extended by fraternal succession. The alleged marriage between Mwondha and Kakaire's sister points to the contemporaneity of Mwondha and Kakaire, and the similarity in generation-depth of the abaiseWakooli and the abaiseMenha ruling lineages tends to confirm the indication of a depth of six extended generations, and this time-depth would seem in co-ordination with that accorded to Kagulu's reign.[43]

The evidence suggests, then, that Mwondha displaced Naminha, not only over the same apparent issue that forced Kagulu to flee his office in Buganda, but at approximately the same time as well. While the possibility of a connection between Kagulu's Buganda and Mayole is indicated by the chronological evidence, one must search elsewhere for evidence pointing to a link across which the practice, or a tradition of the practice, may have passed. There is some evidence of occasional contact between the kings of Buganda and the rulers of Soga states from the first half of the eighteenth century. Kabaka Mawanda, who succeeded Kikulwe, brother of Kagulu, unleashed an invasion of Busoga,[44] and there may be other, perhaps earlier, associations. In the rather confused and eclectic tradition of the abaiseMusuubo,[45] the family which preceded the abaiseMenha as

[43] An abaiseNaminha tradition, quoted in CTBTH, Text 672, relates that Naminha Wangubi, the first Naminha killed in the battles over the transfer of power from Naminha's house to Mwondha, ruled eight generations back from 1899.

[44] Kaggwa, *Kings*, p. 51.

[45] This abaiseMusuubo tradition, quoted in CTBTH, Texts 614, 615, 616, and in Lubogo, pp. 128–9, was apparently assembled in the early twentieth century for the edification of leaders considering the installation of the *Kyabazinga*, the paramount ruler of twentieth-century Busoga. The abaiseMusuubo, hoping to establish themselves in a prominent office in the Kyabazinga's administration, recalled

rulers of Bugweri, there is reference to a mission, sponsored by the early rulers in the centre of Busoga including Musuubo, to the Kabaka to discuss the problem they were having with the penetration of Mukama into Busoga. In the tradition, Mukama is called *Ibanda* and the Kabaka is referred to as *Cwa*, and, while these specific identifications are out of line chronologically and are surely only impressionistic, it is possible that the early rulers of the central part of Busoga, Musuubo, and Naminha among them, may have sent emissaries to Buganda to seek assistance in holding back the advances of the abaiseWakooli pastoralists into Mayole and the abaiseMenha pastoralists into Kizenguli. Such a visit would have taken them to the Buganda of either Kabaka Ndawula, Kagulu, Kikulwe, or Mawanda, all ruling between approximately 1700 and 1760.

Further possible evidence of this link between Naminha and Kagulu, the link suggested by the identity of the two experiences of cruelty in the royal palaces, concerns the secondary totem, or *kaibiro*, of the abaiseNaminha. Unlike the other groups of Lwo origins in Bukooli, the abaiseNaminha avoid, as their secondary totem, the Edible Rat. According to Kaggwa,[46] this very period—at the time of the reigns of Ndawula, Kagulu, Kikulwe, and Mawanda—was when the Edible Rat clan was emerging as an important clan at the capital of the Kabaka. It is possible that the abaiseNaminha or their emissaries became acquainted with important figures of the Edible Rat clan at the same time as their emissaries were becoming aware of the custom of receiving visitors in Kagulu's palace on the mats of spikes.

While the story of the spikes suggests the climate of opinion within which the transfer of Naminha's power to the abaiseWakooli occurred and suggests some linkage between Mayole and Buganda, the story of the finding of Naminha's beads portrays the transfer of power in terms unmistakenly Lwo. In the tradition of the lost beads,

---

their role as a commoner family in the installation of the abaiseNgobi as 'state founders' in northern Busoga. The abaiseNgobi, as the largest and most powerful of the clans in Busoga, would clearly get the office of Kyabazinga. The abaise-Musuubo sought, as a commoner clan, a subsidiary role, yet they sought it aggressively. The tradition appears to be of recent fabrication, though there may be certain grains of truth within it. The tradition reflects the confusion and uncertainty among the early 'historians' of Busoga who attempted, for whatever purpose, to organize the diffuse traditions into all encompassing 'constructions' of Soga history.

[46] Kaggwa, *Clans* [MS. translation], 'Omusu'.

it was Mwondha, the mwiseWakooli herdsman, who managed to displace the abaiseNaminha rulers of Mayole.

Mwondha Mukwaya became the chief as a Wakooli in this way: Mwondha was a herdsman of Naminha's cattle. When Naminha had gone to war, on his return he found that his wife had died. I do not remember her name. She had beads on her hands and on her legs. When she died, she left the beads to someone else. This person put the beads into a pot and put it under a stone. He also died. Naminha found all the people at home dead. There was no one to ask for the things that he had left with them at home. He announced that the one who found the beads would be given a cow.

Beads are the symbol of hereditary authority in the culture of the Lwo. CTBTH, Text 41, explains the importance of these beads to the ruling house of Bukooli: 'They cannot bury one of those of the royal clan unless they bring that bead. There are only a few who know about those grains because they were made by God ... like those Europeans who have very expensive beads, and like the Indians who have expensive jewels. Those are the beads which they must have to bury those of the royal clan.' The story of Mwondha and the beads continues,

Now then, Mukwaya Mwondha was herding cattle together with Bandha. Bandha was a doctor and he cured people, blind people, and deaf people, and he cured war wounds. He rested under a tree. When Mwondha saw something under a tree he called his friend . . .
Whenever Naminha called [Mukwaya, instead of answering 'Wangi' [an expression of deference to a superior], Mukwaya used to say 'Waitu' [a familiar response to an equal].
And when he came back and someone called him 'Mwondha', he answered 'Mukwaya'. It went on for a long time like that with him answering that way.
Naminha asked him, 'Why do you call out "Mukwaya" like that?' The boy did not answer. One day, he [Naminha] called many people to whom he said, 'I have called you here to ask that boy of mine why he answers "Mukwaya" whenever I call him. We want to know the meaning of the word "Mukwaya". If he cannot tell you, spear him with reeds until he dies.'
The boy stood before the meeting and was asked the question: 'Why do you always answer "Mukwaya" when someone calls you?'
Mwondha answered, 'There are many important things in the bush; I saw things in the forest.'
They said, 'Take him. He must show you what he saw that made him call out "Mukwaya"' ['the one who finds']. They tied his hands behind his back and he was escorted by two askaris. In the past, askaris were called

Abambowa. He took them to the stone and showed them the pot. They said, 'Release his arms but tie a rope around his waist.' They tied a rope around his waist. They took the pot before Naminha. When Naminha opened it, he found the beads he was looking for. Naminha gave orders, 'Lift him high. Carry him on your shoulders.' He called for all his girls and wives and the drums were beaten which said, 'Naminha is at Kitumba' [the clan drumbeat slogan]. These drums were beaten because Mwondha had seen the beads. They took him around the palace and the Naminha said, 'Put him down and bring him to me.' They brought a stool and he was seated. Naminha said, 'I have seen it, and now I declare that it was right for Mwondha to answer "Mukwaya". That is what he saw.'

From then, Mwondha was not allowed to herd cattle. He said, 'Mwondha is now a prince. He cannot herd cattle.' He gave a speech and said, 'All present must hear this. When I die, there is nobody else to rule after me except Mukwaya. I have approved him and his name is Mukwaya. Do you understand?'

They said, 'Yes we have heard.'

He said, 'Have you princesses heard that?'

'Yes, we have heard that.'

When the time came, he died, and on his death-bed he said it again, 'I have called you here to reiterate what I said before. I know this illness will kill me but when I die Mukwaya will succeed me.'

It was so—when Naminha died, they said, 'Is there any other person to succeed him?'

They called out, 'The will gives the *ssaza* to Mukwaya! We therefore confirm him.'

That is how Mwondha got the *ssaza* and became the first Wakooli.[47]

As the abaiseWakooli were eclipsing the abaiseNaminha rulers of Mayole, other clans of Lwo origin were emerging from the camps on the Malaba and Kibimba Rivers and were gradually becoming absorbed in the Bantu-speaking world. The abaiseKiruyi, a Lwo group evidently related to the abaiseWakooli, spread from Kayogera near the Kibimba where they had found the abaiseMusobya of the

[47] STBTH, i. 6–8. This tradition is quoted from a mwiseBandha source. Variations of the same tradition are related in CTBTH, Texts 41, 672, 793. An abaiseNaminha version, quoted in Text 672, is somewhat similar, at least to the point where the beads are found. Picking up the story from this point, the Naminha tradition relates, 'Naminha told him [Mukwaya], "I can now trust you as a very good man and a fine hunter. . . . You may have been my herdsman but now I appoint you here to be my *Katikkiro*." He served him and was a good, hardworking man worthy of trust. After a time, he [Mukwaya] ran away, and made arrangements with doctors. He then became an enemy. He killed Naminha Wangubi as well as Naminha Mugonvu and Naminha Kiryensenhe. . . . By his cruelty, he drove Naminha from his *ssaza* together with his people.'

Small Mudfish. From Kayogera, Kiruyi, the clan founder, distributed his sons around the north-eastern part of present-day Bukooli, to Madoha, to Namukonge, to Kasookwe, and to Nsango on the eastern side of the Kibimba River.[48]

Another group of Lwo origins, the abaiseKiranda, travelled from their camp at the Namasere River near Buhuni[49] and established a permanent settlement at Namago,[50] several miles to the north-west. Namago, firmly within the early domain of the abaiseWakooli ruling family of Bukooli, was the site of the *nkuni* of the abaiseKiranda and was the centre of their later dispersal throughout Busoga.[51]

In the early eighteenth century, the abaiseKibiga were emerging as a dominant clan in the area to the south of Budoola, in the region of Banda. The abaiseKibiga were a segment of the abaiseMudoola and broke off and migrated south, establishing a permanent settlement at Lubira south of the Lugada River,[52] which was, in later times, to mark the border between the Banda and Bukooli states. At Lubira[53] was located the Mukama *nkuni* of the abaiseKibiga. Each Mwoda, the ruler of Banda, enclosed his *mbuga* within a steep trench and the abaiseKibiga drumbeat is the same as that of the abaise-Mudoola, reflecting the importance of the trenches in the defence of their communities. The drum beats the slogan, 'Do not play with holes; otherwise something scratches you. Your fellow man is like a leopard.'[54]

Within a few generations, the abaiseWakooli ruling lineage was to become the dominant Lwo family in the Bukooli area. Mwondha Mukwaya built an enclosure at Namakoko, seven miles north-west of Kitumba. From Namakoko, the early Wakoolis expanded their domain and enhanced their power over an ever widening region. By the nineteenth century, the abaiseWakooli rulers of Bukooli, though troubled by endemic civil war, were still able to wage campaigns more than fifty miles from their seat of power at Namakoko. There is a song that reflects the advance of centralized power around the Namakoko seat. The song, *Baise Omuyayu Ow'enkoko alekule* celebrates the 'fierce rulers of Bukooli who caught hold of the country as a "wildcat [*Kayayu*] catches hold of the hens [*enkoko*]".'[55]

[48] STBTH, i. 97–8.   [49] 33° 47·5′E, 0° 27·5′N.
[50] 33° 44′E, 0° 31′N.   [51] CTBTH, Texts 202–16.
[52] 33° 53′E, 0° 23·4′N.   [53] 33° 49′E, 0° 16·3′N.
[54] *Osogosa enkompe, Mulimba alikwagule, Musadha mwino mpala.* CTBTH, Text 349; STBTH, i. 85.
[55] CTBTH, Text 791.

The several Lwo groups had, from their initial arrivals on the western side of Malaba, 'caught hold of the country', and, while gradually being absorbed into the Bantu-speaking world, they gave

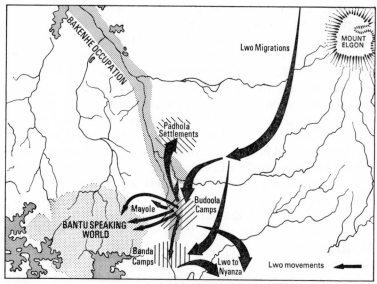

MAP VIII. Lwo Movements in Eastern Uganda

the country the gift and tradition of Mukama. The Lwo groups arriving in eastern Bukooli[56] constitute one of the streams of Mukama tradition in Busoga.

[56] Movements of the Lwo in Bukooli are outlined in Map VIII.

CHAPTER VIII

The Arrival of Kakaire

As the abaiseWakooli were eclipsing the power of the abaiseNaminha rulers of Mayole, the abaiseMenha, another Lwo group, were displacing the abaiseMusuubo of Kikalangufu Hill as rulers of their Kizenguli domain, eight miles west of Mayole. One popular tradition records that the abaiseMenha arrived at Wangobo[1] at the confluence of the Namaloe and Naigombwa Rivers in what is now north-western Bukooli. In the tradition, Kakaire, the leader of the abaiseMenha, is recalled as a hunter.

After arriving at Wangobo, they saw these hills [in the Kizenguli or Busimo area—what is now the southern part of Bugweri County]. As it is known that a hunter cannot be restrained, he [Kakaire] travelled with his dogs and reached Bukohe. The clan he met in that part was that of abaiseMusuubo. Musuubo had made something like a swing on which small children play and he was just swinging without caring about his subjects' favour, nor did he gift them lavishly, nor do anything else besides swinging. Kakaire, after his *mbuga* had been built, called the people, conversed with them and gifted them lavishly, and the people were moved to say, 'We should not refuse to present ourselves to this man who can do us a favour. We want to go and live with the owner of the other *mbuga*. Kakaire is the only one who can give us a drink. And the other one just goes on swinging.' He then claimed the chieftainship and deposed Musuubo.[2]

But this arrival of Kakaire at Busimo was laden with more significance than the mere transfer of power. Unlike the abaiseWakooli and the other groups of Bukooli Lwo, the abaiseMenha did not travel around the northern shores of Lake Kyoga and Lake Kwania from the Lwo camps near the Nile in northern Uganda. Rather, they appear to have emerged from a complex of Lwo and other groups whose movements took them from Pawiir, through Buruli, Bunyala, and northern Busoga, all lying to the south of Lake Kyoga and the Nile as it flows west from Lake Kyoga. The arrival of the abaiseMenha at Bukohe Hill in the domain of the abaiseMusuubo was apparently one part of an extension deep into the centre of Busoga

---

[1] 33° 41′E, 0° 42·5′N.   [2] CTBTH, Text 331.

of this complex of occupation which spanned the region from Pawiir in the west to Bugwere in the east.

The Pawiir region, encompassing the corridor between Lake Kyoga and Lake Albert, was an area of significant contact among pastoralist and cultivating groups expanding southwards and Bantu cultivating groups pushing northwards from the first millennium A.D. When Lwo pastoralists crossed the Nile into Pawiir in the fifteenth century, they evidently met groups of Bantu, Madi, and Western Lango[3] (and possibly Hima as well) who had confronted one another during pre–Lwo times. As advancing Lwo groups piled up on the southern side of the Nile, they transformed the worlds of the pre-Lwo occupants of Pawiir. The peoples of Pawiir were largely 'Lwooized'. They came to respect the Lwo leaders and worship the spirits of the Lwo. They very likely carried the message of Lwo power and Lwo prestige to neighbouring lands.

From the time of the first Lwo arrivals to the south of the Nile right up to the present generation, Pawiir was a region of almost continuous immigration and emigration. Perhaps within a generation or two of first reaching there, Lwo groups pushed south towards the centre of the Chwezi empire. Chwezi power soon collapsed and these Lwo heirs to royal office in Bunyoro–Kitara were largely absorbed into the Bantu-speaking world.

In the sixteenth century, many Lwo groups, very likely finding grazing lands in too great demand, began pushing north back across the Nile and west into Alurland; others went north to Acholiland, and still others pressed east into modern Lango country to the north of Lake Kwania. Many of the groups which reached Budoola, Padhola, and Nyanza emerged from these Lwo segments departing from Pawiir and moving eastwards along the northern side of Lake Kwania.

While some Lwo groups from Pawiir pushed east across the Nile and into the grasslands to the north of Lake Kyoga and Lake Kwania, other Pawiir groups were evidently moving south and then east through Buruli and Bunyala into northern Busoga and even across the Mpologoma River into Bugwere. Other Lwo groups

[3] Crazzolara has suggested that a group of Nilo-Hamitic origins, which he has designated the Western Lango, occupied present Acholiland in the first millennium A.D., later expanding southwards into present-day West Nile and Lango Districts. J. P. Crazzolara, 'Notes on the Lango–Omiru and the Labwoor and Nyakwai', *Anthropos*, 55 (1960), 177–8.

crossed Lake Kyoga from the Masindi area on the Nile, from Bululu and Kaweri on the Kaberamaido peninsula, and from Namasole to various points on the southern shores of Kyoga—Kasambya, Galiraya, Bukungu, Kigingi, Ikanda, and Iyingo. Kiwanuka, in discussing the history of eastern Buganda, joins the evidence from Buganda with Crazzolara's reconstruction and indicates that Jo-Pawiir were settling in northern Bugerere. He suggests, for instance, that a prominent group of Pawiir Lwo, under Chola, crossed Lake Kyoga, settling in Bugerere. There they emerged as the dominant family in the area some ten generations ago, perhaps in the late seventeenth century.[4]

As the Lwo groups pushed east through the swamp and grassland to the south of Lake Kyoga, they met Banyala groups settled near the effluence of the Nile into Lake Kyoga, Bakenhe groups along the coastlands of Lake Kyoga and along the banks of the Mpologoma River, and Banyama hunting groups in the interior of northern Busoga.

The Banyala appear to have been a heterogeneous assemblage of groups initially a part of the Madi or Western Lango thrust south of the Nile and Lake Kyoga. Later, these Banyala came under successive waves of Bantu and Lwo speakers. Groups in Busoga such as the abaiseMbupi and abaiseMugaya, whose traditions take them back to the area of the Nile effluence,[5] are, on etymological evidence, of apparent Madi origin. Crazzolara suggests that the *Gaya* and *Bub* or *Bobi* groups which occupied Pawiir and Kaberamaido, and to which the abaiseMbupi and abaiseMugaya are apparently related, are of Madi origin.[6]

A group apparently closely related to the abaiseMbupi were the abaiseMudope of Busoga, a Bakenhe clan which dispersed around the shores of Lake Kyoga and along the Mpologoma River.[7]

[4] Mathias Kiwanuka, 'The Traditional History of the Buganda Kingdom', pp. 309–10.

[5] CTBTH, Text 325; also, Lubogo, p. 115. Text 122 records the passage of Mugaya from Kyamatende which is situated near the effluence of the Nile into Lake Kyoga.

[6] *The Lwoo*, p. 450. He has also suggested that the presence of the Lamogi name in northern Busoga is indicative of a Western Lango presence south of Lake Kyoga (p. 334). If so, Western Lango groups may have also been present in Bunyala and Buruli.

[7] One mwiseMbupi source relates that the abaiseMudope and the abaiseMbupi are related (CTBTH, Text 324). Several sources, including Texts 324, 326, 328, record the abaiseMbupi *nkuni* as Kadope or Idope.

Crazzolara, in listing the prominent groups of the Jo–Pawiir of Pawiir, names the Kidopo and the Pawodopi,[8] which are very likely related to the abaiseMudope of Busoga.

While the abaiseMudope have traditions which centre on activities on the eastern side of Busoga and the abaiseMbupi traditions record activities mainly on the western side, the two clans acknowledge as their totems the Rhinoceros and Guinea Fowl, both relatively un-common in Busoga, but prominent among the groups living on the western side of the Nile River between Kyaggwe and Lake Kyoga.

What is suggested here is a pattern of occupation of the Lake Kyoga basin by this mixed Bantu, Madi, and perhaps Western Lango assemblage. These patterns of occupation and contact were evidently repeated to the north and east of Lake Kyoga in Lango and Teso country; encompassed within them were apparently the furthest northwards expansion of Bantu speakers. Lake Kyoga was, as today, very unlikely to have constituted a barrier to contact between and among groups living on its margins. With the arrivals of Lwo groups on the northern shores of Lake Kyoga in Kaberamaido, many of these Banyala groups may have left for safer areas on the southern side of the Lake near the Nile effluence, among the papyrus islands along the eastern side of Busoga, and along the northern shores of Busoga. A. O. Jenkins quotes a tradition which has the Banyala crossing Lake Kyoga from Teso and settling in Bunyala.[9] Crazzolara quotes a tradition of Jo–Pawiir of Kaberamaido which reports that when the Jo–Pawiir reached Bululu,[10] the Banyala were just leaving there for Bugerere across Lake Kyoga.[11]

This postulated complex of Banyala occupation, probably con-strained and pushed back by the Lwo advance into Kaberamaido, was very likely continuous with the patterns of Bakenhe and Ban-yama occupation in northern Busoga.[12]

The traditions of Busoga recall the *Bapakooyo* of northern Busoga. Lubogo writes,

[8] pp. 450–1.
[9] 'A note on the Saza of Bugerere, Buganda Kingdom', *Uganda Journal*, vi, 4 (1939), 204.
[10] 33° 16'E, 1° 39'N.
[11] Crazzolara, pp. 79–80.
[12] See above, Chapter VI, pp. 137–9.

The people who lived within Kitimbo's kingdom, the present Bugabula, were known by ancient names of 'Pa-Jo', 'Pa-Lwo' or 'Pakoyo'. It is widely known now that the original name of the people of Bugabula was Pakoyo, which is derived from Jo-Pa Lwo—the people whose origin is Bunyoro.[13]

There is a Soga clan called abaiseMukooyo which is of the Bushbuck totem, which has a tradition of coming from Bunyoro, and which settled at Ikanda[14] on Lake Kyoga where their *nkuni* is located and where their founder Ikanda died.[15] Another source, a mwiseMugwere, gives the founder of his clan as Mupakooyo, son of Mugwere,[16] suggesting a relationship between the Mugwere group and the Pakooyo complex.

The Bapakooyo community—stretching perhaps from the Nile River, right across northern Busoga, to the Mpologoma River and beyond into what is now Bugwere County—appears to have been the outgrowth of the movements of peoples of Lwo origin through Buruli, Bunyala, and northern Busoga, and across Lake Kyoga to the northern Busoga shores. In this region, the Lwo apparently interacted with, and eventually dominated, the pre–Lwo groups whom they met.

In reconstructing the history of Busoga, one finds the Bapakooyo constituting a link between the stream of Lwo moving south and east from Pawiir and a number of groups of Lwo origin settled in Busoga today. While the traditions of Busoga reveal little about this period of Bapakooyo occupation of northern Busoga, the traditions do reflect a pattern of emergence of prestigious pastoral and hunting families, of evidently Lwo origins, from the milieu of diverse groups wandering about and settling in northern Busoga.

Perhaps the most prominent of the Lwo groups which passed through the region to the south of Lake Kyoga was the Bagweri group which included the abaiseMenha, who ultimately became the ruling house of Bugweri in the centre of Busoga and the abaise-Mugwere group who became dominant in the lands of Bugwere on the eastern side of the Mpologoma River. Tradition records that Kakaire, the abaiseMenha founder, came to Busoga with his brothers Magoola and Ndhoki, his sister Kitimbo, and his wife Kawaga, a mwiseMbupi, along with people of a number of other clans.[17] Magoola, the elder, apparently died somewhere between Bunyoro

[13] Lubogo, p. 49.
[14] 33° 11′E, 1° 17′N.
[15] CTBTH, Texts 454–5.
[16] CTBTH, Text 403.
[17] STBTH, i. 128–9, 137.

and Wangobo, and Kakaire took up the reins of leadership. As they journeyed close to the Mpologoma River, Ndhoki may have left Kakaire's group and crossed the Mpologoma River, reaching Kitantalo[18] and Tademeeri.[19] Ndhoki is variously referred to as the 'first Mugwere',[20] the son of 'Muwoya, the abaiseMugwere clan founder',[21] or princely brother of Kakaire.[22] While there is considerable evidence that Ndhoki left Kakaire's party before Wangobo, there is other evidence indicating that Ndhoki left Kakaire after Kakaire had established himself as the ruler of Bugweri. Only then did he venture to the east across the Mpologoma River, stopping at Bumenya in Bunyole on the way to Bugwere.[23] It is possible that both stories record actual events, together suggesting that the migrating Bagwere split at several points, two groups eventually joining together again in Bugwere in eastern Uganda.[24]

The abaiseMenha have a tradition which describes the route they took in their migration to Bukohe Hill; additionally the tradition asserts that the abaiseMenha travelled with Okali of Bukooli:

... This prince Kakaire together with his brother Magoola and another Mugweri brother, Okali of Bukooli, left Bunyolo to go to Busoga. Magoola died in Bunyole before they crossed the sea. He was buried in Bunyolo. But Kakaire and Okali together with another Mugweri prince reached Busoga. They came in a canoe to Iyingo harbour [on Lake Kyoga, 33° 19'E, 1° 18·5'N]. It is said that the canoe and the paddle they used turned into muvule. They are in Iyingo harbour ... Kakaire and his group from Iyingo travelled ... passing a village which I now cannot remember. But it is between Irundu [33° 23'E, 1° 14'N] and the sea, and marks the boundary between Bulamogi and Bugabula. Later, they left Bugabula and entered Bulamogi travelling to Busiki at Kasedhere [33° 41'E, 0° 46'N]. Kasedhere is in Busiki. They rested there but from there they saw the hills of Bukooli and of Bugweri. They left this place with their group and they passed through Wangobo and they crossed the River Igobero [or Igogero,

[18] 33° 45·5'E, 0° 59·8'N. CTBTH, Texts 396, 399, 404–5, 407.
[19] 33° 58·2'E, 0° 59·2'N. CTBTH, Texts 401, 408–9.
[20] CTBTH, Text 400.   [21] CTBTH, Text 406.   [22] STBTH, i. 128–9.
[23] See the discussion of the later migration from Bugweri to Bunyole and Bugwere, below pp. 167–70.
[24] The abaiseMugwere traditions recorded from fourteen sources reflect several streams of tradition and very extensive clan segmentation. One source, quoted in CTBTH, Text 400, discusses a split in the abaiseMugwere family, a split which caused one large abaiseMugwere family to migrate to Busiki on the western side of the Mpologoma. This is the strongest indication in the Soga traditions of an early division in the abaiseMugwere.

33° 40′E, 0° 42·3′N] and entered Bugweri at Idudi [33° 40′E, 0° 42′N]. They passed to Mbulamuti and Kakaire built an *mbuga* there. Later, that *mbuga* was remembered by all Menhas [title of the abaiseMenha rulers] and each Menha had to rebuild this *mbuga* so as to remember Kakaire's *mbuga*.

From here they went to Bunalwenhi on a hill called Lwino. Here they left their belongings and went to a hill called Luhalambago. From Luhala-mbago, they saw the sea. They asked the people they found in the country, 'Which country is better to live in?'

Those people at Luhalambago which is now in Bukooli told them that 'the best place is Bukohe'. They went back to Bunalwenhi and went to Bukohe. On this hill Bukohe, there was also another hill called Nabuyandha Ikonero. Here, Kakaire was satisfied with the place and he made an *mbuga*.[25]

Other traditions confirm the route taken, but one major difficulty is the place of Okali, the abaiseWakooli forefather, in this migrational story of the abaiseMenha. The abaiseWakooli have no tradition of migration along the route recorded in abaiseMenha traditions. However, there is the tradition of an important marriage tie between the abaiseWakooli and the abaiseMenha which records that Okali took Kitimbo, Kakaire's sister, as his bride.[26] One story relates that the mwiseWakooli leader took Kitimbo from Wangobo where the abaiseMenha group was then camped.[27] This suggests the possibility that the abaiseMenha and the abaiseWakooli could have met in north-western Bukooli in the area of Wangobo and that it was only there that a link was established between the two groups. Lubogo relates that Okali was at Kigobero when he sent for Kitimbo from Kakaire's place.[28] Kigobero is located at the Igobero, or Igo-gero River, which flows less than a mile from Wangobo. Lubogo's version goes on to record that by the time Kitimbo set out to join Okali, Okali was staying at Kisimbiro.[29] Still another version[30] relates that Okali took Kitimbo to cook for him when he was involved with hunting at Luhalambago, a later stop in the journeys of Kakaire.

Whenever the alliance was made or the marriage consummated—and there seems to be no satisfactory evidence of any link whatsoever between the abaiseMenha and abaiseWakooli before Wangobo—the marriage between Kitimbo and Okali is recalled in the traditions of both clans as incestuous. Lubogo has written,

[25] STBTH, i. 128–9.   [26] STBTH, i. 120–1; CTBTH, Text 332; Lubogo, p. 56.
[27] STBTH, i. 120.   [28] p. 56.
[29] ibid., Kisimbiro was one of the early points of settlement recorded in abaise-Wakooli tradition. (See Chapter VII, above, p. 146).
[30] CTBTH, Text 332.

M

After a short time, however, Okali resumed his wanderings, taking his sister with him. They arrived at Namakoko, where Okali incestuously had sexual intercourse with his sister Kitimbo and she became pregnant. News of this was brought to Kakaire who, as a result, became furious and conceived a bitter hatred for Okali. Notwithstanding the circumstances, Okali offered to pay a friendly visit to his brother Kakaire at Bukowe. Kakaire could not bear such an insult, so he collected a big army which he stationed in the valley of the River Kituto to stop the approach of his sinful brother. When news of these precautionary measures became known to Okali, he cancelled his visit but sent men to fetch banana leaves for him from his brother's *mbuga*. Kakaire was so angry that he did not spare them (Okali's men); he ordered his army to arrest them and to put them to death immediately, which they did. The result was that the two brothers became bitter enemies, avoiding each other for the rest of their lives; however, their grandchildren began intermarrying without any knowledge of this ... Kitimbo gave birth to a daughter who was named Kagoya, which is interpreted to mean 'one who sinned against the customs of the clan'.[31]

This story may very well be apocryphal. The evidence of migration taken alone indicates that Okali and Kakaire were not brothers in anything more than a figurative sense. Their relationship probably had its beginnings near the cattle enclosures at Wangobo as the abaiseMenha crossed the Namaloe River into country occupied by abaiseWakooli hunters and pastoralists. There can be little question of Kitimbo's identity being mistaken or of a totemic prohibition of marriage. The abaiseMenha totem is the Female Bushbuck; the abaiseWakooli totem is the Male Bushbuck. The abaiseWakooli customs of birth and death differ considerably from those of the abaiseMenha. They have no common names for male clansmen in their respective genealogies. Significantly they continued to intermarry after the alleged breach of morality.

It is possible that incest may have been given as the explanation for some failure of the marriage, of some failure of Kitimbo to raise a child,[32] or, perhaps, of the mwiseWakooli's failure to complete the marriage by handing over sufficient bride-wealth to Kakaire's group. More importantly though, the story functioned as an explanation

---

[31] pp. 56-7. The fetching of banana leaves from Bugweri was, at a later date, a sign of deference by the abaiseWakooli to the abaiseMenha. It is likely that the fetching of banana leaves began, as a custom, at a later date—it is unlikely that this would have been a custom of the two groups at a time when both were wandering around, apparently preoccupied with herding and hunting.

[32] One source (STBTH, i. 121) relates that 'the child that Kitimbo delivered died before it was given a name.'

of why the two groups, the abaiseWakooli and the abaiseMenha—
both of the Bushbuck totem, both entering the area at the same time,
both displacing the earlier ruling houses of the two domains lying
just two miles apart, both enhanced in their prestige by 'Mukama'
associations, and both active in north-west Bukooli—were not, and
never acted as, brothers. They were evidently from quite diverse
streams of Lwo advance into the Busoga region.

Other groups of Lwo origins, and apparently of the Bapakooyo
stream, pushed south with the abaiseMenha into the heart of Busoga.
The abaiseIdibya, who travelled south with the abaiseMenha and
settled at Bubbala[33] where their *nkuni* is located, were apparently
part of the Lwo thrust into the northern reaches of Busoga. Their
traditions suggest a migration from the northern part of present
Bugabula to Kisiro Island in the Mpologoma River, with one family
leaving the main group and travelling southwards to Bubbala.[34]

The abaiseMpina were also a part of the Lwo movements into
northern Busoga. The *Mpina* name carries the clan back to *Anfina* or
Mpina, the ruler of the Jo–Pa Lwo of Pawiir.[35] Under their leader
Nalwenhi, they travelled with the abaiseMenha to Lwino Hill.[36]
There the abaiseMpina settled with their *nkuni* (Lwino or Bunalwenhi), and this was to become the source of their later dispersals
around Busoga. Nalwenhi emerged as an important chief among the
clients of Kakaire.[37]

The abaiseMuyangu were another Lwo group pressing eastwards
into northern Busoga in the time of the Kakaire migration. One tradition[38] relates that Nangira, a clan founder, travelled with the abaise-
Menha and reached Kikalangufu in Bugweri, having travelled some
of the way from Bunyoro in a canoe. In Bugweri, the abaiseMuyangu
served as warriors of the first Menha, Kakaire. Kakaire gave them a
butaka at Naluswa Hill at Bubbala,[39] where they joined the abaise-
Idibya and another group—the abaiseMwase of the Large Reedbuck
—which also appears to have travelled from the northern reaches of
Busoga with Kakaire. These abaiseMwase have a tradition that
Obala led them to Bugweri from Bunyoro; once in Bugweri, they
settled at Bubbala Hill. Located at Bubbala is *Obala*, the *nkuni* of
the abaiseMwase. The tradition records that the wife of the Obala

[33] 33° 39′E, 0° 40·5′N.   [34] CTBTH, Texts 58–9.
[35] J. Driberg, *The Lango* (London, 1923), pp. 32–3. Also, the Bapina are one
among the pastoralist clans of Bunyoro.
[36] 33° 35·5′E, 0° 29′N.   [37] CTBTH, Texts 333–9.
[38] CTBTH, Text 641.   [39] 33° 39′E, 0° 40·5′N.

nkuni is the Naluswa *nkuni*,[40] and Naluswa is the *nkuni* of the abaise-Muyangu of the Bushbuck totem.[41] The record of a 'marriage' between the *nkuni* figures of two clans living near one another is not uncommon in Busoga. It is suggestive of a very close, preferred marriage alliance between the abaiseMuyangu and the abaiseMwase. The area around Bubbala, including the hills of Obala and Naluswa, is commonly referred to as *Nsoziibiri*, 'Twin Hills', indicative of the prominence of the commonality and alliance very likely involved in the settlement of the two clans there.

The Obala name of the abaiseMwase *nkuni* and forefather of the clan reflects Lwo origins. *Obal*, or *Obara*, is an honorific title among the Lwo and the pastoral Banyoro.[42] But the Large Reedbuck, the totem of the abaiseMwase, is not a typical Lwo totem. The only Reedbuck clan which John Roscoe recorded in Bunyoro is the *Abagere*, a serf clan in Bunyoro as opposed to the free and pastoral categories of Roscoe's list.[43] If they were not Lwo, it is possible that the abaiseMwase were among the groups which came under the strong impact of Lwo advance into the Pawiir or Buruli areas.

Several other clans, apparently not of Lwo origin, joined this movement southwards from the Bupakooyo area into the area of Bugweri. A Guinea Fowl group from the Bunyala–Bugerere area west of the Nile River appears to have travelled with the abaise-Menha into the centre of Busoga. There they became the caretakers of the holy places of the abaiseMenha, and they appear to have been absorbed into the larger abaiseMukuve–Isanga group of the Egret totem, some of whom had come from the south into the domain of the abaiseMusuubo.[44] This apparent linkage between the Guinea Fowl clients of Kakaire and the Egret supporters of the abaiseMusuubo ruling house is one indication of the process by which the authority of the abaiseMusuubo was undermined with the appearance of the abaiseMenha and their supporters on the margins of Kizenguli.

The abaiseMbupi, who gave Kakaire a wife Kawaga,[45] were a

[40] CTBTH, Text 650.

[41] CTBTH, Texts 641, 644. The other abaiseMuyangu sources (Texts 639–40, 642–3, 645) record their *nkuni* as Bbala or Obala.

[42] Crazzolara, p. 449; J. Nyakatura, *Abakama ba Bunyoro-Kitara* (St. Justin, Quebec: 1947), p. 76.

[43] J. Roscoe, *The Bakitara*, pp. 14–18.

[44] CTBTH, Texts 487–97; STBTH, i. 129; Lubogo [Luganda MS.], p. 81.

[45] STBTH, i. 137.

Banyala group. They dispersed through Lake Kyoga and along the Mpologoma River. Some abaiseMbupi families emerged as Bakenhe along the waterways of Busoga. Crazzolara has asserted that the *Bopi* groups of Pawiir are of Madi derivation.[46] It is possible that these abaiseMbupi, whose complex traditions indicate the overlaying of several groups, migrated from Pawiir into Bunyala and from there dispersed across Busoga with one family at least joining Kakaire's thrust southwards.

The abaiseKyewe of the Bean dispersed in pre–Lwo times along the Mpologoma River on the eastern side of present-day Busoga. One segment of the clan, Luma's family, apparently joined the migrating abaiseMenha along the banks of Lake Kyoga and travelled with them through Wangobo to Bukohe.[47]

Another clan, the abaiseIbinga of the Dog totem, were evidently at Kasodo,[48] which lies along the route taken by the abaiseMenha in their travels from Lake Kyoga's shores to Wangobo. Hunters, the abaiseIbinga joined Kakaire and travelled with them to Kizenguli.[49]

Other groups apparently filtered into and through northern Busoga and became part of the Bapakooyo complex but did not travel with Kakaire into the centre of Busoga.[50] The abaiseMukooyo of the Bushbuck totem have a tradition of migration from Bunyoro to Ikanda Hill,[51] perhaps passing through or across Lake Kyoga on the way to Ikanda. From there they dispersed right across the northern face of Busoga.[52] Other groups, including the abaiseMulemeeri of the Pig totem, the abaiseKalijoko of the Oribi Antelope totem, and the abaiseMbeya, appear to have been Bapakooyo clans whose area of occupation extended across the Mpologoma River into the lands which came under the domination of the abaiseMugwere.[53]

There is a tradition among the groups which were in Bugweri at

[46] p. 450.   [47] CTBTH, Text 280; and STBTH, i. 129.
[48] 33° 39′E, 0° 53′N.   [49] CTBTH, Text 52; and STBTH, i. 129.
[50] The process of migration from the west across the Nile into northern Busoga continues today. Since the emergence of the Lwo dominated states in northern Busoga, this migrational track has played an important role in creating links— physical or ideological—between the states of the North and the kingdom of Bunyoro, and thus in refreshing the Nilotic and Nyoro presence in northern Busoga. The northern area of Bugabula County is referred to as 'Bunyoro' by people living in the southern parts of Busoga. And the dialect of the speakers of northern Busoga is called *Lupakooyo*. [51] 33° 11′E, 1° 17′N. [52] CTBTH, Text 454.
[53] CTBTH, Texts 127, 156–7, 523–5. There are traces here, and elements of the Kalijoko group are exemplary, of the early penetration of the region south of the Lake Kyoga basin by groups today associated with the Teso.

the time of the arrival of the abaiseMenha and their companions from the north that it was Kakaire's skill as a hunter which won him the stool of Kizenguli from the abaiseMusuubo. 'Menha came to visit and he went to Bukohe there and lived with his host. Then he killed animals and gave meat to peasants to eat.'[54] However, it was very likely not the hunting alone which gave Kakaire the stool. Kakaire had already built up a great following among the Bapakooyo in the north through his skill as a hunter. These were the people called *Banyama*, or 'Meat People', by the Bakenhe fishermen of the Mpologoma River.[55] The hunting life and hunting prestige assume immense importance among the peoples who recall participation in the events of the broad region stretching from where the Nile flows into Lake Kyoga to Mayole in the south-east.[56] In the traditions, northern Busoga was—in the times when the states of the North were emerging—a difficult wilderness in which one could only survive as a skilled hunter. Tremendous power—built on prestige— flowed to the most skilled hunter and the most generous giver of meat.[57] It was perhaps the prestige that Kakaire and his family had already gained among the supporters who followed him, more than his appeal as a hunter among the Kizenguli groups, which really turned the tide to his advantage in Bugweri. However, events at Bukohe *were* significant.

The hunting tradition continues,

He [Kakaire] met many peasants and he used to give us meat freely. And when some wanted to fight for the meat, he said, 'Don't fight. I shall give you more.' And he did the same the next day. He hunted with bows and arrows, not guns. He gave the meat freely because there were many animals of every kind.

When he said that he wanted to return to his homeland, people prevented him from going and said, 'Stay and judge us when we fight because you are a good man and you give us meat freely.'

He replied, 'You are preventing me from going, but I am a bachelor.'

And they in turn replied, 'We shall give you a wife.' He then asked them, 'Do you know the woman I love?' And they replied, 'Tell us,' and he told them that he loved Nakaziba [a mwiseKaziba girl]. And he said, 'I won't go away.' Kakaire was the one. Nakaziba then became pregnant and gave

[54] STBTH, i. 101.

[55] See the discussion of pre-Lwo northern Busoga in Chapter VI, above.

[56] Traditions do not reflect such hunting prestige in the values of the peoples of South Busoga.

[57] See the traditions of the abaiseWakooli, the abaiseNgobi of Bulamogi, Bukono, and Bugabula, and the abaiseIgaga of Busiki in CTBTH.

birth to a baby boy, Menha oweKibedi, and he said, 'When I die, that child [oweKibedi] is the one to succeed me.'[58]

This was a significant marriage. It evidently drew into Kakaire's orbit the family of Nakaziba who had been important clients of the abaiseMusuubo. The abaiseKaziba had dispersed from Maleka[59] in South Busoga and one family had travelled to Bukohe Hill, coming within the domain of the abaiseMusuubo.[60] It was at Bukohe that the abaiseMenha settled and built an *mbuga*, and it was at Bukohe that the marriage alliance between the abaiseMenha and the abaiseKaziba was consummated. It was at Nsumba on Bukohe Hill that the abaise-Kyewe, followers of Kakaire, settled and where they cared for the royal stool and the royal skins.[61] It was at Bukohe where the jaw-bones of several of the early Menhas were kept. It was here where the rituals of accession of the early Menhas were performed. While Kakaire's great following was built up on the way to Bukohe, it was at Bukohe where the important transfer of power actually occurred.

In attempting to understand this transfer of power from the abaiseMusuubo to the abaiseMenha, we can draw upon the tradition of Kakaire's hunting skill and the tradition of the mwiseMusuubo ruler's playful disregard[62] for his royal duties, both of which are proffered to explain the transfer of authority from one ruling house to the other. But behind these explicit traditions, there is the evidence of Kakaire wooing away through marriage important supporters of the abaiseMusuubo; of his followers, such as the Guinea Fowl people, building marriage links with clients of the abaiseMusuubo; and of the great prestige and authority over a large body of followers which he carried into the country. On these blocks his base was built, and the power of the abaiseMusuubo collapsed.

One mwiseMenha source has argued, on the basis of written evidence which came to his attention, that the Bagweri who settled in Busoga and Bugwere in eastern Uganda came from the ancient heart of Bunyoro in what is now Toro. The assertion is based on an interesting story which records that the people who persistently interrupted conversations at the court of the first Mukama were called 'Bagweri'

---

[58] CTBTH, Text 222.   [59] 33° 34'E, 0° 25·3'N.
[60] STBTH, i. 81. Bukohe is located at 33° 35·6'E, 0° 28·2'N.
[61] CTBTH, Texts 280, 459.
[62] This is the tradition which records that he was always playing on a swing. See above, p. 137.

from the word *kugwera*, meaning 'to interrupt'.[63] There is no other evidence to support this assertion. The credibility of the assertion rests on the place and time at which the Lwo who emerged as the Bagweri were 'Bantuized'. If the 'interrupters' story has some basis in fact, these Lwo were 'Bantuized' at the time or before they reached the court of the first Mukama, or an early Mukama, and were part of the penetration of Lwo from the north deep into western Uganda to the heart of old Bunyoro–Kitara. Roscoe does record an Abagweri clan in his list of pastoral clans of Bunyoro.[64]

There is a quite different possibility however. B. A. Ogot, in reconstructing the migrations of the later settlers in Padhola, relates that a Jo–Koch

group eventually found itself in the country of Bugwere [Bugweri] in Busoga, probably around the present village of Segero, where it is said their remnants still live. . . . One of their clan songs is actually in Lusoga, and the explanation offered is that it was the Basoga women they married who translated the original Luo song into Lusoga.[65]

Ogot—on the basis of the work of Okech[66] and Crazzolara—has suggested that the Jo–Koch were one of the Jo–Nam groups which shattered at the Pubungu camp, leaving there in all directions, one perhaps finding its way to Busoga.[67] There are several indications that these Jo–Koch are the source of the abaiseMenha of Busoga, and that the Jo–Koch of Padhola are one segment of the group which reached Bukohe. Crazzolara, in addressing himself to the history of the Jo–Koch, discusses their origins in northern Uganda and their development and movements since then.[68] According to Crazzolara, the Jo–Koch were, like the abaiseMenha, skilled users of the bow and arrow.[69] Among the names in the royal genealogy of the Jo–Koch are *Ikek* and *Koch*,[70] which are perhaps related to the *Kakaire* name. Moreover, Crazzolara records that during a famine many Jo–Koch migrated to Bunyoro where they worked for the Mukama. While most eventually left, some remained in Pawiir near Masindi Port on the Nile.[71]

There is a tradition, quoted by Crazzolara, that a Jo–Koch group visited the Mukama, who gave them the Lwo royal insignia. This Jo–Koch delegation returned to their homeland of Ragem north of

[63] STBTH, i. 127–8.　　　[64] *The Bakitara*, pp. 14–18.
[65] *A History of the Southern Luo*, p. 104.
[66] L. Okech, *Tekwaro Ki Ker Lobo Acholi* (Kampala, 1953), pp. 46–52.
[67] Ogot, pp. 104–5.　　　[68] *The Lwoo*, pp. 303–11.
[69] ibid., p. 306.　　　[70] ibid., pp. 310–11.　　　[71] ibid., pp. 306–8.

Lake Albert where their leader was installed as *Rwot* (King) with the royal emblems. Among the peoples of the Jo–Koch of Ragem were the *Pokwero*, or *Pokweri*,[72] a clan name perhaps related to the *Gweri* root of the abaiseMenha of Bugweri and the abaiseMugwere.

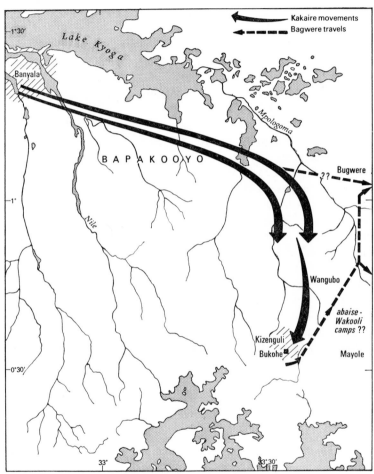

MAP IX. The Kakaire Migration

What is suggested here is that the abaiseMenha of Bugweri may have been part of the Jo–Koch group which reached Pawiir and, while evidently retaining their 'Lwo-ness', won the favour of the

[72] Crazzolara, p. 344.

rulers of Bunyoro. Still carrying their prestige as great warriors and hunters with the bow and arrow, and perhaps with a semblance of royal authority given by the Mukama, the Bagweri migrated east-wards along the southern shores of Lake Kyoga until they reached Iyingo, from which point they gradually advanced southwards into the centre of Busoga. The name Kakaire may simply be a 'Bantu-ized' form of *Koch* or *Ikek*, omnipresent names among the Jo–Koch. Thus, the Jo–Koch group which left Isegero in Bugweri—located about one mile from Bukohe, capital of the abaiseMenha—may have been a segment of the family of abaiseMenha who reached Bukohe from the north. The Isegero segment, however, may have left the centre of abaiseMenha activity before becoming fully absorbed into the Bantu-speaking world. This Isegero group, according to Ogot, travelled from Bugweri to Bunyole in eastern Uganda and from there to Padhola some ten generations ago.[73] This Padhola tradition, recording that the Jo–Koch stopped off in Bunyole before reaching Padhola, would tend to support the abaiseMenha tradition which has a group—the emergent abaiseMugwere—leaving Bugweri under Ndhoki after Kakaire had been installed at Bukohe. This Ndhoki group reached Nabowa[74] in Bugwere before moving on to the centre of Bugwere.[75] An abaiseMugwere tradition records that before the abaiseMugwere reached Bugwere in eastern Uganda, they were at Bumenya in Bunyole.[76] Bumenya may have been the place where the Jo–Koch divided, some going to Padhola and some to Bugwere. The Bumenya place name is an additional indication of the relationship with the abaiseMenha of Bugweri in Busoga.

Kakaire's family, then, very likely a segment of the Jo–Koch Lwo, drove southwards into the centre of Busoga,[77] assumed authority over the settlements at Kizenguli, and gradually expanded this authority northwards. These prestigious Lwo settlers at Bukohe would consti-tute still another thread of the emerging Mukama tradition of Busoga.

[73] This estimate of ten generations would be in accord with the estimated date of 1710–37±32 for the reign of Kakaire, based on the overall chronological pic-ture of Busoga.
[74] 34° 01′E, 1° 02·5′N.
[75] STBTH, i. 129.
[76] CTBTH, Text 400.
[77] The movements of the Kakaire group are traced in Map IX.

CHAPTER IX

The Children of Mukama

A PROMINENT theme in the traditions of northern Busoga identifies the founders of the several abaiseNgobi dynasties as brothers, the sons of Mukama. The idea of a unity of kinship and a common heritage devolving from Mukama through one family of fraternal, though autonomous, dynasties is embedded in many of the traditions relating to the arrival and installation of the abaiseNgobi ruling families in northern Busoga. The popular tradition draws together the many abaiseNgobi ruling lineages—the lineages of Muzaaya Ngobi Mau of Buzaaya, of Kitimbo of Bugabula, of Ngambani Lamogi of Bulamogi, of Ibanda Ngobi of Buzimba and Luuka, of Kibalya Lagwe of Bulole, of Kitimbo Nkono of Bukono, as well as the ruling lineages of eleven other states in the north. One version records, 'Mukama came from Masaaba side . . . from the east. When Mukama came into this country, he went on producing children, the princes. Like those Ngobis, he begat Tabingwa, Zibondo. Those are his children with Nkono and Kitimbo. And so Mukama passed through and departed.'[1]

The Ssaabalangira Ggomotoka found a similar tradition, one which recorded the usually unidentified Mukama figure as 'Nnamutukulu',[2]

Once a man called Mukama Nnamutukulu came from the east on the Bukedi side and crossed over a river called Mpologoma, having his wife with him—her name was Nnawodo. When he crossed over that big river which is traversed by canoe, he came to Kigulu Hill in Busoga and slept there. The very place where he slept is called Nnamusisi, and there is a rock there. Mukama Nnamutukulu was light-skinned. It is said that he came with the following children: (1) Kitimbo; (2) Nkono; (3) Wakooli at Bukooli; (4) Walube at Kigulu; (5) Zibondo at Bulamogi; (6) Tabingwa at Luwuka; (7) Muzaya at Buzaya; and a coterie of many other people.[3]

---

[1] CTBTH, Text 718.
[2] Or Namutukula, Kyebambe III, ruler of the Bunyoro dynasty in the early nineteenth century, too late to be associated with the contribution to Busoga accorded the Mukama of Soga tradition.
[3] Y. T. K. Ggomotoka, 'Ebifa Mu Busoga', *Munno*, March 1926, p. 52.

Lubogo records a similar tradition,

... That on his way from Mount Elgon, Mukama had with him his wife, five children, some men, two dogs, spears, cattle, goats, and many other things. While in Busoga, he had two more children, Ibanda and Kitimbo ... Mukama fell to hunting ... animals. He lived temporarily among the hills of Kamigo at a place called Irera, not very far from where Jinja is. Later on, he went to explore the country around River Mpologoma. He arrived at a place which he called Namakoko, in Bukono, and he built a home there. He had his son Unyi (Kitimbo Nkono) with him. Mukama asked Unyi whether he would like to have that part of the country for himself and Unyi accepted. ... The following were Unyi's brothers: (1) Okali, who was given the part of Bukoli, his title Koli; (2) Ibanda, who was given the part of Kigulu, his title Ngobi; (3) Ngambani, who was given the part of Bulamogi, his title Zibondo; (4) Ngobi Mau of Buzaya, his title Muzaya; (5) Kitimbo, who was given Bugabula and entitled Gabula; Nyiro, who was given Luuka and entitled Tabingwa.[4]

A tradition of the same theme was recorded by D. W. Robertson:

One Mukama, who afterwards became the ruler of the Nyoro kingdom, or his son, came to Busoga from Mount Elgon. ... He stayed some time in Busoga and usually occupied himself with hunting. From time to time, his wife bore his children and to each son he apportioned the part of the country where his birth had taken place. In this way the first born, Akoli received ... Bukoli, Zibondo was given Bulamogi, Nkono received Bukono, Tabingwa received Luuka, and Ngobi received Kigulu.[5]

This theme of the princely brothers of the father Mukama is found again and again in the popular tradition of Busoga. While all the royal Bushbuck families associate themselves with the Mukama presence in Busoga, the idea of a unity of kinship devolving from Mukama is more pronounced among the traditions associated with the abaiseNgobi ruling houses. The theme of abaiseNgobi unity based on a common ancestor is reinforced by the existence today of a functionally united kinship group comprising eighteen royal houses and many non-ruling lineages all referred to as abaiseNgobi. However, this theme of unity is opposed to a considerable body of evidence indicating that the various abaiseNgobi families arriving in the North belonged to at least two diverse streams: first, the stream of Lwo crossing the Mpologoma River directly into Bulamogi and

---

[4] Lubogo, pp. 8–9. In a later chapter (pp. 41–2), Lubogo offers another version of the Mukama family of princes. While the families presented in the two versions are similarly structured, the given routes of migration are quite different.

[5] D. W. Robertson *The Historical Considerations Contributing to the Soga System of Land Tenure*, p. 6.

Bukono; and second, the stream of Lwo from the camps on the eastern side of Bukooli who crossed Busoga to the Nile River, with some continuing west.

Nkono and Zibondo

In the popular traditions of Mukama's activities in Busoga, Ngambani Lamogi and Kitimbo Nkono, founders of the ruling houses of Bulamogi and Bukono, are recalled as two of the several sons of Mukama. Today, the descendants of Ngambani and Kitimbo Nkono have a place among the other families calling themselves, and called by others, abaiseNgobi. Lubogo records that,

On his arrival in Busoga, Mukama had with him the following children: Okali of Bukoli, Ibanda of Kigulu, Ngambani of Bulamogi and Unyi (Nkono) of Bukono. Zibondo Ngambani and Unyi were both left in Bukono after they had crossed River Mpologoma into Busoga with their father, Mukama. The latter roamed about the country hunting wild animals. Ngambani and Unyi were then young, strong men who enjoyed hunting as a sport. They hunted elephants and killed so many animals that their men never starved for lack of food. Besides hunting, these two young men were skilled craftsmen; they knew pottery, carpentry and many other forms of handiwork.

Soon their reputation spread over the land, which is now Bulamogi, across a now non-existent Lake Ntakwe which then separated Bukono from Bulamogi. The people of that land heard of the wonderful things which were being done by the people who had come from Elgon. They sent some envoys to Bukono to see what these wonderful things were. Nantamu and Musosa (Mugosa) were the envoys to Bukono and they were greatly impressed by the respect which people paid to the two young men. The outcome was to invite one of these young men to cross over into Bulamogi. Unyi encouraged his brother Ngambani to accept the invitation and (Ngambani) followed the envoys to Bulamogi.[6]

There is a considerable body of inexplicit evidence supporting the theme of Ngambani Lamogi and Kitimbo Nkono as brothers, yet this same body of evidence sets them off as dramatically distinct from the other ruling lineages which today call themselves, and are called by others, abaiseNgobi. First, the *nkuni* of the ruling families of Bulamogi and Bukono is Waama,[7] while the ruling houses of Bugabula, Luuka, Buzimba (Kigulu), Buzaaya and Bulole, all families of the abaiseNgobi clan, respect only their Butimbito *nkuni* and do not

[6] Lubogo, p. 18.
[7] CTBTH, Texts 562, 720–1, 725, 727–9, 731–2, 734, 736.

recognize Waama.[8] Second, the drumbeat slogan of the abaiseNgobi houses of Bulamogi and Bukono is, 'I have no child',[9] while that of the other abaiseNgobi families is 'The Eye of the Chief'.[10] Third, the royal families of Bukono and Bulamogi had among their regalia the prestigious *kinakyeri* drum and *kimasa* harp, while the other abaise-Ngobi groups did not have them.[11]

Traditions reflecting on the migrations of the Lwo groups reaching Bulamogi and Bukono underscore this sharp distinction between the Bulamogi and Bukono abaiseNgobi and the other abaiseNgobi groups in Busoga. Both the abaiseNgobi of Bukono and the abaise-Ngobi of Bulamogi recall crossing from the eastern side of the Mpologoma in the area of Lake Lemwa to the western side of the River. One tradition records the Bukono founder's passage from Bugwere on the eastern side of the Mpologoma to Kikalu harbour on the western side where he and his followers established an early settlement.[12] Another source records that the first Nkono of Bukono passed from Kakolo on Lake Lemwa—situated on the northern side of Bugwere—to Kikalu on the western side of the Mpologoma.[13]

The Bulamogi traditions record not only a passage from the Kakolo harbour on the eastern side of the Mpologoma to the western bank, but suggest, as well, that the ruling family of Bulamogi continued to have strong ties with their early home on the eastern side. The ruling family of Bulamogi carried their dead back across the river to Kakolo where the corpses were buried.[14] The Nankodo and Kakolo traditions are not in conflict; Nankodo, in Bugwere, is just across Lake Lemwa from Kakolo in Pallisa.[15]

Fallers recorded a detailed description of the funeral rites for a deceased Bulamogi ruler, and the same tradition of a return to the east is found within it:

In the second generation after the death, in the time of the grandson of the deceased one, they went to take away the jaw-bone. . . . The baiwa and the important chiefs and princes went secretly at night to get the jaw. They cleaned it and rubbed it with butter and decorated it with cowrie shells. . . .

[8] CTBTH, Text 562.
[9] '*Nambula mwana*', CTBTH, Texts 722–3, 731, 736.
[10] '*Liiso ikulu*', CTBTH, Texts 715–16, 562, 737–41, 745–7.
[11] CTBTH, Text 731.   [12] STBTH, i. 71.
[13] CTBTH, Text 603.   [14] CTBTH, Text 133.

[15] The source of Text 133, while naming Nankodo as the site of the burial ground, asserts that it is found in Pallisa. He may, in fact, mean adjacent Kakolo. In any event, the two are separated by only a mile of water.

The jaw and a milking cow were put into the hut with a wife of the deceased one to guard them. These things were left in the hut for two years. Then a bull, a male goat, a male sheep and a cock were prepared and a leg was taken from each. They might also catch a woman who was walking along the road. All these things were taken secretly at night to a forest at Nankodo in Gwere country. They left those things there and ran away. This was done because the first Lamogi, when he left Mukama, built his first palace in that place.[16]

This evidence of a westwards migration of the Bulamogi and Bukono royal families from the Lake Lemwa area is in conflict with the traditions of the other abaiseNgobi groups which recall migrations through Budoola into Bukooli and across the centre of Busoga.[17]

Yet, while the evidence indicates both that the Bukono and Bulamogi ruling houses were quite distinct historically from the other abaiseNgobi families in northern Busoga and that the Bukono and Bulamogi families were themselves closely related, the genealogical evidence indicates a considerable disparity in time between the arrival of Ngambani in Bulamogi and the arrival of the first Nkono in Bukono. The Bulamogi ruling line is seven generations deep counting back from Kisira who died in September 1898 to Ngambani, the founder.[18] On the basis of the seven generations, Ngambani was probably established in Bulamogi by 1737 ± 32 years. The ruling lineage of Bukono appears to be considerably deeper, reaching back from 1897, when Kyebambe Kitamwa was removed by British arms,

[16] Fallers, pp. 133–4.

[17] There is but one tradition which contradicts this construction of the westwards migration of the Bulamogi and Bukono royal families across the Mpologoma River. Recorded by Lubogo, pp. 8–9, and quoted in this chapter (above, p. 172) this has Mukama—father of Unyi Kitimbo Nkono, the founder of the lineage of Nkono of Bukono—reaching Bukono from the south-west, from the area of Irera in the Kamigo Hills a few miles from Jinja. As Lubogo tells the story, Unyi, while not mentioned until Mukama reaches the River Mpologoma in his wanderings through Busoga, is left in Bukono by his father. There is no other evidence, explicit or inexplicit, which would tend to support this description of Mukama's journey, and the weight of the evidence is strong on the other side. The tradition appears to have come from S. W. Nkondho, a prominent figure in the abaiseMusooko clan, and an early historian in Busoga, who attempted to develop a synthesis of abaiseNgobi traditions and who worked as an assistant to Lubogo in Lubogo's research. Nkondho's clan, the abaiseMusooko, are, interestingly, linked to the Kamigo site in their own traditions.

[18] Lubogo, pp. 18–27. Lubogo asserts that there were other rulers in the royal line but that their names are not remembered. These 'rulers' may very well have been princes who managed to secure brief periods of independence from the legitimate line, and perhaps hegemony, during a period of intensive strife following the death of Bwoye in the fourth generation back. CTBTH, Text 562, lists a few of these sometimes autonomous princes.

through ten generations to the founder, Kitimbo Nkono.[19] On the basis of ten generations, the Bukono founder was established at Kikalu Hill by perhaps 1656 ± 38 years. Thus, while the popular traditions record the two founders as both contemporaries and brothers, the evidence of chronology suggests the possibility that, though probably of related lineages, they were not contemporaries.

The Bushbuck totems, the pastoral traditions, and the names of the two ruling families of Bukono and Bulamogi affirm that they were part of the Lwo expansion southwards. However, evidence of more specific 'origins' or derivation is weak. The Bulamogi founder Ngambani is called Lamogi in a number of traditions, and the Lamogi root is found in the Bulamogi place name. The Lamogi name figures prominently in the traditions of the northern peoples of Uganda and among the Lwo in particular. Crazzolara has postulated that the Balamogi of Busoga are related to a larger Lamogi group that expanded from a homeland in the Agooro Range in northern Uganda in the first millennium A.D.[20] These migrating Lamogi groups were gradually absorbed into the later Madi and Lwo expansions.

Lamogi, or Ramogi, is, as well, the name of one of the Lwo groups migrating southwards around the eastern side of Lake Kyoga and along the western slopes of Mount Elgon into the eastern Uganda area in the sixteenth or early seventeenth century. These Lwo migrants, who were to be among the pioneer settlers in Padhola, crossed the corridor lying between the Elgon foothills and the Malaba River, seeking a more secure home on the western side. Some settled temporarily in Bunyole and then moved across the Malaba River into eastern Bukooli. If the search for security was the primary drive of the Lwo in their travels through the corridor between Mount Elgon and eastern Bukooli, some Lwo may have left Bunyole in a northwards direction, crossing the Namatala River into present Bugwere County. The Ramogi clan was one of the Lwo groups which settled temporarily in Bugwere.[21] Ogot has recorded conflicting testimony concerning the possible relationship between the Ramogi of Padhola and the Ramogi of Bulamogi. One tradition recalls the Ramogi settling in Bugwere for a short time, only to be pushed southwards into Padhola by the arrival of Bagwere groups from Busoga in the previously sparsely occupied Bugwere.[22] The arrival of 'Bagwere from Busoga' is very likely contemporaneous with the foundation of the

[19] CTBTH, Text 731.   [20] Crazzolara, *The Lwoo*, pp. 329–34.
[21] Ogot, *A History of the Southern Luo*, p. 81.   [22] ibid., pp. 80–1.

Bugweri state in Busoga by abaiseMenha some seven generations back from 1900.[23] It is possible that some of the Ramogi clan may have been cut off, fleeing north to the area of Lake Lemwa on the northern side of Bugwere, while the main party retreated southwards to Padhola. Lake Lemwa was the immediate point of origin of the Nkono and Ngambani families crossing the Mpologoma to Kikalu Hill and Bulamogi. Both Nkono[24] and Ngambani may very well have been related to these groups of Lwo pressing southwards through the western foothills of Mount Elgon.

A third group, not of the Bushbuck totem, has a tradition recalling a parallel migration across the Mpologoma from the east to the western bank, there establishing a new seat of power in Busoga. These are the abaiseIgaga of Busiki who may or may not be related to the other abaiseIgaga groups in Busoga.[25] The founder of the Busiki state is recorded as Nemwe and the evidence suggests that Nemwe arrived at Namagero from the east, from across the Mpologoma River. The several Kisikis who immediately followed Nemwe[26] all had their capitals on the eastern side of Busiki along the river, only gradually extending their power into the interior of Busoga.[27] Like the Bulamogi ruling house, the abaiseIgaga rulers of Busiki continued to have ties with the eastern bank. One Kisiki had a *mbuga* on Kisiro Island in the River and the 'treasures' of the Kisikis were stored on Namakakale Island which abuts the Bunyole mainland.[28]

All these groups—the ruling house of Bukono, the ruling house of Bulamogi, the ruling house of Busiki, along with several of the Padhola groups—possess a sacred drum called *achiel*, or *ekinakyeri* in Lusoga suggesting, with the other evidence, that, perhaps some ten to

[23] See above, pp. 167–9.

[24] Several sources including Lubogo (pp. 8–9) record Unhi Nkono as the founder of the Bukono ruling house. The Unhi name may be associated with the Owiny group of Lwoo who, with the Ramogi, were in the vanguard of Lwo arrivals in the area between Mount Elgon and eastern Bukooli. For a discussion of another Unhi (or Wunhi) figure see below, pp. 181–2.

[25] The traditions of the various abaiseIgaga groups in Busoga defy synthesis in any more than a general way. There appears to be one major scission between the abaiseIgaga of Busiki and those of Busambira at Nhenda Hill, and one secondary cleavage between the Busambira group and the Nantamu group of Bulamogi. There is today no functional unity among the several groups calling themselves abaiseIgaga. While the problem is much discussed by the various abaiseIgaga, there is no clear evidence of segmentation within *one* parent family.

[26] Nemwe is reckoned to have lived some eight generations back from 1899, perhaps 1683 ± 36 years.

[27] See Map X.   [28] STBTH, i. 50.

N

twelve generations back from 1900, groups of Lwo pastoralists and
non-Lwo groups living along the rivers of the Mpologoma system
had begun to form an integrated complex of settlement and culture,
and that from this complex emerged the royal families of Bulamogi,
Bukono, Busiki, and, perhaps Bugwere. It was perhaps within such a
complex that the earliest measure of political control over client
groups appeared, eventually to be carried over to the western banks
of the Mpologoma.

Whatever the patterns of settlement and culture were on the eastern
side, the Lwo families crossing the Mpologoma River into Bulamogi
and Bukono were probably not unfamiliar with the conditions and
opportunities on the western side. Traditions record these Lwo as
enthusiastic and skilled hunters, and they may have crossed the
Mpologoma on brief hunting forays well before they crossed to stay.
They very likely became one new element among the old *Banyama*,
'Meat People', the hunting, and presumably pastoralist, population
in the interior of Busoga who were so clearly set off from their neigh-

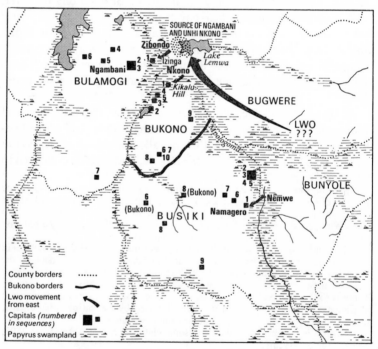

MAP x. Capital Sites in North-East Busoga

bours—the Bakenhe fishermen of the rivers—by their own 'meat' economy.

The Bakenhe on the rivers very likely played an important role in the initial movements of Lwo families across the Mpologoma. The Bakenhe in the Bulamogi and Bukono area included the families of Nantamu and Mugosa, both mentioned by Lubogo[29] as inviting Ngambani to settle permanently in Bulamogi. There is a tradition that Nantamu, a mwiseIgaga, migrated to the Mpologoma River bank in north-eastern Bulamogi where he found among other groups Kafamba's family of abaiseMukose. Nantamu is recalled as having given a woman to Kafamba and as having won Kafamba's heart. When Kafamba died, Nantamu succeeded him as headman in the area. Later, the mwiseNgobi Lamogi (Ngambani) arrived from the eastern side of the Mpologoma and 'took over from Nantamu without fighting'. Nantamu gave a woman, Nakuya, to Lamogi, and Lamogi settled at Lubulo, near Gadumire.[30]

Nantamu's group occupied Izinga on the Mpologoma River directly across from the old Lwo camping grounds at Nankodo and Kakolo, later the location of the hallowed funereal shrine of Ngambani Lamogi on the eastern side. Izinga lies on a direct line between Kakolo and Lubulo Hill near Gadumire where Ngambani built his first enclosure on the western side of the River. Nantamu's family was therefore in an ideal position to assist Ngambani's transfer to Busoga. Throughout the history of the Bulamogi state, the Nantamu lineage was permitted considerable autonomy within its Izinga estate, a status perhaps attributable to the crucial role which they played in the migration and settlement of the Ngambani Lamogi group in Busoga.[31]

While the passage of Kitimbo Nkono to the western bank probably antedated Ngambani's arrival at Izinga by at least a generation, the processes involved in the migrations and in the establishment of

---

[29] p. 18. The Bulamogi and Bukono Bakenhe also included the abaiseIruba, but they are not mentioned in this tradition of Ngambani's arrival.

[30] STBTH, i. 44. Lubogo (p. 18–19), records that 'when Ngambani first arrived in Bulamogi, he settled at Izinga, Nantamu's area, but he later moved his *mbuga* to Buguge near Gadumire Hill. He made Nantama [Nantamu] one of his principal chiefs. Nantamu's authority prevailed over a small island of Izinga measuring about two square miles.'

[31] Lubogo, p. 18, records the names of several of the followers of Ngambani Lamogi. Mostly Lwo and all with origins on the eastern side of the river, they included Muwoya (or Muhoya), Twoli (or Tooli), Nyoro, and Nankola. All settled close to Ngambani at Gadumire.

hegemony over groups along the western bank of the Mpologoma appear similar. While the Lamogi group crossed to Izinga—then occupied by Nantamu and his family—the Kitimbo group crossed to Kikalu Hill, then occupied by abaiseIruba. The abaiseIruba had themselves migrated from the eastern side of the River and among them were a number of Bakenhe families. The abaiseIruba are of the Rabbit totem. Rabbit totem groups, including the abaiseIruba and the abaiseMuganza, were significant among the settled Bakenhe along the Mpologoma River in the Bukono area and were perhaps part of the postulated complex of settlement and culture on the western bank. Further south, the abaiseIgaga, crossing the Mpologoma under their leader Nemwe, found Bakenhe groups living in the area of Namagero, less than a half mile from the River and there, among them, Nemwe established his first home on the western bank.

What is suggested by the slim evidence relating to these three groups which traversed the Mpologoma is that the crossings made no immediate impact on the state of affairs of Busoga. They brought no sudden revolution in government or demography, perhaps no im- mediate change in economy or language. What was significant was that the crossing had been made. Settlements of Lwo, and groups influenced by the Lwo, were planted on the western bank. If these colonists were at first hesitant, if strong ties still remained with their homes and perhaps their relatives on the eastern bank, they were none the less there. Gradually their impact would become felt and the settlements at Lubulo Hill, at Kikalu, and at Namagero would attract followers and clients from the interior of Busoga. Allied to the Bakenhe of the River while maintaining an economy in which pastoralism and hunting were pronounced, these first colonists were in a position to build a bridge between the river and the interior. As hesitancy gave way before new-found confidence, the centres of settlement would shift boldly away from the river to the interior.

The Central Thread of Mukama Tradition

While the founders of the abaiseNgobi ruling houses of Bukono and Bulamogi appear to have been part of a hesitant movement across the Mpologoma River from the Lake Lemwa area, all the other abaiseNgobi families of northern Busoga are associated with a quite distinct migration—the bold journey of Lwo and followers along a route from east to west, from the Mount Elgon area into eastern Bukooli and across central Busoga to the Nile and beyond.[32] This route through the centre of Busoga is in accord with the popular tradition of Mukama's travels through Busoga. According to one tradition,

Mukama came from the Bukooli side and reached Naibiri and built a *mbuga* called Naibiri. The gate of the Lubiri was called Kazigo. He then went from Naibiri to Nsambya near Bunafu ... and he stayed there for some time. From Nsambya, Luuka, he went to Kebagani where he divided the land among his children. Then he went to Bunyoro. From there, his son Kitimbo came back this way.[33]

In Soga tradition, the recollected itineraries of the Mukama figure in this journey across Busoga vary in detail, yet all record an entry point at Budoola on the Malaba River in the east and an exit point near Nankandulo on the Nile to the west, and most record such stopping places as Nang'oma Hill in eastern Bukooli and Nhenda Hill, Busambira.[34]

The name of Mukama, so prominent in the traditions and in the religious culture of northern Busoga, may be no more than a symbol of a group and no less ambiguous than a praise name, yet attempts have been made to identify the Mukama of Soga tradition as a particular Mukama or King of Bunyoro. Ggomotoka[35] identified the Mukama as Nnamutukula, Mukama of Bunyoro in the early nineteenth century.[36] Another possibility has been proffered by Tito Winyi[37] who recorded that Mukama Olimi I, who reigned some fourteen generations back from 1900, '... went to Busoga, for there the princes were causing trouble and rebelling. He turned them out of their chieftainships and installed others in their places. He then invaded parts of Kavirondo, Nandi and Masai.' On the basis of an eclipse associated with Kabaka Nakibinge of Buganda, a contemporary, Olimi I's reign is reckoned to have been in the first quarter of the sixteenth century. Other sources record that the Mukama of Soga tradition was the son of a Mukama Wunhi (Winyi).[38] Nyoro traditions record three rulers named Winyi ruling before the nineteenth

[32] See Map XI.   [33] STBTH, i. 71.
[34] Budoola is located at 33° 53·8'E, 0° 27'N. Nankandulo is located at 33° 04'E, 0° 41·5'N. Nang'oma Hill is located at 33° 52'E, 0° 25·3'N. Nhenda Hill, Busambira, is located at 33° 30'E, 0° 33'N.
[35] Ggomotoka, 'Ebifa mu Busoga', p. 52.
[36] According to the genealogy presented by K. W. [Tito Winyi, Mukama of Bunyoro-Kitara], 'Kings of Bunyoro-Kitara', *Uganda Journal*, iii (1935), and iv (1936).
[37] ibid., iv (1936), 79.   [38] CTBTH, Texts 463, 603, 715.

century, one in the fifteenth generation back from 1900, one in the twelfth generation back, and one in the eighth generation back.

These possibilities do not accord well with the traditions of the Soga dynasties which recall the Mukama parent and the Mukama journey. The dynasties of northern Busoga associated with the Mukama tradition are all some seven generations deep counting back from 1899 through the founder's generation. Ggomotoka's Nnamutukula would then be too recent as he apparently reigned in the nineteenth century. The possibility of Olimi I, a son of a Winyi, would have to be excluded because he was too early.[39] The Winyi of the twelfth generation back was succeeded by his son Olimi II who probably reigned in the early seventeenth century. Olimi II is then a possibility and cannot be ruled out on the basis of this genealogical evidence alone. The Winyi of the eighth generation back was succeeded by a son Nyaika who apparently reigned in the early eighteenth century. While possibly too late, he cannot be ruled out absolutely on the basis of the genealogical evidence alone. But there is no evidence that these two Mukamas, Olimi II and Nyaika, ventured eastward into Busoga, or more specifically, ventured across Busoga from east to west, a still more improbable journey. The evidence seems to run in the other direction; both Olimi II and Nyaika reigned during periods of retrenchment, with the frontiers of Bunyoro under attack, with the Nyoro kings taking defensive rather than offensive stances. Under these conditions, it is unlikely that they would have been able to participate in distant foreign adventures.

The reference in Nyoro traditions to the campaign of Olimi I in Busoga in the sixteenth century is interesting and would be quite significant if the reference to 'Busoga' meant in the past what the geographical reference means today; that is, the district stretching from the Nile to the Mpologoma River, from Lake Kyoga to Lake Victoria. In earlier times—particularly before the Ganda armies began regularly attacking across the Nile—'Busoga' referred to little more than the state in the south-west, near today's Jinja, called Busoga and ruled by the lineage of Ntembe of the Reedbuck. From an early date, the dynasty of Ntembe was involved in the adventures of the Bunyoro and Buganda monarchs in the areas of Kyaggwe and Bugerere to the west of the Nile. The Busoga of Ntembe may have found its way into Nyoro tradition as it did into Ganda tradi-

---

[39] The eclipse in Olimi's reign has been reckoned at 1520. Richard Gray, 'Annular Eclipse Maps', *Journal of African History*, ix, 1 (1968), 148–9.

tion, and only later did the meaning of the word come to encompass more than that small area along the Nile across from Kyaggwe. Journeys and campaigns in Busoga are likely to have been little more than activities in the lands to the west and east of the Nile near its source.[40]

While the evidence suggests that the Mukama of Soga tradition may not have been of the Nyoro ruling line, the problem of identifying Mukama remains. Mukama is a praise name and title throughout much of the Interlacustrine region. By itself, the Mukama name reveals little of the specific origins of the heroic figure of northern Busoga. But there is evidence which places the origins of Mukama, or of a group represented by that name, among the early Lwo settlers crossing the River Malaba into eastern Bukooli in the late sixteenth and early seventeenth centuries. Among these Lwo were the founders of the abaiseMudoola of Busoga who apparently emerged as early leaders in the Lwo camping grounds on the eastern side of Bukooli. Today, the abaiseMudoola of that area recall that their clan forefather was Kigenhi.[41] The abaiseNgobi ruling families of Buzimba (Kigulu) and Luuka record Kigenhi or Kigenyu as an ancestor of the Mukama who passed through Busoga and who left sons as princes to rule the country some seven generations back from 1899. Kigenhi, in these recollected genealogies, antedated Mukama by three generations and their ancestor and founder Ngobi by some four generations.[42] The timing of Kigenhi in abaiseNgobi traditions—eleven or twelve generations back from 1899—is in accord with the timing of the early Lwo settlements in eastern Bukooli, settlements which Ogot has dated in the late sixteenth and early seventeenth centuries, or some eleven or twelve generations back from 1899.[43]

Other evidence supports this postulated connection between the Mukama of Soga tradition and the abaiseMudoola of Budoola.

[40] One can perhaps compare the Soga use of the term 'Bunyoro'. To Basoga, 'Bunyoro' refers to the area of north-western Busoga, Bugerere, and Buruli as much as to the distant centre of the Bito kingdom.

[41] CTBTH, Text 349. While Kigenhi is a popular nickname for the 'foreigner' or 'visitor', no other figure named Kigenhi is recalled by the descendants of the early Lwo of eastern Bukooli.

[42] Daudi Waiswa, 'A History of Busoga', 'Book of the abaiseNgobi of Kigulu and Luuka', both in CTBTH.

[43] Ogot records that the 'Owiny and Adhola groups . . . claim to have settled in the upper part of the Bukooli County—in Budola, Buduma, and Butema areas—for some two to three generations, before moving away to their respective homes about twelve to thirteen generations ago [Ogot counts back from 1966], and therefore between 1570 and 1630 A.D.' (p. 74).

Various sources relate that Mukama, in his travels through Busoga, first stopped at Nang'oma Hill.[44] Nang'oma Hill was at the centre of the abaiseMudoola camps and became the site of their royal enclosure. The abaiseMudoola at Nang'oma Hill may be associated with the Adhola figure, who, in Padhola traditions, was the founder of Padhola society and the one who led the migration from eastern Bukooli back across the Malaba River to Lul on the western side of present-day West Budama County.[45] Adhola's group was camped at Budoola. Lwo traditions record that the Adhola group emerged from the Owiny assemblage. The Owiny group broke apart in the camps on the eastern side of Bukooli. An Owiny segment went eastwards into Nyanza and an Adhola segment eventually recrossed the Malaba into Budama. The Wunhi of Soga tradition, purported father of Mukama, may be associated with this Owiny presence in the Budoola camps.[46]

Nang'oma Hill and the abaiseMudoola forefathers appear to have been at the epicentre of political developments crucial to the whole region of eastern Uganda and western Kenya. From there, the Adhola and Owiny figures emerged, carrying with them enormous prestige into western Kenya and back across the Malaba to Budama. The abaiseMudoola assumed a dominant position among the Lwo camped in the Budoola area, perhaps picking up the reins of leadership from Adhola and Owiny. Budoola was the point of departure of similarly prestigious Lwo setting off for the west across the centre of Busoga, leaving in their tracks a series of political nodes ruled by dynasties of the abaiseNgobi.

Mukama and his followers—the founders and guardians of the abaiseNgobi dynasties of central Busoga—were not the first to forsake the area of intensive Lwo occupation on the western side of the Malaba for the Bantu-speaking interior of Busoga. The abaise-Naminha, associated through their founder Kimumwe with the Nan-

[44] Nang'oma Hill is located at 33° 52′E, 0° 25·3′N. Lubogo, p. 140: 'On his arrival in Busoga, Mukama first went to Nangoma Hill in Bukoli.'

[45] Ogot, p. 75.

[46] Ogot, p. 75, notes a passage from the unpublished 'Tribal Notes' of Captain Persse which records a tradition that the 'Padhola migrated from Nagongera in modern West Budama to Budola under the leadership of Mufuta, Kasede, and Owiny. In Budola, they separated, Owiny went to Nyanza, Kasede went back to Budama; and Mufuta remained in Budola and his descendants were later assimilated.' Ogot adds the note that 'Kasede is the founder of a subclan—Amor-Kasede, one of the Padhola clans that claims to have lived in Budola before returning to Budama.' To compound the thesis still further, one must note that Mufuta is the title of the traditional leader of the abaiseMudoola.

g'oma site and the abaiseMudoola group, travelled west to establish a settlement at Kitumba Hill, emerging briefly as a ruling clan among the groups settled there. The abaiseBandha also travelled west from the same Budoola area, settling at Kisaho. The abaiseWakooli likewise pushed west from the Lwo camps in eastern Bukooli, reaching the area of Namakoko and unseating their predecessors, the abaise-Naminha, as rulers of the western region of Bukooli.[47] Little by little, the Lwo of the Budoola camps were making contact with the Bantu-speaking world to the west. Gradually, they would become embedded in the Bantu world, yet would dominate politically the non-Lwo families whom they would find, or who would join them in the North.

As the prestigious Mukama figure left Budoola and passed through the centre of Busoga, he attracted followers, clients, and wives to his entourage. The abaiseMususwa of the Hyena were—at the time of the Lwo settlements in Budoola—settled at Isegero Hill some sixteen miles to the west. There their leader was Nabala. The abaiseMususwa have a tradition that

Mukama, when he was at the hill at Namakoko [lying midway between Nang'oma and Isegero Hills], wanted to know a yokel who was in that part. He was told that there was a man living there and so he asked for him to be brought before him. He had always been there, that man, our ancestor. But Mukama wanted to see him. They then selected a page to go and fetch him. When the page reached there, our ancestor was skinning a young goat. At that time, we had started to learn the Lupakoyo language. They used to say that when it was spoken it resembled Lusiki or Lulamogi or Lugwere languages. We use to say . . . as the other one said, 'I am the one who is skinning the young goat.' [*Nze nsusa kabbuli kange*]. Therefore, Mukama was informed that, 'He is skinning his young goat.' [*Asusa kabbuli ke*]. Mukama then called him, '*Nsusa kabbuli kange*.' It developed into our clan name, and from this it became abaiseMususwa.[48]

Nabala, the leader of the abaiseMususwa, and several kinsmen joined Mukama in Bukooli and later, on the western side of Busoga, found themselves among the followers chosen to escort the sons of Mukama through Busoga.[49]

[47] These early Lwo of Bukooli are discussed in Chapter VII, above.

[48] CTBTH, Text 610. This is one of the few traditions among the 'Collected Texts' which reflects on the changing linguistic patterns within Busoga.

[49] There is some evidence that the Mukama figure took a wife from the abaise-Mususwa. e.g., Lubogo, p. 52, writes, 'At the beginnings of his wanderings, Mukama had a number of followers: among them were Kitandwe, Musoko, and Nabala (Mukama's wife).'

The abaiseMusobya also joined the entourage. They travelled with Mukama to Nhenda Hill and there established their clan shrine, a shrine that remains today, though the control of the hill passed to the abaiseIgaga, who became rulers of Busambira.[50] They accompanied Mukama to the west when the journey began again at Nhenda and eventually they joined the abaiseMususwa and other groups who were asked to guide young Prince Ibanda Ngobi back to Busoga.

The abaiseIgaga of Nhenda played a critical role as the journey of Mukama unfolded. Lubogo relates,

... it is stated that Mukama had with him two dogs, a wife and some followers. Nobody knew the reason for Mukama's travels. He first landed at Bufuta [Budoola] in Bukoli and then travelled to Bunyonga [Buwongo] via a hill known as Busoga. At Buyonga the inhabitants begged him to stay and rule them but Mukama refused and only asked them to follow him, in the hope that he might have a son whom he could give to them as a ruler. The Buyonga inhabitants accepted the offer and followed him; the members of Igaga clan at Nyenda claim to have come from these Buyonga inhabitants.[51]

It was during this segment of the journey that Mukama took as wife Naigaga, a daughter of the abaiseIgaga. Lubogo gives a picture of the abaiseIgaga head, Kisambira, travelling across country to meet Mukama who was in the country purportedly hunting elephants.

... a man called Kisambira from Nyenda Hill came seeking to befriend him. Mukama accepted the friendship. Kisambira was of the Iseigaga clan [abaiseIgaga] and was so convinced by the good intentions of his new friend that he gave Mukama his own daughter for a wife. Her name was Tegulwa (a 'gift'). Mukama accepted the gift and married the girl. While he continued his journey, his new wife was pregnant. ... Soon she found travelling very difficult but Mukama made her a walking-stick from a mubanda tree which grew in a forest at the foot of Kamigo Hills.[52]

Other groups linked themselves to the migrating Mukama. The abaiseNkwalu who had migrated north-eastwards from the shore of

[50] CTBTH, Text 595.
[51] Lubogo, pp. 52–3. Buwongo, at 33° 34·7′E, 0° 29·6′N, was within the domain of Kakaire the mwiseMenha ruler and his descendants of the Bugweri ruling line. If the quoted story of the Buwongo stop is true, it is possible that the Mukama group reached there from the east just before, or just as, the Kakaire group reached the Buwongo area—certainly not long after.
[52] Lubogo, p. 136. The hills of Kamigo are located in the area of 33° 16′E, 0° 38·2′N. It was at Kamigo, according to Lubogo, that Kisambira found Mukama. CTBTH, Text 610, gives Naigaga, and not Tegulwa, as the name of Mukama's bride.

Lake Victoria to Magada, a few miles south of Nhenda, found themselves drawn within Mukama's orbit:

When Mukama left Magada for Nhenda to look for a wife, we left with him and eventually came to Namunsaala ... after Mukama had reached Nhenda and married a mwiseIgaga girl, she said that she wanted to eat millet. So they looked for grinding stones and by then, that girl was pregnant. Mukama then took her away and they went to Kyebando; and she gave birth to a baby boy.[53]

The abaiseNkwanga of the Elephant who came from the east, came with Mukama. 'The first time that Mukama came here, he came with Nkwanga. He went with Nkwanga on his travels around the country until they reached a hill called Kigulu ... Mukama, before he went back, told Nkwanga, "Please take this woman to a hill called Kigulu and let her settle there."'[54] Later, these abaiseNkwanga would act as the guardians of the children of Mukama and would seat the rulers of Buzimba (Kigulu) and Luuka, both abaiseNgobi, on their thrones.

The abaiseNangwe, the abaiseKibande, the abaiseMukooyo, and the abaiseMuganza were prominent among the families joining Mukama. One tradition records that Mukama was accompanied by his mother Namboira and her brother Mboira,[55] and these were apparently abaiseKitandwe. Other traditions record that Mukama travelled with a number of wives. Chief among them were Naigaga, the mwiseIgaga girl, and Nakasanga, a mwiseIsanga girl who apparently joined Mukama in the Buwongo area.[56]

The evidence suggests that—in the course of this journey across Busoga—Mukama had three sons whom he left in the country as princes: Ibanda Ngobi, Muzaaya Ngobi Mau, and Kitimbo. Muzaaya and Kitimbo were evidently full brothers, the sons of Nakasanga, the mwiseIsanga wife of Mukama. Ibanda Ngobi, the most

[53] CTBTH, Text 759. Namunsaala is located eight miles north of Nhenda. The abaiseNkwalu dispersed through Busoga with the abaiseNgobi royal families of the Mukama stream. The location of Kyebando is not clear.

[54] CTBTH, Text 766. Kigulu Hill, shrine of the abaiseNgobi of Buzimba (Kigulu), is located four and one half miles north of Nhenda Hill. Ngobi Ibanda, son of Mukama, apparently moved from Nhenda Hill, the home of his mothers, to Kigulu when he came of age.

[55] CTBTH, Texts 603, 716.

[56] CTBTH, Text 733. The abaiseMukuve had moved into the Buwongo area from the south. They appear to have absorbed an Isanga group from among the groups flowing into the centre of Busoga from the north with Kakaire. See Chapter VIII, above p. 164.

prominent son, was the child of Naigaga, the mwiseIgaga girl from Nhenda Hill.

... along the way there is a stream which I don't know for sure nor do I know whether or not it separates Butamba and Bugabula. There was a stream there which had bamboo shoots in it and it was there where she slipped. As she slipped, she uttered, 'Wi ibanda', and she caught a bamboo shoot and when she pulled herself to shore she gave birth to a child. That child was named Ibanda [Bamboo], and they walked on. ... Now the boy whom she gave birth to at the stream in which there were bamboo shoots remained in Kigulu until his descendants covered the whole of Busoga ...[57]

Lubogo records a similar tradition:

... Mukama travelled along the shores of the River Nile, via Buzaya to Kakindu, from where he crossed the Nile into Bunyoro (Bugerere) which is now part of Buganda. In the course of his journey, Mukama came to a small river which separates Buganda from Bunyoro. Here his wife gave birth to a son whom he named Ngobi.[58]

Similar traditions are numerous. One identifies the bamboo-filled stream as the Lumbuye.[59] Another[60] identifies the river as the Ngobi and locates the river in the area to the west of the Nile as Lubogo did in the passage quoted above. What is significant is that the infant Ibanda Ngobi was taken back to Nhenda Hill by several of Mukama's followers and was raised by the family of the child's mother, Naigaga. The returning party included the Prince; the mother, Naigaga; Mboira (Mukama's uncle); Nankuni, a mwiseNangwe; Ompiti, a mwiseMusobya; Nabala, a mwiseMususwa; and Nkwanga, a mwise-Nkwanga. One tradition records that Mukama instructed them,

'Take the woman to that hill where we were and from where we viewed Bugwere and Masaaba.' He told this to some of his men, 'Take this woman to that hill where we were and where we saw Budama where we came from, the route we took.' There were many lions there so these people built a hut for the prince. They cut many trees and surrounded the huts as a protection against lions. These were abaiseIgaga.[61]

As the infant, Ibanda Ngobi, was taken back to Nhenda Hill to be raised by the family of his mother, Mukama is said to have moved off to the west. But many of his followers, particularly those who had joined Mukama in the area of Nhenda Hill, left Mukama and retraced their footsteps eastward, accompanying Ibanda Ngobi to the area of Nhenda Hill. There at Nhenda they became as intimately

[57] CTBTH, Text 610.   [58] Lubogo, p. 53.   [59] CTBTH, Text 595.
[60] CTBTH, Text 603.   [61] CTBTH, Text 595.

attached to the young prince as they had been attached to Mukama. The abaiseIgaga apparently took the major hand in raising the young prince. Nhenda Hill became theirs; and when Ibanda Ngobi was a young man, he was established in a new enclosure at Kigulu Hill a few miles to the north. The most loyal followers of his father moved with him out of the domain of the mwiseIgaga ruler of Busambira. There at Kigulu Hill, a new centre of power and prestige would emerge among the prince, his clients, and his faithful guardians.

When Ibanda Ngobi was older, he travelled around the centre of Busoga. He raised two sons. One, Nhiro, was raised at Kiroba Hill and founded the ruling line of Luuka. The other, Lugwiri, was born at Kigulu Hill and founded the ruling house of Buzimba (Kigulu). As the prestige and authority of Mukama had passed to Ibanda Ngobi, so it passed to Nhiro and Lugwiri. Each of these young princes attracted followers—or children of the followers—of Mukama and of Mukama's son Ibanda. Two dynasties based on the gift and paternity of Mukama were emerging in the centre of Busoga.

In several of the traditions which record Mukama's journey through Busoga, the birthplace of Prince Ibanda Ngobi is located on the western side of the Nile River. Approaching the Nile from the east, Mukama's party reached the area of Luzinga lying north-east of the Mabira, the great forest which reached right across the Nile and stretched north and south from Nankandulo[62] to Budhagali.[63] Passing westwards from Luzinga, they arrived in the area of Nankandulo and Lwanyama on the Nile's eastern bank. It was here, apparently, that Mukama crossed the Nile and headed west. And it was between Luzinga and Nankandulo that Mukama left his eldest son Muzaaya to brave the wilderness. Lubogo writes,

His birth is rather obscure, people are not sure of his birthplace. What is certain is that he was Mukama's son, and that Mukama gave him a large piece of land near the Nile. His proper name was Ngobi Mau but he was later nicknamed Muzaya, because he stayed in a lonely land infested with mbwa flies. ... Most of the people in this area were Baganda who had crossed the Nile to come and settle in this part of the country. They were the people who nicknamed Ngobi Mau ('skins') because Ngobi used to wear skins.[64]

[62] At 33° 04′E, 0° 41·5′N. Map XI traces the movements of Mukama.
[63] 33° 09·5′E, 0° 29·5′N.
[64] Lubogo, p. 7.

Muzaaya was the son of Nakasanga, the mwiseIsanga girl who joined Mukama in the area of Buwongo Hill east of Nhenda.[65] Though left in a harsh land, Muzaaya was not left alone. He had with him a small coterie of his father's most dedicated followers, including abaiseIsanga, his mother's people; abaiseMususwa; abaiseKitandwe; abaiseMwase, who gave a wife to Muzaaya; and abaise-Muhaya, who also gave a wife to Muzaaya; and abaiseMukooyo.

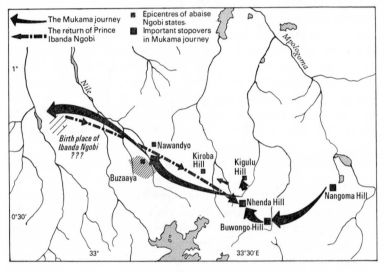

MAP XI. Mukama in Busoga

These families had joined Mukama's entourage east of Nhenda Hill, and many of them may have already been associated with Muzaaya's mother's people, the abaiseIsanga, in the area of Buwongo. It is possible that these families were drawn into the orbit of Mukama at that moment when Mukama reached Buwongo and married Naka-sanga.

Muzaaya's party found Buzaaya a small and difficult land. Bounded on the northern and eastern flanks by the Kiko River, on the southern flank by the heavy forest, and on the western side by the Nile, the environment was less than ideal for the pastoralist with expansive notions. In settling in this forlorn place, Muzaaya did find

[65] CTBTH, Text 737.

such groups as the abaiseMulondo—apparently recent migrants from the western side[66] of the Nile—and the abaiseLwendhu, fishermen on the Nile. The traditions of Buzaaya suggest that few settlers were attracted to the country and that eventual expansion into the forested areas was undertaken at the expense of the noble pastoral culture which Muzaaya's father Mukama and his antecedents had introduced to the centre of Busoga. Yet this was Muzaaya's country, and there among his loyal followers Muzaaya's authority seemed firm. He had the gift of Mukama through paternity. He had his devoted followers who had come to acknowledge his authority, and whose very presence enhanced the prestige of this son of Mukama.

Yet even in this difficult country, he came to face a more dangerous challenge: one from his younger brother Kitimbo, also a son of Mukama and Nakasanga. It came first as a challenge to his authority in his very enclosure and later as a challenge to his ambitions to expand eastwards across the Kiko River.

Tradition records that Kitimbo was raised by Mukama after Mukama left Muzaaya in Buzaaya and crossed the Nile heading west. There is no evidence that Mukama's wanderings ever stopped. The popular tradition of Busoga records that Mukama crossed to Bunyoro and there founded the Bito ruling line. Set against the chronologies of the Nyoro ruling houses and against the Nyoro and Lwo traditions, this proposition seems very unlikely. It is possible that Mukama just wandered in the country between the Nile in the east and the Kagera River in the west, there finding lands more suitable and more open to his pastoral interests.

Popular Soga tradition also records that relations between the Soga princes and Mukama, the father, did not lapse when Mukama crossed the Nile. Lubogo records, 'Mukama then continued his journey to Bunyoro, where he lived until his death. He often sent presents to his children, such as stools, spears and shields which were

[66] The abaiseMulondo are of the Monkey totem. All the abaiseMulondo in Busoga trace their origins to the eastern Buganda area. The Monkey clan is recorded in Ganda tradition as having escorted Prince Kimera into the centre of Buganda. Kimera was not the only prince escorted into the region from the west. Bushbuck figures such as Kiiza, Namuyondho, and Kiki were apparently escorted into the area of eastern Buganda by Monkey groups. They seem to have carried certain Ganda-Nyoro traditions of kingship into Busoga, and by the nineteenth century were seating various rulers on Soga thrones. These thrones came to be called by the name *Mulondo* or *Namulondo*. Bugerere was formerly called Bulondoganyi, indicating the importance of Balondo settlements there.

needed for customary ceremonies.'[67] There are several references in Soga tradition to continuing connections with Mukama. These references tend to be vague rather than specific—we hear of no specific journeys to the Bunyoro court until the late nineteenth century. It is unclear whether these connections were with the departed Mukama and his descendants, whose identity and whose location in the *west* are unidentified; or whether these connections were with the ruling house of Bunyoro either directly with the court kings or through the delegated officers in Buruli and Bugerere; or whether these connections were merely diffuse associations preserved through Lwo groups crossing the Nile from the west into Buzaaya and Bugabula, the two Ngobi states bordering on the Nile.

There is a prominent Soga tradition that records a visit by the first Muzaaya to his father's place in the west on the occasion of his father's death, 'When Mukama died, his sons went to Bunyolo to bury him.'[68] There at Mukama's camp Muzaaya, the eldest, found his younger brother Kitimbo—a full brother, son of Nakasanga and Mukama. The responsibility of finishing Kitimbo's upbringing fell on Muzaaya's shoulders. The tradition continues, 'After the burial ceremony, Muzaaya took up his young brother Kitimbo and brought him to Buzaaya to rear him. Kitimbo was brought up in his elder brother's palace.'[69] Muzaaya was, by this time, already a man. He had at least two wives, one a mwiseMwase, the other a mwiseMuhaya Considering that Mukama had reached Buwongo before he married Nakasanga—Muzaaya's mother—and that Muzaaya was a man when his father Mukama died, it is likely that the heroic journey of Mukama from Budoola to the far side of the Nile had consumed the whole of Mukama's adult life.

Trouble developed in Muzaaya's palace.

When Kitimbo became an adult, he got his brother's wife pregnant. When his elder brother asked his wife who had got her pregnant, she answered, 'It was your young brother from the palace.' Muzaaya said, 'Had I known, I would never have brought you here from your father's grave. Go with your woman. I do not love her any more.'[70]

Kitimbo, some devoted servants including Mugogolo, a mwise-Mukooyo, and Mwase, a mwiseMwase, as well as the young girl—also a mwiseMwase—packed up and left Muzaaya's palace. Some

---

[67] p. 53.   [68] CTBTH, Text 697.
[69] ibid. Text 719 records, 'Kitimbo [Mukama's] last son, was left to Muzaaya'.
[70] CTBTH, Text 697.

traditions record that Kitimbo was sent to his father's people in Bunyoro to collect a fine.[71] In any event, Kitimbo seemed to have attempted to reach his late father's camp.

Now as they were about to cross over to Bunyoro, they lost their way. They followed elephant tracks which led them to Mbulamuti from Buzaaya. They rested here. Their food was mice which were caught by the dogs so that they had meat. From Mbulamuti, they travelled and travelled along the shores of the lake [Lake Kyoga] . . . until they reached Kasato. When they reached Kasato, they viewed the lake and saw it from end to end. Somebody remarked, 'You said that from home to Mukama's burial place is one day's journey but ever since we started our journey, two complete months have passed and we have not sighted a harbour through which we can cross. Now what do you think?' He replied, 'How can I think anything? We are lost.'
'What was it that your father used to say?' 'He told me that he came from the East. You can also see that this lake is from the East. Let us give up our intention of going to the graves. Let us follow the lake east and find the way father came.'
That is why they left Kasato Hill and travelled to reach Itamya . . . and built huts there. They stayed there a bit longer resting their legs. From here, they travelled along the lake shore until they reached Ikanda. And they built there a house. They stayed there longer, resting their legs. From here, they descended until they reached Kagulu. By the time they reached Kagulu, they were exhausted, and the woman was about to deliver. She went behind the house and delivered a son. This child was born at Kiherere. That is why the child was called Maherere. They stayed there waiting for the woman to gain strength and for the baby to grow some. They were there about three months. Then Kitimbo prepared for the journey and asked his friends to prepare also. 'Our companion, for whom we have been waiting, has now gained some strength. So let us go on.' Mugogolo then said, 'Our friend, you have made us travel in the jungle for months and months. We started walking when this woman was pregnant only two months and now she has delivered. Why do you lead us to lands that you do not know? You cannot show us the way to the graves, and you cannot find the way back to Bunyoro. If you came from Bunyoro and you cannot find the way back, how can you guide us through these lands where you were not born? We are not going to go there now. What we tell you to do is this: Allow us to go to your elder brother so that you may apologise. If he wants to kill us it is better to die among people than to die alone in the bush.'[72]

[71] CTBTH, Text 615 records, 'Kitimbo was left to Muzaaya but Kitimbo made a mistake. He committed an offence against Muzaaya's wife. He was asked to pay a fine. He was told to go to Unhi to collect the amount to pay the fine. The offence was against a woman. He got a woman pregnant.'
[72] CTBTH, Text 697. Map XII traces these movements of Kitimbo.

o

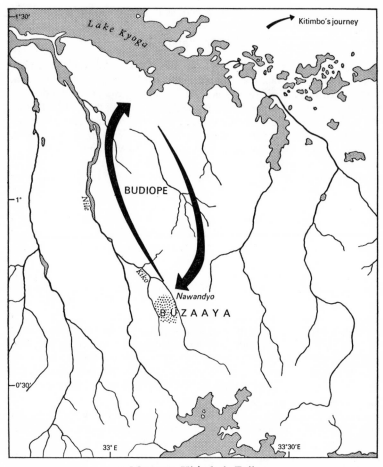

MAP XII. Kitimbo's Exile

Kitimbo apparently agreed. They turned south and within two days they reached the vicinity of Muzaaya's palace. At Nawango,[73] they could hear Muzaaya's drum. Kitimbo was frightened and halted the march. Eventually he managed the courage to send Mugogolo and Mwase to visit Muzaaya. When they reached Muzaaya's, they told Muzaaya's councillors, 'Our friend has sent us to you to beg mercy. He will never do such a thing. "You are my father, mother, and my grandfather. I do not understand anything. Please forgive me".... He

[73] Nawango is located at 33° 12′E, 0° 54′N.

has asked us to carry to our chief this humble request.'[74] When he received the message, Muzaaya was restive but not vindictive.

... he asked the *Katikkiro* to get prisoners to carry food and an axe to go and build him [Kitimbo] a house in the bush where he was.
'I do not want to see him now. I will respond when I am ready with an idea, but I am still very angry.' He again ordered for more prisoners to get food and knives and to go to Naminage to build a house for Kitimbo. . . . After about two weeks, Muzaaya ordered his *Katikkiro*, 'Get food and send it to that fool.'[75]

Muzaaya gave more help to Kitimbo in the following years. When Muzaaya died, Kitimbo went to his funeral.

People said, 'We want Kitimbo to succeed his brother.' Some other people said, 'He cannot succeed because the deceased has not been on friendly terms with him. Now, how can he succeed him in office? Get another heir.' They elected the son of Muzaaya. Then Kitimbo said, 'I do not want to become the heir. I will stay in my land where I have long suffered. I will get settlers.'[76]

So Kitimbo left and returned to his palace at Nawango. Soon he moved and established a new centre at Nawandyo near the Kiko River. He placed settlers there which was along the border of Buzaaya near the Kiko River, apparently to halt the eastwards expansion of the Buzaaya state.

It was there at Nawandyo less than a mile from the Kiko Valley and just across from the palace of Muzaaya of Buzaaya that Kitimbo established his authority over an independent domain. Kitimbo's occupation of Nawandyo created contention with Muzaaya. Muzaaya is reported to have told him, 'No, my friend, this part of the country was given to me.'[77] Kitimbo eventually moved northwards several miles to Naminage. But he left some of his most loyal supporters there, thereby effectively establishing his control over the Nawandyo area and at the same time his authority over the families who travelled with him through the bush and the families who came over to him from Muzaaya's. These devoted supporters included abaiseIsanga, abaiseMwase, abaiseKitandwe, and the abaise-Mukooyo, all but the last followers of his father Mukama, and all followers of his elder brother Muzaaya. Again, it appears, the authority and prestige of the prince had devolved from the father. The

[74] CTBTH, Text 697.
[75] CTBTH, Text 697.
[76] CTBTH, Text 697.
[77] CTBTH, Text 716.

lasting ties between Mukama and his men had been made long before the princes were even born. While Muzaaya was weakened, Kitimbo's authority was firmly planted. When he travelled north to settle new areas, the future of the Bugabula[78] state was set. The descendants of Kitimbo would rule the largest state in Busoga.[79]

The spiritual presence of Mukama is felt among all the royal groups of northern Busoga, including the abaiseNgobi, the abaise-Wakooli, the abaiseMenha, and to some extent the abaiseIgaga of Busiki. The popular traditions relating to these groups also record an earthly presence in terms of both migration and paternity. However, this earthly presence is evidently associated with only one of the several streams of Lwo penetration into northern Busoga; that is, the journey of Mukama—descendant of Kigenhi, the mwiseMudoola—across Busoga. His prestige and his authority among his followers were transmitted to his three sons—Ibanda Ngobi, Muzaaya Ngobi Mau, and Kitimbo, each of whom would emerge as a state founder in the early eighteenth century—and through them to their descendants and their descendant lineages across some, but not all, of northern Busoga. The journey of Mukama and his followers through the centre of Busoga is one key element in the emerging tradition of Mukama. The other key is the devolution of the gift of Mukama through the male line. These two elements are at the core of the Mukama tradition, and the lineages of Ibanda Ngobi, Muzaaya, and Kitimbo constitute this core of the abaiseNgobi family. From this central thread the idea of a Mukama journey and the idea of a Mukama paternity flowed to unrelated or distantly related Lwo families in the North. These groups, as Lwo, were certainly part of the ethos surrounding Mukama—the 'milker', the Lwo—and had been part of that ethos, but they were outside the historical context of Mukama. This historical context— the passage of groups from east to west through the centre of Busoga —is the source of the Mukama tradition, the tradition which, in its popular versions, gives legitimacy and unity to the northern royal houses and, with the parallel Kintu tradition, constitutes the culmination of the historical experience for which the Kintu and Mukama events are the points of departure.

[78] Initially called Butimbito, later Budiope, and then still later Bugabula.

[79] Kitimbo, according to Lubogo, p. 16, placed a son, Kibalya Kaigwa—sometimes called Kiti—at Nakabale a few miles north-east of Nawandyo *mbuga*. Within two generations the descendants of Kibalya had established themselves as an independent dynasty over Bulole. Their domain was small, squeezed by the expanding Luuka and Bugabula states.

APPENDIX A

The Questionnaire

[Lusoga]

ssaza.....................erina.....................ekika ....
ggombolola.....................mutala.....................omuziro.................
nkuni.................ibaale, muti, oba lusozi?.....................kiri ha? ....
1. omubala ....
2. amakulu gagwo ....
3. ekika kyava ha?.....................kyabita kitya (oba lyato lyogere)
....
nani eyakireeta?.....................Bika ki byekyaidha nabyo? ....
....
Mwatuukira ha mu Busoga?.....................Mukutuuka mwayagana bani?
....
4. Obutaka bwaimwe mu Busoga buli ha?..................... Nani
eyabubaha?.....................Mwakolanga mulimu ki eri mukama
waimwe?...
5. Obanga buno tinobutaka mwaidhaho muyta?.....................Nani
eyakireetaho?.....................Hano mwatuuka ku mwami ki?.................
.....................Mulimu ki gwe mwakoleranga omwami ono?.................
....
6. Eyatandika ekika nga ni.....................latawe nga ni.....................
Inhina nga mwise.....................Mukaziwe nga mwise.....................
Mutabane we omukulu nga nani...
.....................Mutabane eyasika omutandisi we kika ni.................
.... Yasikirwa mutabane we................. Yasikirwa mutabane
we............... Yasikirwa mutabane we................. Yasikirwa mutabane
we............... Yasikirwa mutabane we................. Yasikirwa mutabane
we............... Yasikirwa mutabane we................. Yasikirwa mutabane
we............... Yasikirwa mutabane we................. Yasikirwa mutabane
we............... Yasikirwa mutabane we................. Yasikirwa mutabane
we............... Yasikirwa mutabane we...
7. Latawe ni.................Amuzaala ni...
Azaala oyo ni.................Azaala oyo ni.....................Azaala
oyo ni.....................Azaala oyo ni.....................Azaala oyo
ni .... Azaala oyo ni.....................Azaala oyo
ni .... Azaala oyo ni.....................Azaala oyo
ni .... Azaala oyo ni.....................Azaala oyo
ni .... Azaala oyo ni.....................Azaala oyo
ni .... Azaala oyo ni ....

8. *Amagombe mulinza*..............................*Omukulu wekika mwisaza lino
ni...........................*atyama*...
Omukunganya wa Busoga ni..*atyama*......
....

9. *Okubuuza: ku bitabo kyebika ne bye byafaayo bya Busoga*

(*interviewer*)
(*date*)

[English]

county.......................name........................clan ....
sub-county............................village......................totem ....
nkuni .... stone, tree, or hill? .... where is it located?
....

1. *drumbeat slogan*...
2. *the meaning of the drumbeat slogan*..
3. *Where did your clan come from?*...................................*How did it
   travel? (if canoe, the name of the canoe)* ....
   ....
   Who led the clan in its travels?...
   What clans accompanied you? ....
   ....
   Where did you arrive in Busoga?....................................*Whom did
   you meet upon your arrival?*..
4. *Where is your butaka in Busoga?*...............................*Who gave this
   estate to you?*..............................*What service did you provide for
   your ruler?* ....
5. *If this place here is not your estate, how did you reach here?*.................
   Who led you to this place?...
   When you arrived here, who was ruling?..
   What service did you provide for this ruler?....................................
   ....
6. *Who was the founder of your clan?*...................*His father was*...........
   His mother was a mwise...............*His wife was a mwise*...................
   His eldest son was..
   The son who succeeded the founder of the clan was............................
   He was succeeded by his son........................*He was succeeded by
   his son*...........He was succeeded by his son............He was succeeded by
   his son*...........He was succeeded by his son............He was succeeded by
   his son*...........He was succeeded by his son............He was succeeded by
   his son*...........He was succeeded by his son............He was succeeded by
   his son*...........He was succeeded by his son............He was succeeded by
   his son*...........He was succeeded by his son............He was succeeded by
   his son*...........He was succeeded by his son...............
7. *Your father is*...........................*His father was*.......................
   The father of that one was......The father of that one was......The father
   of that one was.........The father of that one was.........The father of that
   one was............ The father of that one was............ The father of that*

one was............ The father of that one was............ The father of that
one was............ The father of that one was............ The father of that
one was............ The father of that one was............ The father of that
one was............ The father of that one was ....

8. *The family graves align towards.......................The present head of the clan in this county is.......................living at.............................. The head of the clan in all of Busoga is.......................living at............ ....*

9. *General query on clan books and books and manuscripts recording Busoga's past...*

(interviewer)
(date)

APPENDIX B

The Royal Genealogies of Bugweri and Buzimba

I. The Royal Genealogy of the abaiseMenha of Bugweri
Generations

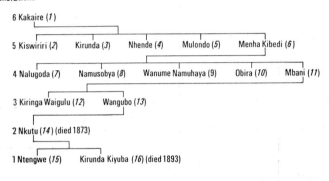

II. The Royal Genealogy of the abaiseNgobi of Buzimba
Generations

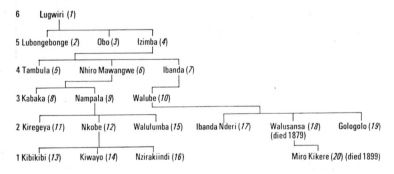

Notes: Numbers in italics are succession numbers. Lines denote kinship ties: the senior figures of each generation are on the left and the figures become more junior moving to the right.

APPENDIX C

Gen. / Date	Bunha	Bukwanga Kiki	Buima	Buzimba	Buzaaya	Bugabula	Luu...
Gen.7	Lume I	Kiki			Ngobi Mau 392 | 398 / 372		Iband Ngob
1737±32				Ibanda Ngobi		375 →	
						Kitimbo	
Gen.6					Lufuka		
1764±30	Kisoma II	Wakwiri		Lugwiri		Mawerere	Nhir...
					Kabega		
Gen.5	Mutyabule II 97		→ Kaima	Lubongebonge			
1791±28	Nandigobe	Kisuha		Obo 98 ←			Inhens...
		Maiso m			Galya		
Gen.4	Mukedi	Kansani		Izimba			
	Munulo	Kagya 507 ←		Tambula		Nadiope m 46 ←	
1818±26	Kituma	506	Kibugo Igodi	Nhiro Mawangwe / Ibanda / Kabaka		341 →	Wamb...
		Mukalula ← 342	Mpango	Nampala			
Gen.3				Walube			
				Kiregeya	Kyangwa		
			Nampala			Kagoda ←	
1845±24		Ngirebisa Kaguya / Kairu	Luhalira			517	
	Lwai II m 516 ←	Kabolu	Kabolu	Nkobe 409 / 511			Kakuk...
Gen.2	Lume II	Unhi II	Kabambwe	Kibikibi 439	Kiwayo / Walulumba / Nzirakiindi / Ibanda Nderi	Kitamirike I 51 / 52	Kalogo m
			Magaya				
	Mpagi II		Nkwewembye / Nhago				Kibaly
1872±22		Muwongwa Musuubo	Tukube 525 ←		Gwanotyo 404 ← → Kadhumbula I		
			Kabugute				
			Waiswa	Walusansa m 268	Nkofukaire		Mudungu
Gen.1			Mwiru	432	Otini 408 → Mutiibwa		454
	Nhago 532 ←		Kisolo	Gologolo 416			
		Bazanya Mukoova	Kyebambe 197 ← / 67	1892r 533		1894 d	Nabwar
1899				Miro 1899 d	Kaluba-Mulije		
	Bunha	Bukwanga Kiki	Buima	Buzimba	Buzaaya	Bugabula	Luu...

Numbers refer to tie-ins
Arrows indicate tie-ins

- - - - - Estimated reign-ends and reign-beginnings
Gen. numbers = Buganda generation estimates

The Chronology Chart

Buganda	Bunyoro	Bukooli	Bugweri / Bufutulu	Busiki	Bukono	Bulamogi	Gen / Date
…kulwe / —r	Kyebambe II	Mwondha	235 / 238 / Kakaire	Kairu	Najomi		Gen.7
		Nandhubu	Kiswiriri	Kahanguzi			1737 ± 32
…wanda / …anga 1 m (m) / …mugala	Olimi III	Mutumba	Kirunda		Nkenga	Ngambani	Gen.6
			Nhende	Isiko			1764 ± 30
…abaggu / m		Nkutu / Nkaye / 'Nanganni	Mulondo	Mumesula	Kisozi	Namubongo	Gen.5
							1791 ± 28
Junju (547→) / m / …emakokiro / 554 / 537	547 ←Duhaga I d / Olimi IV (m 442)	Serwanga / Migero / Mulindwa / Wambuzi / 442	Menha Kibedi / Nalugoda				Gen.4
		442 Kisangiri r	Wanume	503 Muinda / 442	18 ←Ntumba	17 Isoba	1818 ± 26
…manya / 6 / Mulago	538 →Kyebambe III	Mukoova (l) / Kigoigo / Kiyemba	Obira / Mbani / Kiringa Waigulu		Mutyaba	Bwoye / Mukunya I	Gen.3
76 / Suna C (90)		Kibubuka (76)	248 Wangubo m	Nabongo	5 / 400 ←Kabusera		1845 ± 24
…abulagala / 356 Suna d / Nakatema / C Bbanda / C Nnakawa	Olimi V (m 514) / Kamurasi / 550 ←Nyabongo II	550 Nyabongo II		K Mulyampiti / Kalange / Musene / Nabongo II / Jaluswa	7 ←Muzetya / Pande Kembo / Mugalya 1863 d	Wako I	Gen.2
esa 1 / 1870 d			248 Nkutu m / 276 Ntengwe m				1872 ± 22
C Nabulagala / Kabodha / 75 C Lubaga / C Kikandwa / C Nabulagala / C Mutesa 1 d / Mwanga 11	Lubaga / Kabarega	Kaunhe	Kirunda Kiyuba	94 →Dhatemwa / 950 Nalwatu / Kairu Nkonte	Kyebambe Kitamwa	Kisira	Gen.1
Kalema / Mwanga 11 / Mwanga 11 r / Chwa 11	1899 r	Mutanda / 1891 m / 1899 r	1893 / Kakaire Naigambi 1896 / 1897 Munulo r / Nkolo	Kirya Mpahulo / Nkulabwire / Kirya Mankati	1897 r	1898 d / 1899	1899

C = Capital site   d = died
m = murdered   r = removed from office

Bibliographical Note

THE Interlacustrine region is relatively rich in published material. The largest portion of this material is not historical but none the less provides an essential background to historical thinking and historical research. Within the region, Busoga is relatively rich in such published material.

The most prominent work on Busoga is Lloyd Faller's study, *Bantu Bureaucracy*,[1] which, while primarily concerned with conflict and change in Busoga's traditional political institutions under modern conditions, presents a good account of Soga social structure. In the early 1950s, Fallers researched intensively in two small areas of Busoga. While suggesting a number of useful historical hypotheses, he provides little solid data for reconstructing the pre–colonial history of Busoga. However, his discussion of Soga kinship and political structures is, as with any good descriptive or analytical ethnography, of significant value to the 'ethno-historian'.

Busoga is also included in the *Ethnographic Survey of Africa*. The writings of John Roscoe, as well as articles by Bruton, Condon, and Gray, are also valuable sources on the social and political backgrounds of Busoga.

There are two published works which discuss Busoga history. D. W. Robertson, in his *Historical Considerations Contributing to the Soga System of Land Tenure*, puts forward a sketchy outline of Busoga history. Robertson depends upon what must have been a limited quantity of primary data and from this has drawn a number of very tenuous hypotheses and rather unsupported conclusions. He traces the shifting patterns of land control and tenure from localized clan communities early established in the southern part of Busoga, through to the establishment of political despotism in relation to land control, and the predicament of modern chiefly authority. He provides little useful data on the early history of Busoga. Robertson was pessimistic about the possibilities of putting together a clearer picture of the early history of Busoga. He asserts that the clans were all but defunct when he conducted his research; and he estimated that there were some fifty clans in Busoga, a figure which far underestimates the actual figure of over 200. This itself suggests that Robertson's research was skimpy and that his pessimistic assessment of Soga sources was premature. Robertson was a District Officer of the Protectorate and this limited the possibility of researching commoner as well as royal traditions.

The most important published source of evidence on the history of Busoga is Y. K. Lubogo's *A History of Busoga*. Though first published in 1960, Lubogo worked on the volume from time to time between 1920 and 1938. When he began the work, Lubogo, born in Bulamogi County,

---

[1] For details on the sources cited here, see Select Bibliography below.

was a young government chief and veteran of the First World War. Lubogo retired from government service in 1938 after serving a number of years as Treasurer of the Busoga Local Government. He was more recently Mayor of Jinja.

His research was conducted in two rather distinct ways. He first took a personal interest in the history of Busoga, perhaps stimulated by his extensive travels as a young man. This initial approach involved occasional journeys about the country listening to a few old men at a time, taking notes on their testimony. Later, he was appointed by the Busoga District Council to complete an authoritative study of Busoga history. This commission seems to have seriously restricted the freedom of his work. Large meetings were held at which stories were told, discussed, and then voted on. Lubogo accepted the stories which were approved by the full meeting. He has described some of the meetings as consisting of 500 people. He was also limited to taking stories from chiefs and was unable to take into consideration old family and political disputes which are rife in Busoga. His research dealt primarily with royal, or ruling, clans. Upon completion, his manuscript was read before the Busoga District Council, and it was met with considerable criticism. Today, what is remembered of the controversy arising from the Luganda manuscript is the question of whether or not the original commission had specified that Council members were to receive free copies of the book. Though now published, Lubogo's volume, which appears only in English translation, has been read by virtually no one in Busoga.

Lubogo's book consists of seventy-three chapters. Forty-three of these are concerned with traditional political units in Busoga, one discusses the problem of the traditional folk heroes Mukama and Kintu, and the last twenty-nine chapters discuss the traditional culture of Busoga. Of the first forty-three chapters, Lubogo devotes each chapter to one political unit. Some chapters are quite extensive in detail concerning the migrations and settlements of particular ruling families in Busoga and the histories of those families up to the 1930s. Others are repetitive, and quite a number are merely lists of rulers. There are no maps in the book to identify the locations of several hundred place names mentioned by the author.

Lubogo seemingly presents the data as it was given him. He rarely intrudes into the narratives. He does not attempt to substantiate or reject certain details by considering the data of one chapter in the light of another He does not test genealogies by examining correlations between dynasties nor does he point out apparent contradictions and erroneous statements appearing in the narratives.

Lubogo ignored a number of traditional states and only briefly mentions a few others. He does not discuss the histories of the commoner clans of Busoga though he does mention them occasionally. He lists some of them at the end of the volume.

Lubogo had no final control over the translation of his manuscript from Luganda to English. A careful comparison of the original manuscript and

P

the translation reveals a number of errors and omissions in the translation. One chapter is omitted completely, and one chapter appears twice in the published translation.[2]

These then are the significant published sources on Busoga. In the course of the field research, a number of unpublished writings on aspects of Soga history were found. A 'History of Busoga' was found in notebook form. The author of this work, Daudi Waiswa, hereditary chief of a former state, apparently relied on the testimony of three men who had travelled through Busoga from state to state in the late nineteenth century, serving various rulers as retainers. Several written clan narratives were also found, and a number of clan books containing clan genealogies and records relating to clan organization in this century were viewed. Wherever possible, these were photographed or copied and included in 'Collected Texts, Busoga Traditional History'. The 'Collected Texts' which the present writer recorded during field work in Busoga in 1966 and early 1967 constitute the major source on the pre–colonial history of Busoga.[3] While the 'Collected Texts' include a number of written materials found in Busoga, the largest proportion of textual material was of an oral nature and was recorded on tape or on questionnaires.

The discussion of sources on Busoga cannot be confined to those relating directly to Busoga alone. Extensive material is available on the traditional history of other parts of the region, and these are crucial sources in the reconstruction of the early history of Busoga. The works of Sir Apolo Kaggwa on the Baganda are of major significance. Also significant are the unpublished Ggomotoka papers on the history of the Buvuma Islands of Lake Victoria, the works of Crazzolara on Lwo clans and history, and the recent work of B. A. Ogot on the Padhola of eastern Uganda and the Luo of Kenya.

[2] The present writer has been able to obtain a copy of Lubogo's Luganda manuscript and certain details found therein which depart from the English translation are occasionally noted in the present work.

[3] Eventually, the full collection will be reproduced in annotated English translation.

Select Bibliography

BATULABUDE, S. K. 'Ekitabo Kye Kika Kye Mamba'. 1917. Makerere University College Library, Africana Collection.

BAPERE, J. M. J. 'Kintu n'abantu be yali nabo e Bukedi ku lusozi Masaba'. *Munno*, April 1929.

BEATTIE, J. M. 'Bunyoro, an African Feudality', *Journal of African History*, v, i (1964), 25–36.

BIKUNYA, PETERO. *Ky'Abakama ba Bunyoro*. London, 1927.

BRUTON, C. L. 'Some Notes on the Basoga', *Uganda Journal*, ii, 4 (1935), 291–6.

BULIGGWANGA, E. *Ekitabo kye Kika kye Mamba*. Kamapala, 1916.

CARPENTER, G. D. Hale. *A Naturalist in Lake Victoria*. London, 1920.

CERULLI, ERNESTA. 'Peoples of Southwest Ethiopia and its Borderland', *Ethnographic Survey of Africa, North-East Africa*, Part III, ed. Daryll Forde. London, 1956.

COHEN, DAVID WILLIAM. 'Collected Texts, Busoga Traditional History'.
—— 'Selected Texts, Busoga Traditional History,' i, ii, and iii. (Deposited in the Library of Indiana University, the Library of the School of Oriental and African Studies, London University, and the Makerere University Library, Kampala. Microfilms of these volumes are available from the CAMP project, Center for Research Libraries, 5721 Cottage Grove Avenue, Chicago, Illinois 60637, U.S.A.)
—— 'The Cwezi Cult', *Journal of African History*, ix, 4 (1968), 651–7.
—— 'The River-Lake Nilotes from the Fifteenth to the Nineteenth Century', *Zamani: A Survey of East African History*, ed. B. A. Ogot and J. A. Kieran. Nairobi, 1968.
—— 'A Survey of Interlacustrine Chronology', *Journal of African History*, xi, 2 (1970), 177–201.

CONDON, M. A. 'Contribution to the Ethnography of the Basoga-Batamba', *Anthropos*, v (1910), 366–84; vi (1911), 934–56.

CORY, H. *History of Bukoba District*. Dar es Salaam, 1958.
—— *The Ntemi: Traditional Rites of a Sukuma Chief in Tanganyika*. London, 1951.

COX, A. H. 'The Growth and Expansion of Buganda', *Uganda Journal*, xiv (1950).

CRAZZOLARA, J. P. *The Lwoo*. Three parts, Verona, 1950, 1951, and 1954.
—— 'Notes on the Lango-Omiru and the Labwoorand Nyakwai', *Anthropos*, lv (1960).

CUNNINGHAM, J. F. *Uganda and its Peoples*. London, 1905.

DE HEUSCH, LUC. *Le Rwanda et la civilisation interlacustre*. Brussels, 1966.

DRIBERG, J. H. *Engato the Lion Cub*. London, 1933.

DRIBERG, J. H. *The Lango*. London, 1923.

EHRET, CHRISTOPHER. 'Cattle-keeping and Milking in Eastern and Southern African History: The Linguistic Evidence', *Journal of African History*, viii, 1 (1967), 1–17.

EVANS-PRITCHARD, E. E. *The Nuer*. London, 1940.

FAGAN, BRIAN M. 'Radiocarbon dates for sub-Saharan Africa: VI', *Journal of African History*, x, 1 (1969).

FALLERS, LLOYD. *Bantu Bureaucracy*. Chicago & London, 1965.

FALLERS, MARGARET CHAVE. 'The Eastern Lacustrine Bantu (Ganda and Soga)', *Ethnographic Survey of Africa, East Central Africa*, Part XI, ed. Daryll Forde. London, 1960.

FISHER, Mrs. A. B. *Twilight Tales of the Black Baganda*. London, 1911.

FORD, J., and HALL, R. *The History of Karagwe*. Dar es Salaam, 1947.

GGOMOTOKA, Y. T. K. 'Ebifa mu Busoga', *Munno*, March 1926; April 1926.

—— 'History of the Buvuma Islands'. Makerere University College Library, Africana Collection. Translation in CTBTH.

GORJU, JULIEN. *Entre le Victoria, l'Albert et l'Edouard*. Rennes, 1920.

GRAY, J. M. 'The Basoga', *Uganda Journal*, iii, 4 (1936), 308–12.

—— 'Kibuka', *Uganda Journal*, xx, 1 (1956).

GRAY, RICHARD. 'Annular Eclipse Maps', *Journal of African History*, ix, 1 (1968), 147–57.

GUTHRIE, MALCOLM, 'Some Developments in the Pre-History of the Bantu Languages', *Journal of African History*, iii, 2 (1962), 273–82.

—— *The Classification of the Bantu Languages*. London, 1948 and 1967.

HIERNAUX, JEAN. 'Bantu Expansion: The Evidence from Physical Anthropology Confronted with Linguistic and Archaeological Evidence', *Journal of African History*, ix, 4 (1968), 506–10.

HIGENYI, E. W. 'History of the Banyole' [manuscript]. Trans. M. Twaddle; copy in possession of translator.

HUNTINGFORD, G. W. B. 'The Galla of Ethiopia: The Kingdoms of Kafa and Janjero', *Ethnographic Survey of Africa, North-East Africa*, Part II, ed. Daryll Forde. London, 1965.

HUREL, P. E. 'Religion et vie domestique des Bakerewe', *Anthropos*, vi (1911), 62–94, 276–301.

JENKINS, A. O. 'A note of the Saza of Bugerere, Buganda Kingdom', *Uganda Journal*, vi, 4 (1939).

JOHNSTON, SIR HARRY. *The Uganda Protectorate*. London, 1962.

KAGGWA, SIR APOLO. *The Customs of the Baganda*, trans. E. B. Kalibala, ed. M. Mandelbaum Edel. New York, 1934.

—— *Ekitabo kya Basekabaka be Buganda (Kings)*. Kampala and London, 1901, 1912, 1927, and 1953.

—— *Ekitabo kye Bika bya Baganda (Clans)*. Kampala, 1908 and 1949.

—— *Ekitabo kye Mpisa za Baganda (Customs)*. Kampala, 1905 and 1952.

KANYAMUNYU, P. K. 'The Tradition of the Coming of the Abalisa clan to Buhwezu, Ankole', *Uganda Journal*, xv, 2 (1951).

KIRWAN, BRYAN. 'Place Names, Proverbs, Idioms and Songs as a Check on Traditional History', *Prelude to East African History*, ed. Merrick Posnansky. London, 1966.

KITCHING, A. L. *On the Backwaters of the Nile*. London, 1912.

KIWANUKA, M. S. 'The Traditional History of the Buganda Kingdom: With Special Reference to the Historical Writings of Sir Apolo Kaggwa', Ph.D. Thesis, London University, 1965.

K. W. [Tito Winyi, Mukama of Bunyoro-Kitara], 'The Kings of Bunyoro-Kitara', Part 1, *Uganda Journal*, iii, 2 (1935); Part 2, ibid., iv, 1 (1936); Part 3, ibid., v, 2 (1937).

KIZITO TOBI, W. 'The History of the Pre–Kintu period and the Origins of Kintu', *Munno*, 1915 and 1916.

LA FONTAINE, J. S. 'The Gisu of Uganda', *Ethnographic Survey of Africa, East Central Africa*, Part X, ed. Daryll Forde. London, 1959.

LANNING, E. C. 'Masaka Hill: Ancient Centre of Worship', *Uganda Journal* xviii, 1 (1954).

LAWRANCE, J. C. D. 'A History of Teso to 1937', *Uganda Journal*, xix, 1 (1955).

LEAKEY, M. D., OWEN, W. E., and LEAKEY, L. S. B. 'Dimple-based Pottery from Central Kavirondo', *Coryndon Memorial Museum, Occasional Paper 2*. Nairobi, 1948.

LUBINA, E. 'Ssese ey'oButaka'. Makerere University College, Africana Collection.

LUBOGO, Y. K. *A History of Busoga*. Jinja, 1960.

—— Luganda typescript of a 'History of Busoga'. Makerere University College Library, Africana Collection.

LUGARD, F. D. *The Rise of Our East African Empire*. London, 1893.

MACDONALD, J. R. *Soldiering and Surveying in British East Africa*. London, 1897.

MAIR, LUCY. *Primitive Government*. Baltimore, 1962.

MCMASTER, DAVID N. *A Subsistence Crop Geography of Uganda*. Bude, Cornwall, England, 1962.

MORRIS, H. F. *A History of Ankole*. Kampala and Nairobi, 1962.

—— 'Historic Sites in Ankole', *Uganda Journal*, xx, 2 (1956).

—— 'The Kingdom of Mpororo', *Uganda Journal*, xvii, 2 (1955).

NSIMBI, MICHAEL. *Amannya Amaganda n'Ennono Zaago*. Kampala, 1956.

NYAKATURA, JOHN. *Abakama ba Bunyoro-Kitara*. St. Justin, Quebec, 1947.

OGOT, B. A. *A History of the Southern Luo: Migration and Settlement*. Nairobi, 1967.

OLIVER, ROLAND. 'Ancient Capital Sites of Ankole', *Uganda Journal*, xxiii, 1 (1959).

—— 'A Question about the Bachwezi', *Uganda Journal*, xvii, 2 (1953).

—— and Mathew, Gervase. *History of East Africa, I*. Oxford, 1963.

—— 'The Baganda and the Bakonjo', *Uganda Journal*, xviii, 1 (1954).

—— 'The Problem of the Bantu Expansion', *Journal of African History*, vii, 3 (1966).

—— 'The Riddle of Zimbabwe', *The Dawn of African History*, ed. Roland Oliver. London, 1961.

—— 'The Royal Tombs of Buganda', *Uganda Journal*, xxiii, 2 (1959).

—— 'The Traditional Histories of Buganda, Bunyoro, and Ankole', *Journal of the Royal Anthropological Institute, 185* (1955).

OSOGO, J. *A History of the Baluyia*. Nairobi, 1966.

PERSSE. E. M. 'The Bagwe', *Uganda Journal*, iii, 3 (1936).

PORTAL, SIR GERALD. *The British Mission to Uganda*. London, 1894.

POSNANSKY, MERRICK. 'Bantu Genesis—Archaeological Reflexions', *Journal of African History*, ix, 1 (1968).

—— 'Kingship, Archaeology and Historical Myth', *Uganda Journal*, xxx, 1 (1960).

—— 'Pottery types from archaeological sites in East Africa', *Journal of African History*, ii, 2 (1961).

—— ed. *Prelude to East African History*. London, 1966.

—— 'The Traditional History of the Kingdoms of the Western Lacustrine Bantu', *The History of the Central African Peoples*, Rhodes-Livingstone Institute, 17th Conference. Lusaka, 1963.

—— 'Towards an Historical Geography of Uganda', *East African Geographical Review*, 1, April 1963.

ROBERTS, A. D. 'The Sub-Imperialism of the Baganda', *Journal of African History*, iii, 3 (1962).

ROBERTSON, D. W. *The Historical Considerations Contributing to the Soga System of Land Tenure*. Entebbe, 1940.

ROSCOE, JOHN. *The Baganda*. Cambridge, 1911; 2nd edn, London 1965.

—— *The Bagesu and Other Tribes of the Uganda Protectorate*. Cambridge, 1924.

—— *The Bakitara*. Cambridge, 1923.

—— *The Northern Bantu*. Cambridge, 1915.

SUTTON, J. E. G. 'The Archaeology and Early Peoples of the Highlands of Kenya and Northern Tanzania', *Azania*, 1966.

TAYLOR, B. K. 'The Western Lacustrine Bantu', *Ethnographic Survey of Africa, East Central Africa*, Part XIII, ed. Daryll Forde. London, 1962.

TUCKER, A. R. *Eighteen Years in Uganda and East Africa*. London, 1908.

VANSINA, JAN. *Oral Tradition: A Study in Historical Methodology*. Trans. H. M. Wright. London, 1965.

—— *L'évolution du royaume rwanda des origines à 1900*. Brussels, 1962.

—— 'Recording the Oral History of the Bakuba', *Journal of African History* i, 1 (1960); i, 2 (1960).

WAGNER, G. *The Bantu of North Kavirondo*, 2 vols. London, 1949.

WAINWRIGHT, G. A. 'The Coming of the Banana to Uganda', *Uganda Journal*, xvi, 2 (1952).

WAKO, E. T. 'Basoga Death and Burial Rites', *Uganda Journal*, ii, 2 (1934).
WATTS, SUSAN J. 'The South Busoga Resettlement Scheme', *Occasional Paper No. 17, Program of Eastern African Studies*. Syracuse, N.Y., 1966.
WERE, GIDEON. *A History of the Abaluyia*. Nairobi, 1967.
WOODWARD, E. M. *The Uganda Protectorate*. London, 1902.

Index

The clans of Busoga are arranged according to their eponyms; thus, abaiseIbinga is listed as 'Ibinga, abaise-' and is found immediately after 'Ibanda Ngobi'. Totems are noted in italics and are followed by the Luganda equivalents.

Ikoba, abaise-, 52, 97, 105, 120, 122

interviewing, 31 ff.

Iramu Hill, 132

iron, 5, 30; and Bantu expansion, 73–6; -working in Buganda, 106–7; -working in Samia, 99

Iruba, abaise-, 129, 132, 138–9, 179 n., 180

Isegero (33° 37·7′E, 0° 28′N), 136, 146, 168, 170, 185

Isime Island (33° 35′E, 0° 09·5′N), 133

Itego, abaise-, 132

Iumbwe, abaise-, 45, 89–92, 105, 119; expansion of domain, 120 ff.

Kaberamaido, 127, 157–8

Kaggwa, Apolo, 84–5, 87, 90, 93, 95, 107, 135 n., 148, 150, 206

Kagongwe, abaise-, 131–2

Kagulu Tibuchwereke, Kabaka, 148–50

Kakaire, 149, 155 ff., 168, 170, 187

Kakolo (33° 38·4′E, 1° 08′N), 174, 179

Kalenjin, 95, 101–2, 104

Kalenzi, abaise-, 113, 120–1

Kalijoko, abaise-, 165

Kaliro, abaise-, 131–2

Kaluuba, abaise-, 46

Kasango Iumbwe, 92, 118

Kasodo (33° 36′E, 0° 53′N), 165

Kateregga, Kabaka, 86, 88

Kavirondo, 70, 100. *See also* 'Nyanza'

Kayogera, 152–3

Kayozi, 83

Kaziba, abaise-, 136, 166–7

Kibande, abaise-, 187

Kibiga, abaise-, 113, 141 n., 142, 153

Kibimba River, 128–34, 137, 139, 142, 152–3

Kibumba, 23, 116

Kibwika, 82, 112–13, 121–3

Kidoido, abaise-, 134, 145 n., 146

Kigenhi (Kigenyu), 143, 183

Kigulu, 140, 143, 183, 187

Kigulu (Bukooli) (33° 51′E, 0° 36′N), 131

Kigulu Hill (33° 28·9′E, 0° 38·7′N), 187, 189

Kikalangufu (33° 36·1′E, 0° 28·5′N), 134, 136, 155, 163

Kikalu Hill (33° 39′E, 1° 02·5′N), 138, 174, 176, 180

Kiko River, 2, 191

Kimera, Kabaka, 83, 104–5, 109

Kimira (33° 51′E, 0° 37·4′N), 131–2

Kimumwe, 143

Kinakyeri, 50, 174, 177

Kinhama, abaise-, 52, 113

Kintu, 1, 2, 87 ff., 109, 121–2, 137; associated groups, 68, 84; and banana, 4, 103; dating, 104 ff., 119; eastern theme of, 73, 82–4; and Igulu, 110, 112 ff; impact on Buganda of, 106 ff.; at Mangira, 93; migration, 70, 85, 87, 97, 110; 'origins' of, 94–104; popular tradition of, viii, 56, 69, 71–3, 83–5, 117 ff., 124, 197; western theme of, 73, 76, 83

Kiranda, abaise-, 142, 153

Kirinya Hill (33° 13·7′E, 0° 25′N), 93

Kirongo (33° 36·5′E, 0° 20·5′N), 118

Kiruyi, abaise-, 129, 142, 152–3

Kisendo, abaise-, 4 n., 136

Kisige, abaise-, 46

Kisaho (33° 43′E, 0° 28′N), 144, 185

Kisimbiro Hill (33° 42·2′E, 0° 33′N), 134, 145 n., 146–7, 161

Kisui, abaise-, 105, 119

Kitandwe, abaise-, 187, 196

Kitimbo (of Bugabula), 171, 187, 191–6

Kitimbo (sister of Kakaire), 159, 161–2

Kitimbo Nkono, 171, 173 ff.

Kitumba (33° 44·5′E, 0° 26′N), 143–4, 146–7, 153

Kitumbezi River, 2, 136, 146

Kiwanuka, M. S., 72 n., 85–6, 157

Kiyuuka, abaise-, 52, 88

Kizenguli, 134, 137, 139, 155, 164–6

Kizibu, abaise-, 122

Koch, Jo-, 168–70

Kyabaggu, Kabaka, 135

Kyaggwe, 3, 93, 97, 105, 120, 128–9, 158, 182

Kyanvuma (Luuka) (33° 15·7′E, 0° 45·7′N), 45

Kyema, 91, 119

Kyema, abaise-, 88, 121

Kyewe, abaise-, 138, 165, 167

Kyoga Hill (33° 36′E, 0° 24′N), 114

Lake Kyoga, 2, 76, 125, 127, 130, 137, 139–40, 155–9, 165–6, 169, 176

Lake Lemwa, 174–5, 177, 180